from Dr. Mishlove's webpage, used with permission.

"I think Ted Owens was a most remarkable man, and although I'm damned if I know whether he was really in touch with "Space Intelligences," I think there seems to be no reasonable doubt that he had astonishing capacity for causing changes in the weather . . . "
  —COLIN WILSON
    Author, The Outsider, The Occult, Mysteries *and many other books*

"Dr. Jeffrey Mishlove's *The PK Man* is a courageous commentary on the mysterious power of consciousness. This story of a man with extraordinary abilities is bound to elicit controversy and challenge the limits of the human mind."
  —JUDITH ORLOFF, M.D.
    Author, Second Sight
    Assistant clinical professor of psychiatry, UCLA

"Thanks to Mishlove's study, I have begun to ponder the sobering aspects of mind over matter. It will hopefully become a wake-up call to a new morality that could ensure a sustainable future for all of us traveling on space-ship Earth on the threshold of relating with our greater purpose."
  —BRIAN O'LEARY, PH.D.
    Former astronaut and author of The Second Coming of Science

"In my own experience, and in that of other investigators, the Ted Owens case is not an isolated case. It is only the most extraordinary modern case out of many others. Where we find the maximum strangeness we also may find the maximum chance of finding new truths.
  —JAMES HARDER, PH.D., *professor of hydraulic engineering, U.C., Berkeley*
    Former research director, aerial phenomena research organization

"Ted Owens was one of the most outrageous characters ever to emerge in modern ufology. Calling himself "PK Man," he claimed to control the weather and other large-scale events with the aid of Space Intelligences. The profound implications are expertly explored by Jeffrey Mishlove, who challenges us to expand our minds into new realms of science. It's a fascinating read."

—ALAN VAUGHAN, PH.D.
Author of Incredible Coincidence

"This is a masterful presentation of a most peculiar story. In another place, at another time, men like Ted Owens were considered shamans, magicians, or mages. But in the twentieth century West, he lived in a cultural and scientific limbo that is well portrayed here, and the tension this produced makes the events even more dramatic."

—STEPHAN SCHWARTZ
Author, The Secret Vaults of Time *and* The Alexandria Project

"Owens became a kind of an outcast who embodied the American archetype of the villain-hero renegade memorialized in countless movies. He was Jesse James, Clyde Barrow, and Dillinger using weather disturbances instead of guns."

—JAMES P. DRISCOLL, Ph.D.
Author, The Unfolding God of Jung and Milton

"Mishlove has always been on the leading edge of frontier science and he provides an engaging blend of intellectual integrity, scholarship, and open-mindedness in challenging our belief about the perennial puzzle of untapped human potential."

—LEE PULOS, Ph.D.
Author, Miracles and Other Realities

THE PK MAN

A True Story of Mind Over Matter

JEFFREY MISHLOVE, Ph.D.

With an introduction by John E. Mack, M.D.,
author of *Abductions* and *Passport to the Cosmos*

HAMPTON ROADS
PUBLISHING COMPANY, INC.

for the evolving human spirit

ALSO BY
JEFFREY MISHLOVE, PH.D.

The Roots of Consciousness

Psi Development Systems

THE
PK
MAN

For information write:

Hampton Roads Publishing Company, Inc.
1125 Stoney Ridge Road
Charlottesville, VA 22902

Or call: 804-296-2772
FAX: 804-296-5096

e-mail: hrpc@hrpub.com
Website: www.hrpub.com

If you are unable to order this book from your local
bookseller, you may order directly from the publisher.
Quantity discounts for organizations are available.
Call 1-800-766-8009, toll-free.

Library of Congress Catalog Card Number: 99-91472

ISBN 1-57174-183-6

10 9 8 7 6 5 4 3 2 1

Printed on acid-free paper in the Canada

DEDICATION

This book is dedicated to the whole human race, in the hope that we may learn to wisely wield the dual powers of awareness and intention that we experience every waking and dreaming moment.

TABLE OF CONTENTS

FOREWORD

By John E. Mack, M.D.,
Professor of Psychiatry, Harvard University Medical School

One evening late in December 1985 Ted Owens phoned Jeffrey Mishlove to warn him in an angry voice that the U.S. government must cancel the next space shuttle flight. "This is the most important call you will ever receive," Owens said, "The S.I.s (Space Intelligences) really mean business. They will destroy the shuttle. It's up to you to prevent it." A month later, on January 28, 1986, Mishlove was "shaken to my bones" when the Challenger space shuttle exploded, killing its seven crew members, including thirty-seven-year-old teacher Christa McAuliffe. "I realized that I had been ignoring Owens too long," Mishlove writes in this remarkable story. His book raises for me the question of whether we have all ignored for "too long" the powerful ways that what we call consciousness or "mind" can impact directly the material world.

This book may well be a milestone, a kind of turning point in the long debate over whether the human mind can affect the physical world. For the examples Mishlove provides of Owens' powers are so dramatic, and so thoroughly and meticulously documented, including the use of independent testimony in many instances, that it would be difficult for even a hardened skeptic to find conventional explanations for much of what has occurred. Indeed, Mishlove documents so many instances, and goes so far to accommodate his potential critics and consider alternative explanations, that it seems at times like extravagant overkill.

Ted Owens, who was born in Bedford, Indiana, in 1920, had early encounters with what in our culture is called the paranormal. His grandfather taught him the mysterious art of dowsing, and his great-grandmother seems to have had psychic powers, demonstrating her skills at the Ouija board, along with her ability to find lost objects and to predict deaths. As a child Owens himself says he had the power to levitate his body.

As an adult, Owens seems to have possessed, or been able to mobilize, truly extraordinary powers. Mishlove discusses painstakingly whether Owens' powers were merely precognitive, reflecting the capacity to anticipate events that would have occurred anyway, or if he could actually cause these phenomena to occur. In any event, thunder and lightning, snowstorms, earthquakes, droughts and hot spells, drought-relieving or freezing rains, floods, tornados, power failures, volcanic eruptions, the technical failure of human machinery, strange turnings of sports events, and the summoning on command of UFOs into the vision fields of spectators—all have appeared to have occurred in hundreds of instances over a period of three decades (Owens died in 1987) immediately or soon after Owens' predictions or declarations of causal intent. The likelihood that more is involved here than precognition (mysterious enough in itself) is suggested by the fact that in some instances Owens' performances were invited by others, as in the case of his drought-relieving initiatives in Florida and Australia. But none of these events, according to Owens, were simply the result of the powers of his own mind. They were brought about by Space Beings or Space Intelligences (SIs) with whom he was in intimate contact.

This book is best approached, I believe, in the light of the controversy that has surrounded the whole question of whether there is a significant truth to be learned of the entire realm or realms that are considered paranormal, including psi or parapsychological phenomena, action at a distance (non-locality), spiritual healing, the power of prayer, etc.—all those phenomena that reflect the workings of a force field without an apparent material substrate. Many scientists seem to believe that rather than to add immensely to our understanding of the universe and our place in it, the establishment of the reality of such matters would undermine the entire carefully built edifice of scientific materialism that they (and we) are expected to maintain at all costs. Able researchers such as Rupert Sheldrake and Dean Radin have shown that on average the quality of studies in parapsychology has been higher than in other more accepted sciences. One needs only to review the work of Stanley Krippner, Robert Jahn, Charles Tart, and Larry Dossey—to name a few—to discover that this is so.

But the problem underlying the acceptance or rejection of these matters is not scientific, or not primarily so. It is about fundamental cosmologies or worldviews, relating to what Mishlove calls the "metaphysical war of ideas" that "has been taking place throughout Western culture during the past century." At the heart of this war of the worldviews lies the question of the power of consciousness or unseen intelligence to affect feeling, behavior, and events in the material world. On one side is the several-hundred-year quest of our culture to conquer and control the material world through ever more wondrous technology, while voiding the universe of any inherent intelligence apart from the projections of our brains. The cost of this worldview has been to turn our planet into a giant marketplace, where no moral or spiritual values beyond immediate human appetites seem to prevail. Almost every major social problem this planet now faces, including the desecration of the environment, the extremes of poverty, the epidemic diseases and other hardships that are its consequences, and the threat of nuclear war, derive from this materialist hubris, which is not confined to the West.

The opposing worldview, which is gaining momentum slowly throughout the planet, although too late perhaps to preserve most of its life forms, is the one that most peoples throughout history and in most places on the Earth still experience. In this view the universe is replete with intelligence and intelligences, unseen forces and beings or entities of varying density, some of which have the property of manifesting on this plane in a form that many people can perceive. Furthermore, behind or prior to all of this is a luminous ultimate reality or creative principle, manifested as divine light or love, from which all other reality derives. The failure to perceive, or to be able to perceive this reality—the senses by which we might know these things have atrophied, the poet Rilke once wrote—lies at the heart of the crisis that we now confront.

It is in this context, I believe, that the sometimes vastly destructive effects of Owens' demonstrations, resulting sometimes in the loss of lives, should be regarded. In his increasing frustration to have the reality of the powers he could wield recognized, Owens seems like a God of the Old Testament, inflicting plagues of escalating effect upon a stiff-necked populace determined to remain locked in ignorance and denial. He beseeches Mishlove to be a fighter for the truth he knows. "You are sitting on the greatest parapsychological find in history," but are "afraid to do anything about it," Owens berates the author. Wisely, Owens identifies concern with public criticism as the source of the hesitation of Mishlove and others to put forth openly what they have found out about such matters, their self-censorship stemming from fear of criticism "by peers tougher than you are."

There are times that Owens seems to behave like a petulant child, perpetrating the revenge of the misunderstood, striving as Mishlove correctly states, "to intimidate the world into supporting him." But when one considers the stakes, it could be a great error to stress too heavily the personal or egoistic aspect of Owens' personality or to judge his behavior too harshly. "I am not doing it," he said. Another intelligence was working through him. "It is the UFO, Egyptian, and Mayan powers that are currently engaged in these activities."

"I figure that somehow I had managed to contact the essence of the intelligence behind Nature itself," he said after he had "made" a particularly severe storm that almost destroyed Las Vegas. Mishlove even suggests that Owens became a kind of mirror onto which people would project their dark emotions, reaping from him what they had sowed themselves.

Owens' purpose, of course, is to liberate, to awaken us from a slumbering ignorance of the peril we face, to enable us to recognize the power we possess to change our fate, and, above all, to become open to the possibility, in Owens' words, "that we are living in the vicinity of other-dimensional, conscious life-forms who are invisible to our normal senses." Interfacing with these beings, especially the ones referred to as Space Intelligence Masters (SIMs), could bring great rewards to humanity. But Owens suffers terribly in the familiar mode of the prophet ignored in his own time—"They didn't believe I was for real," he said sadly when nobody came to one of his lectures. He certainly did not profit from his powers, and found it always difficult to provide for his family.

We are not now, nor may we ever, be able to "explain" in the terms of a mechanistic science the remarkable phenomena documented by Jeffrey Mishlove in this extraordinary book, but this does not diminish their importance or give us the right to ignore them. The month after the Challenger disaster Mishlove began to take Owens' mind training course, not, as he states, to "influence weather patterns and call down UFOs," but in order to "be very effective in communicating parapsychological information to the public." I can testify personally to Mishlove's success in this regard, for the interview he did with me for *Thinking Allowed* (his national TV program on new thought and consciousness) after the publication of my first book on the UFO abduction phenomenon was the most intelligent and "effective" I experienced. It is clear from this book that Mishlove's capacity over the past fourteen years to become a leader in bringing intelligent discourse to the field of parapsychology owes much to his relationship with Ted Owens.

Mishlove acknowledges that he delayed the publication of *The PK Man* for many years because society was not ready to receive it. One well known skeptic even warned him that "the book could do you professional damage." Mishlove's statement that our ability to explore parapsychology and ufology objectively for the last century or more has been "hampered by social dynamics" may go down as one of the greatest understatements of all time. He anticipates that there will still be skeptics—I prefer the term debunker for those who have, in Jeffrey's words, made "irrevocable social commitments to worldviews that are inconsistent with the data herein presented"—who will "develop some ingenious strategy for delegitimizing the data itself." But Mishlove does not appear to be afraid of this sort of thing anymore, perhaps in part from the courage that Ted Owens helped instill in him quite a few years ago.

Toward the end of the book Mishlove refers to the work of the great sociologist Pitirim A. Sorokin, who as early as 1938 already knew that a predominantly sensate or rationalistic paradigm was dying. For all its material triumphs this worldview is far too limited to encompass the vastness of the human spirit, and has brought us to the brink of ecological and military disaster. Sorokin anticipated that major shifts of cosmology tend, as we have seen, to be accompanied by great social upheaval. Dead as it may be, the dominating perspective of scientific materialism still seems to obstruct the road to the future, like the decomposing carcass of some great ancient mammoth. Jeffrey Mishlove's powerful true story may greatly help to clear the way for new creative human visions and achievements.

References

Sheldrake, Rupert. "Experimenter Effects in Scientific Research: How Widely Are They Neglected?" *Journal of Scientific Exploration*, vol. 12, no. 1, 1998, pp. 73-78.

Radin, Dean. *The Conscious Universe: The Scientific Truth of Psychic Phenomena*. New York: Harper Collins, 1997.

Mack, John E. *Abduction: Human Encounters with Aliens*. New York: Charles Scribner's Sons, 1994.

ACKNOWLEDGEMENTS

Thanks, of course, are due to Ted Owens (1920-1987), the "UFO Prophet" and "PK Man," who gladly provided material needed to complete this study. Special thanks are due to D. Scott Rogo (1950-1990) who collaborated with me in 1979 on an unpublished manuscript called *Earth's Ambassador*, about the Ted Owens case. The present volume represents a revision and further digestion of that original work—and many of Scott Rogo's thoughts appear in this book. Thanks are due to Jack and Winifred Rogo for thier assistance and permission regarding the 1979 manuscript.

Thanks are also extended to those researchers who supplied their files on the Owens case. These include Dr. Leo Sprinkle of the University of Wyoming; Dr. Harold Puthoff and Mr. Russell Targ of the Stanford Research Institute (SRI) International in Menlo Park, California; Dr. Berthold Schwarz; and Mr. Wayne Grover. I am particularly indebted to those researchers who contributed to a special February 1978 meeting about Ted Owens, including Dr. Elizabeth Rauscher, Dr. J. Allen Hynek, and Dr. James Harder and to the Washington Research Center in San Francisco that sponsored this meeting.

Although the material incorporated into this volume has been collated from the files of several researchers and writers, full responsibility for the views and data rest with the author. These views do not reflect those of the researchers whose work is cited. Although Mr. Owens read through the 1979 manuscript for factual accuracy, this does not mean that he endorsed either the conclusions or evaluations.

Finally, I would like to thank and acknowledge all of the individuals who have helped me with the revision of the various manuscripts of this book, including my beloved wife Janelle M. Barlow, Dean Brown, Jim Driscoll, Uri Geller, James Harder, Obadiah Harris, Jean Houston, John Mack, Ted Mann, Robert Masters, Michael Miley, Edgar Mitchell, Henry Monteith, James Mullaney, Brian O'Leary, Judith Orloff, Lee Pulos, Robert Reussig, John Rossner, Stephen Roulac, Jack Sarfatti, Stephan Schwartz, Lars Spivock, Russell Targ and Marcello Truzzi.

Physicist Saul-Paul Sirag deserves special acknowledgment for writing the section titled "A Brief History of Hyperspace" that appears in chapter 12. Awo Fa'lokun Fatunmbi (a.k.a. David Wilson) also contributed significantly to the discussion of shamanism in chapter 12.

A five-hour conversatoin with Kevin Ryerson in January 1998 inspired me to revise the dusty manuscript originally written two decades earlier.

Special thanks are also due to my agent, Rita Rosenkranz, and my editor, Richard Leviton, who both played important roles in midwifing the long-delayed birth of this book.

INTRODUCTION

"PK" is the parapsychological abbreviation for psychokinesis or mind-over-matter. J. B. Rhine, the father of American parapsychology, popularized the term in the 1940s, while working at Duke University. He suggested that every act of human free will, such as raising your arm in the air, necessitates psychokinesis. Indeed, human free will is an enormous problem for science and philosophy. But parapsychologists are especially interested in manifestations of psychokinesis outside of the human body, in which the mind itself exerts a direct influence on distant physical systems, with no known mechanism of mediation. The implications of this ability are staggering in every way—philosophically, scientifically, sociologically, spiritually, and most importantly, in terms of how we know and understand ourselves.

I met Ted Owens, the PK Man, in 1976 and began my study of this fascinating American shaman that continued until his death in 1987. Owens demonstrated his claim to possess psychokinetic powers in the letters he sent me almost every month, informing me in advance of his plans to control a variety of large-scale systems: hurricanes, earthquakes, temperature, and other weather conditions. The results would then be documented in newspapers. Oftentimes, his demonstrations were accompanied by a variety of bizarre events, including lightning, power blackouts, and UFO sightings. The sum total of these demonstrations make the Owens case unique in the entire history of parapsychology and even in the older discipline known as psychical research.

Over the decades, parapsychologists have accumulated a good deal of scientific evidence in support of psychokinesis, generally involving conscious control of small-scale, instrumented systems such as dice, quantum mechanical random event generators, magnetometers, and thermistors. Some fascinating metallurgical studies have been conducted regarding bent spoons and strips of metal. Owens' unique contribution has been to suggest that it is just as easy for the power of psychokinesis to influence a labile large-scale system, such as a hurricane, as it is to influence a small-scale system in the laboratory. At one time, he requested of me that this large-scale type of psychokinesis be labeled "the Owens effect."

Ironically, Owens himself often vacillated when it came to interpreting the effects that he apparently produced. While he did not hesitate to claim psychokinetic powers, he generally suggested that the effects were actually produced by other-dimensional beings he called the Space Intelligences. These entities, Owens suggested, had their own motives, independent of his own. He was their chosen representative on Earth. When he sent them telepathic messages, they generally carried out his instructions. At first, one might think of this as a completely different, alternative explanation. However, parapsychologists are accustomed to thinking of psychokinesis, telepathy, clairvoyance, and precognition as different facets of one mental faculty called "psi." From a scientific perspective, it is nearly impossible to distinguish one from the other. Perhaps, in the future, when more refined tools are available, we will be able to do so.

Ted Owens was a large man with a thick neck. His voice was deep and resonant, like that of a professional broadcaster. He spoke in a clear, Midwestern accent, and his speech was sprinkled with folksy metaphors. He always dressed informally and could often be seen smoking a cigar. During the years when I knew him, his long, white hair was almost shoulder length, and he sported a beard. He had a fondness for beer and whiskey. Ted was also a member of Mensa, the organization exclusively for individuals with a high intelligence.

Ted was a family man. Baby Jerome was born to his wife, Martha, in 1977. At that time, their son Teddy, who was four years old, had a mop of blond hair. My own stepson, Lewis, who was then nine years old, met Teddy and marveled at the fact that he could touch the tip of his nose with his tongue. Their oldest son, Beau, was then sixteen. He seemed like the shy type. This was Ted Owens' second family. As best I could tell, he was estranged from Lornie and Rick, the children of his first wife, Pat.

Ted Owens and his family lived almost like vagabonds. I received mail from his residences in Cape Charles, Virginia; Bernalillo, New Mexico; Silverton, Oregon; Vancouver, Washington; Ocala, Florida; and Fort Ann, New York. Throughout the period of my study, Ted Owens was not gainfully employed in any regular way. He was supported by a small coterie of true believers who accepted his claim that he was the messenger of other-dimensional Space Intelligences—which often guided him to relocate. Occasionally, he earned a little money in the form of donations for his work as a spiritual healer. He was also a teacher of esoteric wisdom, through his Church of SOTA (Secrets of the Ages). Sometimes, he trained students, using a hypnotic process he developed to enable them to contact the Space Intelligences themselves. Although Owens himself lived close to the poverty level, occasionally his clients would include wealthy individuals who would pay all of his expenses on various jaunts to places like Mexico, Puerto Rico, and Egypt.

Like the cinematic character Forrest Gump, Ted Owens had an interesting, synchronistic penchant for being on the scene at the time of historical events. In June 1975, for example, while returning from Egypt, he was flying into New York's Kennedy Airport immediately behind Eastern Airlines Flight 66 from New Orleans. That airplane crashed, apparently struck by lightning while landing. It was the worst aviation disaster in U.S. history at the time. Owens was also in Vancouver, Washington, at the foot of Mount Saint Helens, on the very day in May 1980 when its eruption made it the first active volcano in the forty-eight states for almost sixty years.

While Ted Owens was not a fictional character, I think of him as having been larger than life, akin to such mythical, American folk legends as Paul Bunyan and Pecos Bill. But he was a very real, flesh-and-blood human being. What made Ted Owens unique was his apparent, extraordinary psychokinetic talent. Ted Owens had the rare gift of mind-over-matter. His, and our own, tragic ignorance about such powers is most insightfully displayed by considering the above-mentioned coincidences. On each occasion, Owens was actually, but not intentionally, concentrating on a picture or diagram symbolizing the events that occurred soon thereafter.

While on that flight into Kennedy Airport in June 1975, Owens was seated in first class. He was enjoying the free liquor and was waving about for the stewardesses to see the issue of *Saga* magazine that had just been published with an article featuring his exploits. The article actually contained an illustration portraying a plane crash from an earlier episode in the Chesapeake Bay area (described in chapter 10), with the suggestion that Owens' psychokinetic powers had inadvertently downed Navy jets. So here is Owens in an intoxicated state, concentrating on a picture purporting to illustrate how his abilities can knock airplanes out of the sky at the very time and vicinity when such a rare event actually did occur! The fact that lightning apparently struck the Eastern Airlines jet is also significant since one of Owens' specialties was causing lightning to strike—simply by pointing his finger at the desired location (described in chapter 5).

The story that Owens told me regarding the Mount Saint Helens eruption was that he was at a nearby park, with his children, at the time, showing them how to use his "PK Map" technique. Owens claimed that the PK Map was the primary method he used. It involved drawing a diagram symbolizing effects that he wished to produce and then using that image as the object of his focused concentration. He would mentally send these images to his other-dimensional friends, the Space Intelligences, sitting in invisible UFOs high over the planet, and they would use their advanced powers to actualize Owens' intentions. He was having his children direct PK energy toward Mount Saint Helens hours before it exploded—but he claimed that this was just practice and that he did not intend for it to erupt.

Naturally, these events are not definitive. In and of themselves, they carry no evidential weight in offering proof for something as scientifically extraordinary as psychokinesis, the power of the mind to directly influence distant physical events. However, when taken in the context of hundreds of other dramatic instances, a picture begins to emerge that cannot be so easily dismissed. The great psychical researchers of the nineteenth century, such as William James, one of America's most brilliant thinkers, argued that the evidence should be considered like a bundle of sticks. Each individual stick might be easily broken, but, when tied together into a bundle, they are as strong as steel.

Scientists and scholars will debate the existence of psychokinesis for many decades into the future. There is no escaping the enormous social controversy aroused by claims such as those that appear in this book. However, I suspect that most readers will be more interested in the moral and ethical implications of Ted

Owens' career. The examples cited above suggest strongly that, if Owens' abilities were indeed real, then he used them in a careless, negligent, and even malicious fashion. Even though he was also a healer, he was not above engaging in the practice of hexing.

If we assume that psychokinesis is real and that it can, indeed, be wielded in the manner presented in this book, then what are the ethical and social issues that arise? Up until about 200 years ago, presumed witches were burned at the stake, based on this assumption. This is, certainly, the most deeply troubling aspect of human psychokinesis in general and the PK Man in particular. It is probably a major reason why psychokinesis is rarely a topic of discussion, even among parapsychologists. Throughout this book, I shall attempt to explore these social and ethical issues from different perspectives.

When I worked with Owens between 1976 and 1987, my interest was primarily in exploring how his talents could contribute to our scientific knowledge as well as how they could be harnessed for practical purposes. Owens, himself, seemed eager to work on behalf of humanity, helping to end droughts, engaging in healing, or in helping to diffuse international tensions. He hoped that he could serve as an ambassador between the Space Intelligences and the U.S. government. The problem was that very few people at that time were prepared to acknowledge the existence of psychokinesis. The few who were sufficiently open-minded were aghast at the possibility of working with such an unpredictable character as Owens. The noted UFO researcher, J. Allen Hynek, exemplified this attitude at a scientific meeting about the Owens case that I convened in 1978, when he said that he considered Owens' powers to be subconscious in nature and that, therefore, he wouldn't "go near him with a ten-foot pole."

It is necessary that I am clear with the reader about my own biases. For some reason, it has not been within my makeup to feel horrified about Ted Owens—although I have, indeed, been apprehensive. In fact, I tend to regard certain moralistic interpretations of his life and career as a throwback to hypocritical, Victorian ethics. The distinction between black magic and white magic, for example, seems all too neat to me. Human history has been far too cluttered with devastating holocausts, witch hunts, and superstitions perpetrated by those who thought they were opposing evil for me to feel much sympathy with that line of rhetoric. This is not to say, of course, that Owens was without sin. To the contrary, his faults were many, and they were large. He, himself, was his own worst enemy—and it would be no exaggeration to say that, if psychokinesis were to become recognized by a court of law, his actions would be criminal.

But the courts do not recognize psychokinesis and are unlikely to do so for the foreseeable future. It would create a legal mess of incalculable proportions. And so, if Owens committed murder and mayhem through the use of psychokinesis—as shall be amply presented here—he was truly beyond the reach of the law. Yet, he need not be beyond the reach of our own judgments and evaluations of his behavior. Above all, I encourage readers to form own opinions regarding both the validity of Owens' psychokinesis and the quality of his character. The situation is complex, and I have generally refrained from offering a single, definitive opinion of my own. I can simply say that we, as a society, must learn how to deal with a powerful tool that is beyond the reach of the law.

Owens used many metaphors to justify the outrageous ends to which he focused his mental powers. He often compared himself to Moses wreaking the ten plagues upon Egypt with the help of God. He compared himself to a dentist, causing pain in the service of long-term hygienic goals. Sometimes he thought of himself as a schoolteacher, insisting that a recalcitrant student receive a painful lesson. All of these metaphors, naturally, can be criticized as being inappropriate and vainglorious.

But one thing is clear. Owens lived and operated within a world that offered him little in the way of support or understanding.

Often his efforts to use psychokinesis for human benefit were met with sarcasm and ridicule. This is a situation that is faced today by thousands of talented intuitives, psychics, shamans, healers, and seers. I have known hundreds of these people personally and consider them my friends. I have a very special place in my heart for them. I understand their suffering, and I see the enormous psychological defenses which they bring to bear against the constant social drumbeat that belittles the legitimacy of their own inner experience. These defenses are most unfortunate.

Ted Owens lashed out at those who treated him with contempt. He felt that they deserved a lesson, and dozens of such lessons shall be documented in this book. In spite of the fact that Owens overreacted, I feel enormous sympathy here. I do not believe that it is right to treat other human beings with disrespect. It has taken decades for blacks, women, and other minorities to establish this principle. Today, homosexual men and women are still struggling to establish a social atmosphere in which their dignity is not subject to constant derision. I regard all of these movements as a liberation of the human spirit. However, I suspect that only after the gay liberation movement has accomplished its goals will there be sufficient impetus to apply the same principles to the mistreatment of those who are gifted with shamanistic, spiritual, and psychic powers.

My sense is that Owens used his psychokinetic powers like a mirror, reflecting back and amplifying the negative thought forms that were directed toward him by a wide variety of critics and skeptics. Many people have condemned him for this, as the results seem to have been loss of property and sometimes even of life. Others regard Owens as a hero standing up for the vast reach and power of the inner psyche, the evolutionary birthright of all humanity. Ironically, both perspectives are accurate.

Like many psychics, Owens also compounded his own diffi-culties by taking credit for a wide variety of events—well beyond those that I, as a sympathetic parapsychologist, found reasonable. After all, the newspapers are full of unusual events. Every day, something unusual occurs, and it is not always the result of psychokinesis.

This leads to yet another problematic aspect of evaluating Owens' life from a moral perspective: the scientific question of causality. If Owens were using psychokinesis, or mind-over-matter, as classically conceived, we should hold him accountable for the results of his intentions. However, what if he were, instead, using precognition to predict various events that he then claimed to be causing? His accountability would be much less. Of course, we cannot ignore Owens' claim that the real culprits in his many mischievous episodes were the Space Intelligences, other-dimensional energy beings aboard invisible UFOs. Teasing out the threads of causality among these competing hypotheses is difficult business, particularly when we are intellectually bound to pay attention to the skeptical claim that all of this may be some sort of an illusion.

This book has two conclusions. In chapter 11, I describe my own experience in taking Ted Owens' training program. That experience served as a catalyst in my transformation from a beleaguered, depressed, and jobless parapsychologist to the host of the weekly *Thinking Allowed* public television TV interview series in production since 1986, a few months after I took Owens' training. It was never my interest nor intention to use psychokinesis to produce lights in the sky or to control weather patterns. My interest has always been to serve as an effective communicator of the realities of the deep, inner psyche. My years of work and then my training with Ted Owens has helped me to better fulfill my own destiny and continues to do so today.

The second conclusion, in chapter 12, provides a broader intellectual context for the life and career of Ted Owens. Owens' life is examined from the perspectives of sociology, anthropology, ufology, physics, and psychology. Within each of these disciplines exists perspectives that allow us to begin to make sense out of that which at first may seem irrational and unbelievable.

CHAPTER 1

SNOW DURING THE CALIFORNIA DROUGHT

The most beautiful thing we can experience is the mysterious. It is the source of all true art and science.

Albert Einstein

They Were Eager to Discuss the Case

In February 1976, I visited the huge, military-industrial think tank, SRI International, in Menlo Park, California, at the invitation of physicists Hal Puthoff and Russell Targ. In addition to their groundbreaking work in remote viewing, or clairvoyance, which later became the basis for a twenty-year military intelligence program, Puthoff and Targ had also achieved fame and notoriety for their experiments with Uri Geller. This work had been published in the prestigious British journal, *Nature*, in 1973. When I arrived at their laboratory, I found the two physicists very excited, even flabbergasted, about another case. They eagerly explained to me that they had been contacted by a strange man named Ted Owens, who signed his letters "PK Man" and proclaimed that he was "the world's greatest psychic." Owens seemed eager to be used as a subject for parapsychological testing. Puthoff and Targ declined the offer but nevertheless for several years continued to receive correspondence from the PK Man that documented his demonstrations.

On January 30, 1976, Owens wrote to Puthoff and Targ telling them that he was going to show them the extent of his powers by causing heavy storms over the San Francisco area and thereby ending the drought that was then approaching disastrous proportions. His letter read:

> Last night on TV the evening news showed a stricken
> California. Crops are dead and dying and the animals
> are in pitiful condition. Now I, Ted Owens, PK Man,
> will change all of that. Within the next 90 days from the
> time of this letter I will pour and pour and pour rains
> onto and into the state of California until it is
> swimming in water and the dangerous drought is
> completely over. There will be storm after storm, light-
> ning after lightning attacks, and high winds. . . .

It didn't take ninety days for Owens' demonstration to come off. A freak snowstorm hit the San Francisco area on February 5. It was the first storm of winter, and many more were to follow. According to an Associated Press (AP) release, "The unexpected snowfall came as part of the first major California storm this year in a season that has brought drought to farm areas and talk of water rationing in many communities." The last snowstorm to strike the San Francisco Bay Area occurred in 1887 and dropped 3.7 inches of snow. The only other snowfall in the area fell in 1962 when mild flurries were seen. The February storm left no less than 3.5 inches of snow on the ground. As though unintentionally acknowledging Owens' complicity in the affair, the AP story also stated that "the storm featured lightning and sleet" and added that "a giant television tower on Mt. San Bruno, south of San Francisco, was hit by lightning." Interestingly, lightning is very rare in the San Francisco area.

The storm hit San Francisco unannounced, delighting residents but mystifying meteorologists who were totally caught off guard by it. In fact, it was so freakish that Claude Holmes, a representative for the National Weather Service, had to admit to the *San Francisco Chronicle* that he was baffled by it. The meteorological aspects leading to the storm were "so complicated," he said, "that I'm not sure I understand all the details myself." Whatever the case may be, the snowfall was only the beginning of the end to the drought. Just as Owens had predicted, the storm heralded several weeks of snow, lightning and winds. An *Oakland Tribune* story on February 5 reported that the storm exhibited "nearly every phenomenon in the weatherman's book throughout the Bay Area" including snow, hail, sleet, thunder, and lightning. Gale warnings were issued in northwestern California. The storm went on for several days and introduced what was to be one of the worst winters in California history. The rainfall was unbelievable for the rest of the season as storm after storm meandered over the state. These continual storm fronts produced formidable problems in Southern California.

Los Angeles nearly became a disaster area when the constant moisture weakened the foothills that surround many areas of the city, and this led to huge mudslides that caused millions of dollars worth of damage as expensive hillside homes were completely destroyed by mud and structural damage. Resultant flooding even took a few lives. The weather eventually became so freakish that, at one point, a tornado watch was called. This was the first time this had ever happened in recent history. Tornadoes are extremely rare in California, and none had ever struck Los Angeles.

Another peculiar aspect of that fateful winter is that there was considerable UFO activity reported in California right before the storms began. During the last week of January, half a dozen law enforcement agencies logged calls about a cigar-shaped object, complete with flashing lights and vapor trail, that was seen traveling through southeastern California. After the storm, on February 8 and 9, two scientists spotted a UFO flying over the Siskiyou Mountains in Northern California. One of these witnesses, Paul Cerny, was a noted UFO investigator quite capable of distinguishing a genuinely mysterious airborne object from a conventional craft. Since UFO activity was not rare in this area, these UFO appearances possibly had nothing to do with Owens' demonstrations. However, as we shall see, UFO phenomena often accompanied these demonstrations.

Puthoff and Targ sent Owens a note congratulating him on his successful prediction and received a telegram response from him stating that it was not a prediction, but that he, Owens, had *caused* the snowstorm! After all, that was why he called himself the PK Man, PK meaning *psychokinesis*, the ability to affect matter with the mind. This was food for thought, and when I visited the physicists some weeks later, they were eager to discuss the case.

Hyperdimensional Entities Affectionately Known as "Twitter" and "Tweeter"

Puthoff and Targ brought out Ted Owens' 1969 book *How to Contact Space People*, and with great interest showed me a drawing of two large, insect-like creatures in the text, whom Owens affectionately called "Twitter" and "Tweeter." The book claimed that Owens had produced many demonstrations of his psychokinetic powers for government officials and even named the officials he had interacted with in each case. For the CIA, Owens had "used his powers" to cause ships to sink. For NASA, he had demonstrated his "control" over lightning. Nevertheless, Owens bitterly complained, these agencies still refused to take him seriously.

Owens also described the visualization techniques that he used to communicate with Space Intelligences (SIs), i.e., hyper-dimensional entities who were continually in his view, monitoring the Earth from UFOs. He saw them as looking into a screen where his thought-forms appeared. Other people could communicate with them using this same method, he stated. I experienced this some ten years later, when I took Owens' training program (see chapter 11). The Space Intelligences, Owens often claimed, were the ones who really had the power. Just as often, however, he attributed his powers to psychokinesis.

Because of the controversy that their research was already generating, Puthoff and Targ did not feel that they could afford to pursue an investigation of Ted Owens. Nevertheless, the recent events had piqued their curiosity. The solution, it seemed to them, was simple: turn the project over to a promising young graduate student. I was their candidate.

Owens liked to tell how the UFO entities captured him and operated on his brain to make him half human and half alien. He had a thick crease at the base of his skull that, he said, resulted from this operation. In August 1976, some months after I learned about Owens, he gave me an opportunity to inspect this crease for myself at the City University of London where we were both attending a conference sponsored by the Parascience Foundation. All of this came about because *Psychic* magazine, a now defunct publication but once of some distinction, ran a news item based on information gleaned from Puthoff and Targ about Owens' possible role in ending the California drought.

How a Drought Ended during the London Parascience Foundation Conference

In May 1976, Owens received a letter from Suzanne Stebbing, a British student of the paranormal and a friend of Professor John Taylor, a well known mathematician at King's

College in Great Britain and an ardent student of parapsychology. England was at the time suffering from its worst drought in 150 years, and Stebbing, having read the *Psychic* magazine item about Owens' powers, was wondering if he could end it. In a return letter dated May 10, Owens informed his admirer that he would begin work on the project but asked that Taylor himself write to him asking for the demonstration. As part of his performance, Owens promised massive rainfall during the next ninety days as well as lightning strikes, high winds, and UFO appearances.

Stebbing wrote back to Owens in early June, explaining that Taylor was too tied up with other work to write to him. However, included in her letter was an invitation for Owens to come to England where he could meet Taylor in order to give an address to a paraphysics conference scheduled to be convened at the University of London. (Paraphysics is to physics as parapsychology is to psychology. Both fields engage in scientific inquiry into the paranormal aspects of nature.) In this same letter, Stebbing advised Owens that the drought had begun to abate slightly but that it was still a serious condition threatening to create havoc across the country. Although some rain fell in June, these showers did little to offset the deleterious effects of the prolonged drought.

Owens finally heard from Taylor towards the end of his self-imposed deadline. Taylor pointed out that, since so little rain had fallen during the last ninety days, he considered Owens' rainmaking attempts to be a clear failure. He reiterated his feelings in a letter to Owens two days after, in which he pointed out that British meteorologists had announced that there was no end to the drought in sight.

This was all quite true. By August, when the paraphysics conference was slated to convene, England was in bad shape. London residents were being asked to reduce water consumption by one third. In some outlying villages, water had to be trucked in. By August 27, the *London Times* had to report that, according to government ministries, there still seemed no end to the drought in sight and it could easily last through September. My friends in London joked that if I wanted to get my picture in the *Times*, all I had to do was appear in Piccadilly Circus with an umbrella!

August 27 was also conspicuous since that was the day Owens arrived in London. Synchronistically, it rained there that very day. It was the first rain in twenty-eight days, and although it did not end the drought, it dampened the entire southeastern section of England. It rained again the following day, and, as typically happened when Owens was around, a mysterious power failure crippled the London subway system and stranded thirty trains during the showers. The rain never stopped. It continued throughout September, and on September 29, the drought was declared officially over by government sources.

Despite the fact that Owens' London demonstration was not a clear-cut success, it was curiously impressive to me, as I was in London at the time and well aware of events in California earlier that year. The rain that ultimately ended the British drought began the day Owens arrived in London, even though no end to it was officially in sight. The fact is that Owens specialized in trying to cause power failures, as shall be shown throughout this book. This, coupled with the fact that such a failure occurred the day of his arrival, was also too synchronistic for comfort.

In any event, no matter what role Owens played in the rains, at least England had been saved from disaster, but whether by Owens, chance, nature, or God, one cannot say.

During my 1976 summer trip to England, I was able, for the first time, to meet Owens at a conference convened at the City University of London by the Institute of Parascience, a small, private parapsychology research facility in London. Owens was an invited speaker on the program, and spoke to a somewhat stunned audience—an impressive speaker with a booming voice that rang through the auditorium. Yet, paradoxically, despite his large frame, he seemed like a child. He even pulled behind him a red toy wagon stacked with newspaper clippings documenting his exploits, and he spoke about the hundreds of demonstrations that he had conducted for scientists. He shocked the audience with his claims that he had direct contact with UFO beings, that they had endowed him with psychic powers, that he was being used by the Space Intelligences to end worldwide drought, and that he could be useful in psychic warfare against the Soviet Union.

Despite Owens' bizarre claims and wild theatrics, I was intrigued by him. His words were clear and articulate. His manner was confident. His eyes sparkled with charisma and precocious genius. He rocked the audience with his claim that he had established telepathic contact with other dimensional Space Intelligences. He described how they, the Space Intelligences, had guided his career from infancy to adulthood through over fifty different occupations—bodyguard, bullwhip artist, judo expert, jazz musician, knife thrower, dance instructor, shorthand expert, high speed typist, parapsychology researcher— so that his mind would be flexible enough to manipulate their complicated symbolic system.

Owens held up a signed letter from Dr. Max L. Fogel, the director of science and education for Mensa, who had testified that he had received a written prediction from Owens, two days prior to the event, accurately forecasting the appearance of a UFO in Chase City, Virginia.

Owens, however, explained to his London audience that he had *caused* the sighting and not merely predicted it. He also produced an affidavit from a radio producer in Dallas, Texas, verifying the accuracy of a claim that Owens would produce a major demonstration of his powers by wreaking havoc with the local weather. Owens' pronouncement was followed by some of the most intense and unseasonable weather in Texas history. An earthquake measuring 4.5 on the Richter scale struck, tornadoes came fast and furious, the coldest temperatures in Texas history followed suit, and fierce, hot winds capped the ordeal by destroying half the Texas wheat crop.

Because the conference was running behind schedule, the moderator asked Owens to finish his talk early. This abrupt news shook his self-assured manner. He left the podium like an obedient but bitter child, without taking advantage of the few minutes remaining.

It was a scientific conference and, in this context, Owens was out of place. He was speaking as a psychic to scientists who are by profession and nature skeptical of all psychic claims beyond those that they have personally investigated or that have been reported in the scholarly literature, and even those claims are subject to intense and often hostile scrutiny. To make matters worse, another psychic preceded Owens on the speaker's podium—Susan Padfield, the wife of noted British physicist Ted Bastin. Padfield, whose psychokinetic abilities had been extensively tested, spoke about "psychic support figures." She claimed that when she first started doing PK, she assumed that UFO intelligences were working through her. Since then, she had come to realize that the powers were her own; and the notion that UFO intelligences provided psychic support might have been initially necessary to satisfy her emotional needs but did not explain her PK abilities. Other psychics who claimed to work with spirit guides, saints, or deities were also satisfying the same emotional need, she claimed.

When Owens got up to speak, the cards were clearly stacked against him. Even if the audience would accept the seemingly outlandish claim that he could cause large-scale weather changes, it was not inclined to believe that he did so through the agency of UFOs. They were not inclined to embrace his desire to use his talents in psychic warfare with the Soviet Union; and they were not inclined to accept his messianic claim that he was the supreme Earth ambassador of UFO intelligences. Owens was a liar or a madman, an evil magician or an egotistical crackpot. Few people saw him as a fellow human struggling to share with them the methods by which he had cultivated powers so rare they seem either chimerical or demonic.

The Parascience Foundation Conference was not prepared to handle a character like Owens. Those attending the London conference had mixed reactions to him, ranging from exasperation and incredulity to fascination. Many felt that if Owens wasn't an outright liar, then he was a dangerous character. His claims were difficult to accept, yet the documentation was there for all to view.

Colin Wilson, the well known British novelist, essayist, and writer on the occult, was also in the audience that day. In typical British understatement, he subsequently wrote of Owens, "His manner, of course, lacked the kind of nervous modesty that British audiences take to be a guarantee of honesty." Wilson admitted that he took Owens' claims seriously.

During a break in the scientific program, I took the opportunity to meet Owens personally and to tell him that I had been following his work with interest and that I wanted to interview him for a radio broadcast in America. In the middle of our discussion, the conference organizers interrupted to announce that one of the scheduled speakers had not arrived and that time could now be made available to Owens to make up for the previous disruption of his talk. As we walked together into the auditorium, I sensed Owens' precarious position at the conference and volunteered to make a brief introductory remark stating my knowledge of the San Francisco snowstorm demonstration. Perhaps this move helped to increase Owens' credibility; unfortunately, he was again cut short when the scheduled speaker arrived late. Flustered and apparently humiliated once again, Owens left the podium, this time amid a loud mixture of both hissing and applause.

Later that day, Owens told me how the Space Intelligences had taught him 150 different techniques for telepathic transmission and psychokinetic weather control. The most important of these, one that he used every day, he claimed, was visualizing of the "rainbow UFO." Coincidentally, at that moment I was wearing a pin with the image of a UFO, or the ringed planet Saturn, in front of a rainbow. My girlfriend in those days had given it to me, and I wore it without paying much attention to the symbolism. Owens expressed a strong desire to have that pin and, with considerable reluctance, I finally gave it to him. In exchange, he later sent me a fancy Swiss watch with two dials on it that, he claimed, had accompanied him on his various adventures. Since then, Owens and I enjoyed a good, albeit sometimes stormy, working rapport based on mutual respect.

As I returned from London to San Francisco, my mind pondered the puzzle of Ted Owens. If his claims were real, he might prove to be the most powerful psychic in the history of paranormal research. I had by then become aware that a fair amount of documentation supported Owens' story. During a subsequent visit to SRI International, I obtained from Puthoff and Targ their accumulated correspondence from and documentation about Ted Owens: a stack of letters, affidavits, and newspaper clippings more than six inches thick. I knew then that I was about to embark upon one of the great adventures of my life. But I did not know the price to be paid for opening up this seeming Pandora's box of mystical powers. It is only now, a quarter century later, that the full story can be told—and, I hope, understood.

Science and the Paranormal in the Life of a Graduate Student

As a graduate student at the University of California at Berkeley in February 1976, I was aware that a metaphysical war of ideas had been taking place throughout Western culture during the past century. At stake was the very soul of human society. Scientists were probing spiritual realities, and I did not want to miss out on the adventure. I had arranged to sponsor the first major public appearance in the United States of Uri Geller, the sensational Israeli psychic whose extrasensory perception and psychokinetic metal-bending feats, observed under controlled conditions at Stanford Research Institute (now SRI International) had been written about in the prestigious British magazine, *Nature*. Retorts from skeptical detractors were also subsequently published in *Nature* and elsewhere, containing many wild and inaccurate speculations about Geller. But I knew that the debunkers were overreaching. In one instance, "The Amazing Randi" falsely accused my friend, Jean Millay, an SRI laboratory assistant, of being a Geller associate and helping him cheat! Nevertheless, the debunkers had in their camp many powerful figures such as Leon Jaroff, science editor for *Time* magazine. Their accusations of fraud began to shape the debate and detract from the scientific issues.

My world had become a hub of explosive ideas bandied about by charismatic personalities. I had brought Uri Geller literally into the Berkeley physics department at LeConte Hall, where I witnessed him bend the gold ring of physics professor Forrest Mozer, ostensibly using mind power or psychokinesis. Mozer, then a young professor, and I were each standing next to Geller with our eyeballs no more than two feet away from the bending ring. After his ring was returned to him, Mozer held it up and pronounced before the assembled gathering, "If anyone else were to tell me that they had witnessed what I just saw, I would tell them that they were overworked and should take a vacation. But, I did just see this. It really happened."

Shortly thereafter, Mozer did take a vacation. He went to Alaska. When he returned from the cold north, I spoke to him again about the incident we both had witnessed. He informed me that, upon reflection, he had become convinced that Geller actually accomplished the trick through the use of a hidden pliers. The whole thing, he was certain, had been faked.

While I could not disprove the hypothesis that Geller faked his metal-bending demonstrations, I certainly saw no grounds for assuming with such finality that the matter was settled. After all, I had also witnessed Geller bend a ring on the stage of the Zellerbach Auditorium at UC-Berkeley while the ring was held tightly inside the palm of its owner, Jean Barish. Barish, whom I came to know and who was certainly not a confederate with Geller, told me that she could feel the ring bend inside her hand, as Geller cupped his hands over hers. How could he have used a pliers in that circumstance? As further confirmation, the event was videotaped.

I was also present when Uri Geller bent the car key of physicist Edwin May. This key was bent so much that May had to hire a locksmith to fix the key in order to drive his Audi back home. May was severely annoyed by the demonstration. Even so, since that time, he has become a leading researcher within the parapsychology community. Ironically, while gathering data on extrasensory perception and precognition, May still refuses to accept the reality of psychokinesis. As far as he is concerned, the key-bending incident proved nothing, since it did not occur under well controlled, experimental conditions. I accept Ed May as a scientist of integrity. He is honest about his distaste of fraudulent psychokinesis and fair in his demand that it be demonstrated under the strictest standards of empirical science before he feels compelled to acknowledge its existence. Ed has even gone so far as to show how many dozens of experiments that purport to demonstrate psychokinesis can be explained away, either by conventional physical causes or through such exotic mechanisms as precognitive data sorting, which is not psychokinesis at all but rather precognition.

Ed May is correct in pointing out the uncanny relationship between ostensible psychokinesis and precognition. In many instances, it is not so easy to determine whether an event was caused or predicted. In fact, my dissertation chairman at

Berkeley, the noted philosopher of science, Michael Scriven, showed me that the very concept of causation is riddled with problems. In normal language, we assume causation to function like glue, linking one event to the next. Philosophically, however, the concept is vulnerable to much criticism. Our concept of time is also not as neat and tidy as it seems when we sit watching the clock.

My best friend in those heady years was Saul-Paul Sirag, a college dropout who is also a brilliant theoretical physicist. On one occasion, Saul-Paul visited Uri Geller with a surprise of his own. He handed Geller a bean sprout and told him to "make the clock run backwards." Geller, taken off guard, had no opportunity to prepare any sleight of hand. He closed his fist over the bean sprout and concentrated for a few minutes. When he opened up his fist, he handed Saul-Paul a sproutless mung bean!

I found it very interesting that Geller claimed his unusual talents had some connection with UFO-related experiences. The book *Uri*, written by physician and researcher Andrija Puharich, describes how, under hypnosis, Geller recalled contacts with alien intelligences associated with UFOs. Many additional UFO sightings were reported by researchers working with Geller. (All of this is now documented on the Internet at http://www.urigeller.com.)

A similar claim had also been made by the charismatic physicist, Jack Sarfatti, who had written a subsection about the physics of consciousness for the first edition of my book, *The Roots of Consciousness* (1975). Sarfatti had focused on Bell's theorem based on the Einstein-Rosen-Podolsky thought experiment of 1931, in which Einstein had tried to disprove quantum mechanics by arguing that, if followed to its logical conclusion, quantum theory resulted in the absurd result that subatomic particles were in telepathic communication with each other. The data was now in, Sarfatti triumphantly announced, and Einstein was correct with respect to the implications of quantum theory. Particles did seem connected with each other "nonlocally" in a manner reminiscent of telepathy. However, Einstein was wrong to assume that such an absurd conclusion could not have reality. It was established fact. This might be the handle upon which modern science would begin to integrate the paradoxical findings of parapsychology.

Not only did Jack Sarfatti champion the integration of quantum mechanics with the paranormal but he was also the walking embodiment of many mysteries. Descended from medieval cabalistic masters, Sarfatti lived a life filled—like my own—with synchronicity. More than that, however, like Uri Geller, Sarfatti also claimed to have a UFO connection. In a 1974 radio interview I conducted with Jack (later published in *The Roots of Consciousness*), he had the courage to present the story of his own apparent communications with alien beings, dating back to his childhood.

> In 1952 and 1953 when I was about twelve or thirteen years old, I received a phone call . . . in which a mechanical sounding voice at the other end said that it was a computer on board a flying saucer. They wanted to teach me something and would I be willing? This was my free choice. Would I be willing to be taught—to communicate with them?
>
> I remember a shiver going up my spine, because I said, "Hey, man, this is real." Of course, I was a kid . . . but I said, "yes."
>
> I ran out of . . . my apartment in Brooklyn. My mother wasn't there. I ran down to my little buddies on the street, and I said, "Hey, a flying saucer just called me up. Come on over to my house. They're coming and they're going to come through the window and take me away." We were sort of "dead-end kids." This was a gang of kids right out of *The Lords of Flatbush*. We went upstairs and, of course, nothing happened. This was a big joke.

But what's interesting is that my mother remembers this experience very well. It turns out that I had forgotten most of it. This was really something that occurred over several weeks. Apparently what happened, which is completely blanked from my memory but not from hers, was that I continually received phone calls, many phone calls from the same source. My mother says I was walking around really strange. She began to get worried about me. Finally, one day she picked up the phone, and she heard this computer. She remembers the voices. . . . She said, "Leave my boy alone!"

The Jewish mother talking to the flying saucer or whatever they were. My mother has a strong personality. And that was the end of it. We never got a phone call, apparently, after that.

Because of experiences such as those reported by Geller and Sarfatti, which both individuals still believe to this day, I was convinced in 1976 that the mystery of extrasensory perception was inextricably intertwined with the mystery of UFOs. I had written as much in *The Roots of Consciousness* while I was still a graduate student. It seemed self-evident to me, but the idea was threatening to other parapsychological researchers. They had enough trouble with one paranormal field, all by itself, and did not want to suffer the additional stigma of being associated with a second.

CHAPTER 2

MY SAN FRANCISCO EXPERIMENT

Science is the search for truth—it is not a game in which one tries to beat his opponent.

Linus Pauling

Will Owens Produce a UFO for Me?

After meeting Ted Owens at the 1976 Parascience Foundation Conference in England, I decided to design and monitor an experiment with him. I was sufficiently curious that, in spite of the pressures to focus on my doctoral dissertation at Berkeley, I began working directly with this strange character who liked to call himself PK Man. I was particularly interested in the signed statement from Mensa Director of Science and Education, Max L. Fogel, Ph.D., stating that Owens had produced a bona fide UFO sighting on demand. Owens had written to Fogel on

October 23, 1973, claiming that he was about to contact the Space Intelligences and make a UFO appear to police within 100 miles of Cape Charles, Virginia. Two days later, a UFO appeared directly over the head of a Chase City, Virginia, policeman.

This seemed to me to get right to the heart of two questions: did Owens have unusual powers, and was he in communication with UFO entities? So I asked him if he could repeat such a demonstration for me.

I suggested to Owens that he try to replicate this type of demonstration in the San Francisco area. At the time, I did not realize just what I was getting into. Owens wrote back to me on November 7, promising a performance more provocative than a simple UFO appearance:

> In the interest of science, I am going to give a demonstration of my psi force abilities to the people who live in the San Francisco area 100 miles in circumference, using San Francisco as the bull's-eye of my target.
>
> As of today, and daily for the following ninety days, I will telepath to living entities in another dimension for them to appear in the above target area, so that they may be seen by police, scientists, or other responsible observers who are qualified to report the sightings, also for them to cause electromagnetic and magnetic anomalies within the above-described area. It is my intent to produce not one, but at least three major UFO sightings, as described above, within the above-named time period . . . to be reported in the newspapers in order for the experiment to be a valid one.

Owens went on to promise that the San Francisco area would also suffer "power blackouts, perhaps massive ones" and "small and large power failures." He also wrote that alien life-forms would be seen in the target area.

I was a little taken aback by this announcement since I had asked for a much less extravagant, and more easily analyzable, demonstration. I had not expected Owens to devise an *immediate* and major demonstration, as I had merely asked for a UFO appearance. Owens had given me no time to design a properly controlled experiment. When I asked the psychic to defer the test until I had more time to work out an experimental design, he responded that, once he had set his PK forces in motion, nothing could be done to abort their manifestation. It seemed then that I had to play the game by Owens' rules or not at all.

Scientific Considerations: The San Diego Control Group

To begin with, I mailed out announcements to seventy scientists and other interested parties acquainting them with the ninety-day project. This was done in order to establish advance notification and in hopes that it would help me gather information such as news clippings and personal reports regarding any possible events conforming to Owens' predictions.

Because I was a doctoral student at the time, I decided to consult with my research advisors, Charles Tart, a psychologist and parapsychologist at the University of California-Davis, and Dr. James Harder, a noted ufologist and professor of hydraulic engineering at the University of California-Berkeley. They warned me that it would be hard to assess the demonstration even if Owens' predictions proved correct. It was Harder's view that the UFO predictions could easily come about by coincidence, since he had already investigated two cases within the target area during the previous sixty days. It would not be surprising if a few more cropped up between November and February, Harder maintained. Tart's attitude toward the experiment was just as empirical. He urged me to gather data bases regarding electromagnetic and meteorological anomalies in the San Francisco area so that I could objectively evaluate how truly unusual any event reflecting Owens' psychic intentions might be.

Of course, I was not totally oblivious to the great difficulties I had to face in assessing this experiment. Even if a flurry of unusual events did occur in the target area during the time period set, I would need to have some sort of control condition. Therefore, I arranged for a group of graduate students at the University of California at San Diego (UCSD) to send out an announcement similar to my own to seventy local scientists and government officials in their area.

San Diego is a West Coast city with a population close to that of San Francisco. The letter from the UCSD group went out on January 11, more than midway through the experiment. This letter asked the seventy contacts to report any information they might have concerning blackouts, UFO sightings, and electromagnetic effects during the November 17 to February 7 period.

Although the plan was a good one, I realized that this effort would be an imperfect control. I could not rely on the San Diego people to laboriously check the past two months of news reports. And one might expect a larger number of reports to be recorded from San Francisco and its surrounding communities since they have a larger population, although the statistical database of UFO sightings suggests that most occur in rural areas with a low population density. In any case, not one single incident was reported from my San Diego contacts. This result seemed curious in light of what took place in Northern California during this time.

A Power Outage Frightens Me

The San Francisco experiment began formally on November 7, 1976. The first anomaly to strike the Bay Area came about two and one-half weeks later when a wind storm struck the city, resulting in a massive blackout. According to a November 27 *San Francisco*

Examiner story, the winds "gusting up to 60 to 70 miles per hour—the fiercest in years—created havoc and widespread damage within the Bay Area . . . " The story went on to relate that over 200 burglar alarms had been activated by the winds and that power outages had darkened as many as 100,000 homes. The winds had struck at an inopportune time as well. Since it was Thanksgiving weekend, many of the Pacific Gas and Electric's workers were out of town, making immediate repair work difficult to accomplish.

A subsequent report on the storm, published in the *Examiner* two days later, reported that 130,000 customers in the Bay Area had finally had their power restored. So this Bay Area blackout was certainly massive, to use Owens' term. The winds, the *Examiner* explained, had been produced by polar Canadian air streaming in from the north. The National Weather Service was cited as the source of this information.

I remember, vividly, standing outside my office that windy evening. The moonlight highlighted the clouds roiling in the strong winds. I felt then that, if a UFO were to land in San Francisco, I would rather not be present. I was, frankly, frightened by the possibility that I might be dealing with forces beyond my comprehension.

The winds and resultant blackout, if considered within the context of the Owens' demonstration, are interesting. It could certainly be argued that his prediction about a massive blackout had been fulfilled. However, it is hard to accept that there was anything truly unusual or mysterious about this blackout. Just how common are blackouts and such destructive winds in the area?

I began by calculating that for massive blackouts to be considered significant for my purposes, they could occur in the Bay Area only once every five years. I thereupon contacted, by both phone and letter, several Pacific Gas and Electric (PG & E) officials, hoping that they could provide me with the necessary information and statistics. Unfortunately, I was uniformly unsuccessful at obtaining any information on the history or rate of blackouts in the San Francisco area from them. It should also be noted that the November blackout was caused by winds and was not an electromagnetic effect as Owens had promised. I pointed this out to Owens, as he was eagerly taking credit for the mishap, but the psychic responded by claiming that the Space Intelligences had obviously produced the winds. He also offered the flimsy explanation that the blackout occurred at the worst possible time, on a holiday weekend, and that this was a trademark the SIs had used in order to focus attention on their work.

In any case, there have been few comparable power blackouts in the San Francisco area in the twenty years subsequent to that time. So, with the benefit of hindsight, I would say that this was a mildly significant event—almost meaningless by itself and interesting only in the context of the larger Owens story.

I soon figured out a way to test Owens' claims. The psychic was maintaining that the gales must have been unexpected since PG & E would have kept reserve repair crews on the alert had they been aware of the upcoming winds. This seemed to be a reasonable point to me because PG & E does have its own weather department. So to explore the possibility that the winds were psychically mediated, I contacted the National Weather Service and inquired about the frequency of gale winds in the San Francisco area. The National Weather Service (NWS) responded on December 1, but their expert opinion did nothing to support Owens' interpretation. The NWS merely pointed out that winds strong enough to cause damage occur in the Bay Area several times a year. The gusts that struck San Francisco on November 27, they added, occur about once every two years. Furthermore, they informed me, the winds that had caused the blackout had been forecast and were due to natural conditions.

It is hard to judge whether there is any significance in the fact that winds expected only once in two years struck right in the middle of Owens' demonstration. Again we are faced with the possibility that he may have somehow intensified winds that were already in the making. But, as I pointed out in my subsequent, privately published report on this experiment, "It was clear that if Owens wanted to count this demonstration as a success, he would have to produce greater quality and quantity of phenomena."

UFO Sighting with Multiple Witnesses, Photographed and Videotaped

Owens' chance for another demonstration came during the first week of December. On December 3, he told me over the phone that one of his predicted UFO sightings was about to occur within the next few days. He made a point of reminding me that the sighting would be seen by many reputable witnesses and even be reported on the front page of a local newspaper.

The fulfillment of this specific prediction came on December 8, when the best documented UFO sighting ever reported from the Bay Area startled hundreds of onlookers. Since Owens had warned me of the upcoming sighting, this incident serves as a conceptual replication of the Cape Charles UFO demonstration for researcher Max Fogel, which is just what I wanted in the first place. The story of the sighting made front page headlines in the *Berkeley Gazette* on December 10. The accompanying story read:

> Stephan Poleskie, who, wind permitting, creates aerial art by flying a stunt plane overhead while leaving trails of colored smoke, was startled Wednesday while performing over Cal-State Sonoma. Poleskie suddenly became aware of a circular white object only 1,000 feet away. The event was also captured on Channel 9 TV cameras, and Poleskie said videotape reruns check out and confirm the existence of a curious copilot in the sky. Poleskie, a visiting art professor at UC-Berkeley, may have attracted a vast new audience for his unique art forms.

There was at least one minor inaccuracy in the story. It is not true that Channel 9 TV had filmed the UFO. The object had been videotaped by one of the onlookers, Bill Morehouse, chairman of the art department at California State College at Sonoma (now known as Sonoma State University). He subsequently lent the tape to the television station, which had shown the footage on its nightly news program.

Even so, the UFO had been widely viewed and filmed. Although it had been videotaped for only a few seconds, the craft was in view of the witnesses for ten to twenty minutes. Hundreds of students and other onlookers attending the aerial art show had observed the UFO as well.

Stephan Poleskie told reporters that the object had been within his air zone at an altitude of from 500 to 3,000 feet above ground. At first, Poleskie thought that the UFO, which was hovering when he first spotted it, was a helicopter. He rejected this theory when he noticed that the craft didn't have a rotor or pontoons. The UFO didn't seem to be any larger than Poleskie's own plane, which sported a wingspan of seventeen feet. The object had first appeared hovering in one location of the sky for about ten minutes and had then reappeared in another location in relation to Poleskie's plane. Yet no one could recall actually seeing the object move between the two points. And after about fifteen minutes, several witnesses claimed that they had seen the mysterious object disappear into thin air.

I was impressed by the incident, especially since UFO sightings witnessed and videotaped by so many onlookers are extremely rare and were even more so in 1976, before the advent of camcorders. Of course, I was intrigued by the possibility that the sighting directly related to Owens' prediction. I wrote in my report:

> I would estimate the probability of such an excellent
> sighting within the space-time limits of the experiment
> to be considerably less than one in a hundred. This

estimate is based on the fact that in the past twenty-five years no such sightings are known to have taken place within the target area. When one considers that such well-documented sightings have not been reported elsewhere in the world, the probabilities become much smaller. Such an estimate, of course, is predicated upon assumptions that will remain unverified until either further research establishes a reliable data base or the UFOs make themselves publicly known.

It was an unusual sighting as well as a stunning one. The fact that it occurred so soon after Owens' specific prediction is especially noteworthy. Now, with the advent of camcorders, filmings of presumed UFOs are much more common. I have a shelf full of videotaped documentaries on this subject. Still, they are rare enough, and I do not know of another sighting as dramatic as this one in the San Francisco Bay Area in the decades following.

This event crystallized my thinking with regard to Owens' claims. I could not determine whether he predicted this UFO sighting or caused it through psychokinesis or arranged for it by telepathically communicating with alien Space Intelligences. But it was clear to me that such a dramatic event was no mere coincidence. It had to involve some combination of the aforementioned three factors.

Short, Grey-Skinned Men with Elongated Skulls and No Hair

In his original communication to me, Owens had predicted three major UFO sightings. He also specifically forecast that alien life-forms would be seen in the target area as well. Just a few days before Owens' February 7 deadline, a second major UFO case came to light in the San Francisco area, one that indeed involved the sighting of an alien life-form.

On February 2, the *Concord Transcript* announced that a bizarre UFO abduction had been reported by a local resident. Concord, a quiet little city east of Berkeley, is well within the fifty mile target radius centering on San Francisco. The *Transcript* reported:

> A 24-year-old Concord man told police early today he was whisked away and examined by five-foot grey beings from a flying saucer.
>
> According to the report, he left a Willow Pass Road restaurant about 4:10 A.M. and was confronted by two short, grey-skinned men with enlarged skulls, no hair and black pupils.
>
> The next thing he knew, he said, was that he had been transported to a field at Willow Creek Elementary School. There he said he was facing a circular craft with a ladder extending toward him.
>
> Suddenly, he was inside the ship. While there, he said he stuck his left hand in a chamber and "all sorts of lights went off."
>
> He asked what was happening and telepathically he was told the aliens were on a "mission to study life habits" on Earth. The beings also noted that their craft was from a larger ship located outside the planet's atmosphere.
>
> The next thing he knew, according to the report, he was outside an apartment complex on Mohr Lane.
>
> For about 15 minutes, he said, he was unable to move.
>
> He called the Concord Police Department at 5:33 A.M.
>
> The Oakland center of the Federal Aviation Administration noted it had no reports this morning of unidentified flying objects.

By coincidence (or was it synchronicity?), I happened to be visiting in the Concord area on the day that the story hit the press. The report hadn't been picked up by any other news media, so before the case could be polluted by publicity, I contacted

Professor James Harder who made arrangements, through the cooperation of the Concord Police Department, to visit the witness. Harder, who has specialized in investigating abduction and close-encounter cases, was impressed with the witness.

The abductee turned out to be a married salesman who made his home in the Concord area. He told us the same story as had been printed in the *Transcript*. He claimed to have had no previous psychic experiences, and had read nothing on the subject of UFOs. Unfortunately, the case could not be further investigated because the witness was wary of publicity, and he resisted Harder's suggestion that hypnotic regression might help him to remember more about his frightening experience.

Despite the unsatisfactory resolution of the case, this report is disturbingly impressive in one respect. Many abduction cases are recorded in the United States each year, and it is surprising how many of the witnesses involved tend to describe very similar entities. The "short, grey-skinned men with elongated skulls [and] no hair," as reported by the Concord salesman, also have been reported from New Mexico, Arizona and New York.

In 1978, long before Whitley Strieber's popular books, such as *Communion*, created a new wave of interest in abductions, my associate D. Scott Rogo helped investigate a series of related UFO close encounters and abductions that took place in Southern California. Several of his witnesses said they were abducted by small, dome-headed, hairless entities. If the Concord witness was genuinely ignorant of UFOs and UFO encounter cases, then the parallels between his report and the many others extant in the literature of the field is remarkable.

Kicking the Hell out of the San Francisco Area

The blackout of November 27 and the two aforementioned UFO encounters, one, indeed, involving an alien life-form, were the major events conforming to Owens' predictions—not quite as spectacular as Owens had boasted but intriguing enough to suggest that something unusual was happening in the Bay Area during the course of the ninety-day test. Also, because Owens had stated that many odd things would occur in the target zone during his ninety-day exhibition, I kept careful note of any anomalies occurring there from November to February. Several did, and these represent an added bit of evidence that Owens was making good on his promise.

On January 7, for instance, as the experiment headed into its final days, a series of earthquakes struck. If these were Owens' doing at the close of his exhibition, the psychic was going out with a bang! Eight quakes rattled the Bay Area in rapid succession, one of which was 5.0 on the Richter scale, the strongest recorded in eleven years. The epicenter of the temblors was located only twenty miles east of San Francisco itself.

It must be remembered that Owens never specifically predicted an earthquake as part of the demonstration. However, I was reluctant to rule out the possibility that the quakes were somehow related to the San Francisco experiment. "Owens himself may not be totally conscious of the phenomenon that are produced during his demonstrations," I noted in my report. After all, a major, unpredicted earthquake had struck in Texas during Owens' demonstration there in 1974, and I found the parallel intriguing. There were also some personal interactions between the two of us during the period immediately preceding the quakes that suggested to me a relationship between the quakes and the psychic. My notes from the period read:

> On December 31, 1976, Owens became furious with me during a telephone conversation in which I told him that, after reading through the files of his

past cases, it was clear to me that he "sometimes failed." He got very angry and promised to "kick the hell out of the San Francisco area." Owens also telephoned me on January 7, 1977, several hours before the earthquakes. The message that he called was recorded on my answering device, but I did not speak to him until several days later.

Had Owens told me on the telephone that he had phoned me on the seventh to warn me about the earthquakes, I would have been somewhat impressed. However, he admitted that he did not specifically know that an earthquake was coming. He did feel that "something" was going to happen very soon as a special message to him from the Space Intelligences. It is a totally open question at this point as to whether that something was the earthquakes.

Another odd coincidence, possibly related to the demonstration, occurred during this time as well. Sometime in early December, Owens had told me over the phone that a giant UFO was en route to San Francisco. While remaining invisible to the eye, it would cover the entire target zone. The result would be "crazy phenomena" all over the place. "Things are going to look like a three-ring circus," the psychic warned.

Since San Francisco can be a crazy town anyway and Berkeley, for instance, is commonly referred to as Berzerkeley, this prediction was less than overwhelmingly impressive. Yet indeed many people started acting peculiarly soon after Owens' announcement—just as they had done in Chicago and Cleveland during prior demonstrations (as described in chapter 5). A crime wave that had been steadily rising in the area reached its peak during the ninety-day experiment. The city's crime statistics were so bad that they were even reported in *Newsweek* on December 20. A rash of bomb threats against PG & E installations in the area were made, and some of these threats were carried out. The bombings were the work of the New World Liberation Front, which also stooped to threatening members of San Francisco's Board of Supervisors. On December 20, a hijacking drama was staged at San Francisco International Airport. And for the first time in history, a San Francisco county sheriff, Richard Hongisto, was given a jail sentence for refusing to obey a court order.

Of course, none of these events can be solely attributed to Owens or the Space Intelligences. People are a strange lot and all too often do strange things. It does seem that the incidents listed above are odder than what might be expected to occur in any large metropolis during a ninety-day period, although this is impossible to measure with precision. One item, however, did catch my special attention: a newspaper account of a hairdresser in Walnut Creek named Owen who experienced ostensible poltergeist phenomena in his house. This seeming coincidence of names also occurred in the Chase City, Virginia, demonstration in which a UFO was seen by a radio dispatcher named Owen.

Was my experiment a success or a failure? The answer to this question is as oblique today as it was twenty-two years ago when the experiment was first initiated. The most impressive aspect of the case was Owens' UFO prediction. This forecast the Poleskie sighting so precisely that one cannot help be impressed by it. In fact, the whole San Francisco experiment is, in one respect, tinged with irony. It could be argued that it was a failure, since it did not come off exactly as Owens had predicted. What did come off extremely well was Owens' one UFO prediction and its subsequent fulfillment. And this was all I had wanted in the first place. So I got what I wanted, but only as part of a ninety-day ordeal. I will say that, in the context of Owens' entire career, the strange phenomena observed during the San Francisco experiment seem entirely normal.

For me, the experiment was more of an initiation ceremony than a controlled demonstration of Owens' powers—something of a preparation for encountering Owens' final gift. And I survived, all the wiser for the experience, although my interest in this case began to trigger concerns among my University of California faculty members about their own professional survival.

My official opinion about the San Francisco experiment is contained in a privately distributed sixty-page report on Owens that I wrote shortly after the end of the demonstration:

> It would be rash to draw any solid conclusions from the Ted Owens material at this time. The historical material is very suggestive of the possibility that Owens does in fact wield enormous psi powers that could possibly be used for significant practical application. While the events that Owens predicted for his ninety-day demonstration period in San Francisco did not happen precisely as Owens suggested they would, the data nevertheless strongly warrant further investigation of Owens' claims. This investigation should be oriented to further practical applications of Owens' apparent abilities and also a deeper theoretical understanding of the phenomena.

Following the San Francisco experiment, the earlier Owens' demonstrations in England and the snowstorm that ended the California drought, I became highly motivated to dig more deeply into the mystery of Ted Owens. I began a process of interviewing him about his life history. His story will be presented in the next two chapters.

CHAPTER 3

TED OWENS RECALLS HIS EARLY YEARS

The irrationality of a thing is no argument
against its existence, rather a condition of it.
                                        Friedrich Nietzsche

"They Called Me 'Tee' in Those Days"

"I was born in Bedford, Indiana, on February 10, 1920," Ted Owens told me. "My family was pretty much of typical Midwestern stock." His father, Harry T. Owens, Sr., was a forceful man who had served in the U.S. Navy during World War I as a chief pharmacist mate. He was also an amateur boxer. His forthrightness is well illustrated in a story Owens liked to tell about him. While in France during the war, the elder Owens met a marine who had been wounded in combat. He recognized him instantly as an old school chum. Harry was so zealous in his devotion to duty that he convinced the marine to exchange gear and IDs so that he, himself, could continue fighting the Germans. The marine was somehow able to bluff his way through as a pharmacist mate, but Harry was gassed while on patrol and ended up being sent back to the States despite the masquerade.

Owens' mother was a no-nonsense type of individual who liked to socialize all the time. Ted, however, was raised by his paternal grandparents, whom he called Grandpa and Queenie. The reason for his living with them was a sad one. After his discharge, Harry Owens became a gambler and was away from home for long periods of time, sometimes remaining in Bedford only one month out of the year. This situation, aggravated by the fact that Ted couldn't get along with his mother, made home life unbearable. His mother often took out her frustrations on the lad, so Ted eventually began living with his grandparents.

Owens' grandparents were no strangers to psychic phenomena. They had been raised in poor surroundings and, like so many Midwesterners during the bleak years of the depression, often engaged in parlor-room psychic games. Queenie's own mother was a whiz at the Ouija board and was known for her ability to find lost objects and predict deaths, while Grandpa Owens was a dowser. He taught his grandson the fine art.

"He taught me as a small child in the yard," Owens recounted in his unpublished notes about his early years. "When Grandpa finally became rich and built his own home, he located his own well enclosed in the back of the home. He found it himself with a twig. He'd go out and find wells for other people, friends of his, whenever they wanted him to. He also could talk to dogs and animals. He taught me how to talk to dogs and animals."

Owens likes to tell the story of how his grandfather cured an Indian employee of compulsive wife beating. One day Grandpa Owens took the employee out of town. Nobody knew where they had gone; the two men simply vanished. When they returned a few days later, the Indian never beat his wife again, gave up drinking, and was devoted to his employer. No one ever discovered what had happened. But it was clear that Grandpa Owens was a man of forceful charisma.

It was while still a child that Owens discovered his own psychic powers. These manifested, by his own claim, in the form of a series of spontaneous levitations. According to Owens:

> One day, Queenie took me to a house where she wanted to visit some woman. I was about four years old and was playing out in the yard. I was standing outside of the house when suddenly I began to float up the side of the house, way up to the top of the house. Then I floated back down again; of course, back then I was so young I had no idea of time. So I don't know how long it took. I definitely floated up in the air. When I got back down, I knocked on the door and told Queenie about it, and she laughed and thought I was making it up.
>
> This same phenomenon happened again when I was about thirteen years old. I was at the country club that was just outside of Bedford where there was a swimming pool. It was in broad daylight. I climbed up on the ten-foot board and did a swan dive up in the air, spreading my arms out. Then I didn't come down. I was so astounded and amazed I couldn't believe it, but I kept my arms outstretched and it was the most wonderful, exhilarating feeling I'd ever had in my life.
>
> I stayed up there what seemed like a long time. Then finally down I went into the water. I might have thought it was my imagination because I couldn't figure it out. I knew that what goes up comes down. But when I climbed out of the pool, Bob Armstrong came up, a redheaded kid with freckles, and he said to

me, "Tee." They called me "Tee" in those days. "I knew you could do card tricks, but how did you stay up in the air all that time?"

Owens also developed an invisible playmate during these years. Unlike what most people interested in psychic phenomena believe, there is nothing necessarily psychic about these apparitions. Recent research has shown that they are mental constructs projected by creative and usually bright children in order to practice learning and verbal skills. Owens' playmate, though, wasn't the typical childlike companion or oversized animal that usually develops. His playmate was an adult, redheaded woman whose job it was to help her young charge learn how to read. Owens soon developed a prodigious ability to read as a result of these interactions and soon astounded his parents with his precociousness. Even at seven, Owens' appetite for reading material usually focused on such fringe topics as hypnosis, witchcraft, voodoo, and other related fields. UFOs were a topic that wasn't within his purview probably because UFO books began to proliferate only after the second World War.

"Even when I was a student at Duke University twenty years later," reported Owens, "I had no notion at all of the Space Intelligences. In fact, as far back as 1965, my son Rick told me that the UFOs were over our home in Washington, DC. He suggested then that it was UFOs I was in contact with instead of 'nature' as I then thought. But I told him he was crazy."

Owens' reading influenced him in the direction of stage hypnosis, an occupation he took up as a teenager by giving demonstrations at parties and gatherings. When he wasn't hypnotizing people, he spent much of his teen years carousing with a gang of toughs he had organized to protect themselves from other juvenile gangs which, sad to say, even then afflicted the streets of so many American towns and cities. Fist fights, gang fights, and homemade blowguns were familiar to Owens, who must have been thankful that his father had often instructed him in the manly art of boxing. Ted always knew where to throw a punch for a quick knockout.

Despite his precociousness, Owens did poorly when he entered Bedford High School and was often the bane of his teachers. But over and above his lack of academic inclination, he did develop a passion for physics and often managed to do well in it while flunking or barely passing everything else. He graduated, in fact, only through a bit of improvised blackmail when he caught his English teacher, who was in a position to prevent his graduation, in a compromising situation. The school basketball team had gone on strike, and the distraught teacher, aggravated because they were headed for the state championship, waylaid the team captain in the schoolyard, fell to her knees, and begged the young man to continue with the season. Owens had witnessed the whole mortifying scene and had the foresight to photograph it! Later, he showed the picture to the teacher with the suggestion that a story about the incident might be of interest to the local paper. A quick deal resulted. The teacher got the negative and Owens got his diploma.

By the time of his graduation, Owens' parents had split up. His mother moved to Evanston, Illinois, and his father left town as well. In order to help put one of his brothers through school, Owens also moved to Evanston where he started working at a candy factory while studying shorthand and typing at a business school. He eventually returned to Bedford in 1940 but didn't stay long. World War II was now raging in Europe, and his father urged him to enlist in the Navy. Owens took the advice and served from 1941 to 1945. Boxing and demonstrations of hypnosis were his main pastimes during these world-wrecking years, but as the Navy had an electronics school at Purdue University in Lafayette, Indiana, he was soon transferred there for special training. This wasn't unusual for the times. During the war, the armed forces had such a need for specialized skills that they often sent servicemen to American universities for such training.

Electronics was a young and growing field during the fitful 1940s, and radar, a recent British invention, had just been released to the States for wartime use. While at Purdue, Owens became involved with organizing entertainment events before being shipped to New Caledonia in the Pacific in 1943, where he experienced another of his spontaneous levitations.

"One day I was outside on the ship's deck," Owens recalled. "I climbed up on a hatch. There must have been fifty to sixty men up there, lying around looking at the ocean. I gave a little jump to go down two or three feet off the hatch—and instead of coming down, I went up into the air and just sort of floated. All of the sailors were pointing and saying 'Look at that!' I was just floating and finally came down near the rail some distance away. It was really weird. I'll never forget it. It was definitely levitation. But I don't know what caused it. The sailors' eyes were all bulging out. I lost all sense of time, just as I had done when it happened in Bedford."

Admittedly, these accounts of spontaneous levitation, not simple out-of-body experiences, stretch Owens' credibility. This is probably because such a phenomenon is extremely rare; but it is not unknown in the annals of psychic science. Saint Joseph of Copertino (1603-1663), while a priest in the little Italian town for which he was named, was often seen to spontaneously levitate in full light, and hundreds of onlookers testified to these miracles. These spiritual flights were frequent, and the testimony substantiating their authenticity was a key factor in the Catholic Church's decision to canonize him. Saint Theresa of Avila (1515-1582) was also seen to levitate on more than one occasion. In our own day, the late and beloved Padre Pio, a priest at the Capuchin Monastery of Madonna delle Grazie at San Giovanni Rotondo in Foggia, Italy, was often seen to levitate. For some reason, these cases may strike the reader as more inherently credible than Owens'. Saint Joseph of Copertino, Saint Theresa, and Padre Pio were all holy people of courageous virtue, and their supernatural feats were recorded in a milieu of mysticism and mystical religion in which the supernatural doesn't seem too out of place. But if these great saints could levitate, there is no logical reason to doubt that some of us living secular lives could similarly be endowed with this same ability. Olivier Leroy, a Roman Catholic writer and expert on the subject, documented several cases of spontaneous levitation in his celebrated volume, *Levitation*, in which he cites cases recorded among primitive peoples, shamans, saints, and psychics.

"I Became Conscious . . . I Had Psychokinetic Abilities of My Own"

While in New Caledonia, Owens began taking an academic interest in the paranormal, reading up on the subject. Soon he was doing mind reading as well as demonstrating hypnosis. His apparent success at controlling his extrasensory perception (ESP) led the young serviceman to write Dr. J. B. Rhine, whose name was then synonymous with the study of ESP. Having gone to Duke University in 1927, by 1935, Rhine was well into the study of everything from telepathy to precognition; he had established a laboratory and was publishing a scientific journal. The result of this correspondence was Rhine's suggestion that perhaps Owens should come to Duke at Durham, North Carolina, after his discharge. He also gave Owens some practical hints on how to conduct more controlled demonstrations of his abilities.

Owens didn't immediately make it to Durham after his release from the Navy in 1945. First he went home to Bedford but soon decided to head down to North Carolina. His timing couldn't have been better. Rhine was working on a new book, *The Reach of the Mind*, eventually published in 1947, and needed someone who could take dictation, do typing, and transcribe wax recording cylinders. Owens left for Durham with the assurance that a job would be waiting for him, and although finding that his mentor could be difficult at times, the young man soon developed a deep affection and respect for Rhine. Aside from his work as an assistant for the Duke parapsychologist, Owens was looked upon as a friend.

Although Rhine often challenged his assistant with impromptu ESP tests, he did not seem to have taken much of an interest in seriously studying the psychic powers Owens had apparently developed. Owens took part as a "sender" in some of Rhine's experiments, but he was never one of his star subjects and he is not mentioned in any of Rhine's books. There may have been an underlying strain between them as well, since Owens was openly critical of Rhine's attitude that hypnosis couldn't be used to enhance ESP ability. Owens' opinion, which he forthrightly stated, was that Rhine had simply been using a lousy hypnotist! But even if Rhine didn't formally test Owens for ESP ability, the young man's PK ability made a startling comeback during his Durham years.

"It was at that time that I became conscious of the fact that I had psychokinetic abilities of my own," Owens told me. "I remember one night in particular. I was sitting there studying in this little room that I rented. I noticed a handkerchief on the table to my left moving clear across the table by itself. The next morning when I woke up, I was wide awake, and the front of my bed was about two or three feet up in the air. My body was slanted and then the bed went down again. I immediately jumped out, got dressed and went to tell Dr. Rhine about it."

Rhine's reaction to Owens' story isn't a matter of public record, so we don't know what he said to Owens. However, during Owens' Duke years, PK often occurred in his presence and was witnessed by various workers at the Duke Parapsychology Laboratory. The lab had a rich crop of bright and dedicated young workers during these years, people who went on to conduct much useful research in the field of experimental parapsychology. Few of them today, though, are willing to discuss the Owens matter.

Both D. Scott Rogo, a parapsychologist who worked with me on the Owens case, and I have tried to validate some of Owens' claims stemming from these years by questioning some of the Duke workers who were there during Owens' stay, but none of them were able to cite any specific example of PK they personally witnessed. However, one of these researchers, who was openly critical of Owens, did admit that "odd things" often happened when Owens was around but refused to elaborate any further. I was urged not to discuss the Rhine lab in connection with Owens. Clearly the Rhines were embarrassed about having once been associated with someone who later became as flamboyant and dubious as Ted Owens.

A Mischievous Spirit Called "Big Lornie"

While at Duke, Owens discovered another aspect of his psychic abilities—making contact with the dead. In retrospect, the following incidents were probably due to Owens' own mind and not to the entity he had conjured up. Through the help of Rhine, Owens had become a psychology student at Duke, and it was during this time that he found himself in contact with a mischievous spirit whom he started calling "Big Lornie." Here is Owens' story in his own words:

> I first discovered Big Lornie when I was a student at Duke. The light I was reading by kept going on and off, on and off. I had a little seance there in the room by myself. I said, "If there is a friendly spirit here, will you please come to me and identify yourself?" Well, what showed up in my mind was this beautiful woman who said that, when she was twenty-nine

years old, she had committed suicide over a love affair. She said that she would stay with me and help me. Then all kinds of things began to happen. I had a bottle of shoe polish with the top tightly screwed down. When I went in my closet in the morning all the shoe polish was on the floor. The top was still screwed on and none of the polish was on the sides of the bottle at all.

I realized then that there were some odd things going on that certainly were paranormal. I couldn't figure out what was causing them. Sometimes on dates, my girl and I would be sitting on the couch and the TV picture and sound would go off and come back on again. I'd walk down the street and all of the street-lights would go off on the side where I was walking—but not on the other side. Once I called up my girl at the sorority house and she said, "Ted, the minute you called up here, all the lights in the sorority house went off." This went on all the time.

I would go on dates and girls' earrings would disappear off of their ears. Another girl would have the pens and pencils disappear out of her purse when she went to the movies with me. One girl went into a movie with tight gloves on. She came out of the movie and the gloves were gone—and she hadn't taken them off. Things were vanishing.

It was so marked that neither J. B. Rhine nor his wife could figure out if I was doing it subconsciously or if I was stealing these things. They wondered if I could get earrings off of a girl's ears without her knowing I had done it. Or was it some form of psychic phenomena? The phenomena kept happening with these people right there by our side. To this day it is still happening.

Owens stayed at Duke until 1947 when he learned that his grandfather had only three months to live. He went back to Bedford where he stayed until the elderly man's death and then went on to Texas to visit one of his brothers. While in Houston, Owens got a job with a construction company, and it was here that he learned he possessed another psychic ability. Owens discovered he had a peculiar control over lightning. He first publicly demonstrated this singular ability one day while talking with some of his fellow employees. A little boy was looking on. They were openly skeptical of his claim so Owens decided to prove it by pointing his finger into the sky and invoking Big Lornie. Immediately, a lightning bolt struck suspiciously close to the company office!

"One secretary fainted," reported Owens. "The other had to go home. The boy's eyes were reeling around in his head like marbles in a skillet. It scared the hell out of them all."

Owens changed jobs soon afterwards and became chief clerk with a railroad company. He also married his first wife, Pat, whom he had known at Duke. Pat was a brilliant woman who had lied about her age in order to enroll at the university. She was much younger than Owens; in fact, she was still a teenager. Pat's parents had never approved of Owens, but the enterprising young man convinced Pat to rendezvous with him in Houston. They were soon married, but the relationship was hardly an ideal one. These were hard times, and Pat couldn't cope with Owens' frequent bouts of poverty. She was born of a wealthy family and often deserted her husband when things got tough. But things changed in 1951. Owens, then thirty-one, benefited from an inheritance his wife received from a rich uncle, and the couple moved to Chicago where he studied judo and music. A one-time amateur drummer, Owens now took up music professionally and organized his own jazz group.

It looked like things were finally going well financially, but the marriage still didn't work out. Ultimately, it ended in divorce but only after two children had been born. Owens eventually remarried and after a while took up residence in Philadelphia with his new wife, Martha, and their newborn baby.

"Rain Came Down in Buckets"

Owens long claimed that he had the ability to use PK to control the weather. He discovered this power long before he had any conscious inkling that the Space Intelligences even existed. The key date was in 1963 when Owens, who had developed a knife-throwing act, was living with Martha in Phoenix, Arizona, where they had taken up residence in a huge old house. It was blisteringly hot that summer, and sometimes the sticky heat rose to 112 degrees Fahrenheit in the shade. Owens and his wife were lounging around one afternoon, wondering what could be done about the weather, when Ted remembered something he had heard during his time at Duke. In a discussion among the parapsychology laboratory workers, someone had brought up the subject of Native American rain dances and their alleged efficacy. Since he had no reason to doubt that PK could be used to produce precipitation, Owens figured that perhaps he possessed the same ability.

As these thoughts came back to him, it dawned on him what he should do. He told Martha that a sudden idea had entered his head, and he went out into the yard behind the house, pointed his finger at the sky, envisioned lightning emanating from it and projected the words "rain, storm, lightning" into the air.

Martha looked on sympathetically, and after Owens engaged in his little exercise for a few minutes, asked him if that was "all there was to it." Owens reported:

> It wasn't too long before the sky grew black, and they had a knock-down, drag-out storm, with lightning hitting everywhere and rain pouring down. It hadn't

rained in months there. So I said to Martha that, on a semiscientific basis, the storm didn't prove anything because it could have been coincidence. So I'll have to wait some more. So I waited two or three days until it got hot and sunny again, and then I went out and repeated my demonstration. I also wrote to the newspapers about my plan, but of course they ignored me.

"Rain came down in buckets," according to Owens, but this time his wife's reaction wasn't awe. She had hung up her wash earlier in the day and was not delighted that her husband's storm had thoroughly drenched it.

Owens, on the other hand, was so pleased with the result that he decided to engage in a series of weather control experiments. He said of these:

> The upshot of the whole thing is that in two weeks I produced I don't know how many storms. I even began to get special effects. For instance, on one occasion there wasn't enough lightning, so I told some friends that I would increase the lightning as the storm ran its course. I superimposed the words, "lightning, more lightning" on the mental imagery I was casting up into the sky. Then there was lightning everywhere. In the paper the next day, they headlined a story about the storm, "Lightning Aerial Display."

But the sudden lightning displays weren't the only odd event of the storm. As the lightning was zigzagging across the sky, there was a sudden knocking at the door. It was the landlord who lived nearby and he had some nephews with him. He seemed excited, and he rushed to see if his tenants were all right for, during the storm, he had seen lightning actually strike the Owens' home on three separate instances.

As he traveled over the country during the next four years, Owens often tried to control storms or produce hurricanes in the Atlantic. He also began diligently informing the U.S. State Department about his apparent abilities and their potential use. It was, in fact, this very discovery that eventually led him to go to Washington, DC. This was a crucial turning point—and set the pattern that was to last for a quarter century until Owens' death in 1987—of persistent, yet unsuccessful, efforts to interest the U.S. government in working with Owens' bizarre talents. For Owens, it became something of a crusade—and one that eventually took on a dark and nasty quality.

Owens' apparent success at storm-raising as well as his lightning control made a deep impression on him. He wrote:

> Electrified by my success, and knowing for certain that I had something, I wrote to government agencies and many important people, but to no avail. No one would believe me. We moved then to Los Angeles, also in the middle of a drought, and I made some tremendous storms there. Then I determined we would go to Washington, DC, and take my weird ability directly to the government agencies there. On our way, we drove through Las Vegas, and I made a terrible storm there, just to keep in practice. It nearly wrecked the town. Now, I figure that somehow I had managed to contact the essence of the intelligence behind Nature herself.
>
> While resting in Myrtle Beach, an idea occurred to me. A hurricane had appeared off Florida, so I called my kids together, drew a map and a course for the hurricane to follow (using Southern Florida as a bull's-eye) or else no one would believe me later on, and wrote to government agencies and scientists about what I was doing. To the amazement of our family, the hurricane (Cleo) followed my map to the letter. If it would start to

deviate from its target, I would communicate with Nature and get it back onto the course I had prescribed. During that season, I successfully directed three hurricanes to our improvised target!

Of course, all of these early accounts are anecdotal. I have only Owens' word that these events did occur. If it were not for the later, documented demonstrations, it would be easy to simply dismiss Owens as a braggart or a crackpot.

"The Best Decision I've Made in My Life"

In his 1969 book, *How to Contact Space People*, Owens gave evidence of his penchant for obtaining documentation of his various feats. He included reprints of four affidavits testifying to his predictive powers. Unfortunately, these documents often did not contain enough information to be of much value. Pat Shannon, a notary public in Los Angeles, validated the accuracy of five of Owens' predictions. She stated, for instance, that he "predicted the '1966 East Coast Fireball' which would fly over Philadelphia," but she did not state (a) the date this was supposed to occur, (b) when his statement was made or (c) Owens' precise wording. Similarly, Shannon testified that Owens "predicted violent lightning in the city of Philadelphia" and that "three such storms occurred within a few days and weeks." Unfortunately, Shannon did not note the date of this prediction, and further weakening the case, lightning storms are not uncommon in the East, especially in winter.

Mrs. Zelda Hansell, an Ardmore, Pennsylvania, resident and friend of Owens, was more specific in a December 1966 statement she provided for the psychic. She covered some of the same predictions as noted by Shannon but was more detailed about them. She asserted that Owens predicted a major hurricane five days before one formed in the Atlantic, a major earthquake in California eleven days prior to the event, and an attack on the U.S. fleet in

Vietnam that came to pass two days later. Mrs. Hansell included the dates for all of these 1966 predictions. Another earthquake prediction for California was made by Owens on April 28, 1965, and was recorded by Mrs. Jeanne Mangels, his Washington, DC, landlady, who supplied him with a signed affidavit to that effect. The earthquake struck the next day.

On May 9, 1967, Owens received a letter from Jim Moseley, editor of *Saucer News* magazine, asking him to produce a UFO event to herald a flying saucer convention slated for New York. Owens wrote back on May 10 stating that he would contact the Space Intelligences and that he was "going to ask them to bring about another Great Power Blackout or something on that scale." Owens wrote again on May 19 and repeated his claim but added that he was asking the Space Intelligences to produce a blackout anytime before June 22.

When a local power failure and resulting blackout struck a section of New York City shortly afterwards, Owens wrote a third time, informing Moseley that this event was only the beginning of the Space Intelligences' work. On June 5, well within Owens' deadline, a major blackout crippled the East Coast. The source of this mishap stemmed from a mysterious power failure in the Pennsylvania-New Jersey-Maryland Interconnection, a linkage that at the time was regarded as a model for electric power nets.

Owens also found himself engaging in more weather control projects at the same time. For instance, in 1967, he wrote to Timothy Green Beckley, the editor of *Searchlight* magazine, claiming that he had asked the Space Intelligences to produce three simultaneous hurricanes during the year. This had happened only five times since the 1880s. But it happened again in 1967. Owens also made this prediction to the U.S. Hurricane Center in Coral Gables, Florida. Hurricanes Beulah, Chloe, and Daphne were all active over one weekend in September, thus fulfilling a claim that had low probability of being realized.

By 1968, Owens' power of weather control had reached a peak, and in that year, he gave several documented demonstrations of his abilities. This was a year when the psychic made a number of successful predictions about weather activities in the East.

Sometime in early June, for instance, Owens wrote to the director of the National Hurricane Center in Florida informing him that he was about to bring a hurricane to Philadelphia, where the psychic was then living. The hurricane didn't materialize immediately, but by June 13 a freak storm stunned the city. The *Philadelphia Daily News* headlined their story on the storm, "Baxter Gives Storm Once-In-A-Century Rating" and reported that the city's water commissioner, Samuel Baxter, had announced that a storm of such intensity occurs only once in a hundred years. Over $100,000,000 worth of damage was caused by this storm.

It is not clear to me what Owens' motives were in these early years. In fact, I doubt if he knew himself. Obviously, he was attempting to attract attention to himself. Often he seemed to do so with reckless disregard for the suffering produced in the wake of his demonstrations. It is indeed possible that Owens' *enfant terrible* behavior represents the puerile manifestation of an emerging evolutionary talent latent in all humanity.

After this apparent success, Owens made a renewed prediction. Before two fellow workers at the law firm for which he worked as a typist, he announced that he would now make a hurricane appear off the coast during the week of June 22. By Sunday, June 24, local Philadelphia papers were announcing that a newly developed tropical storm named Brenda was heading for Bermuda. By that evening, Brenda had become a hurricane, but it headed safely out to sea and spared the coastal areas of Florida. This prediction and its fulfillment may not sound too impressive, but Brenda only sprang into being on Friday, June 21, just one day after Owens had announced his intention of producing one. Even more interesting is the fact that Brenda was the second hurricane of the month. The end of June is early for hurricanes, and not since 1959 had two hurricanes formed in the Atlantic so early in the year. So if Owens was making his announcement in the hope that it would come about by chance, he was way off base. Nor could the hurricane have been predicted through normal inference. Brenda was an unusual storm, and unusualness is Owens' trademark.

The psychic made his next prediction on October 17 when he told one of his contacts, a Philadelphia lawyer named Dennis Kapusin, that he was about to interfere with the course of a hurricane then bellowing off Florida's western coast. He thereupon drew a map of the hurricane area for his friend, showing Gladys, then still only a storm, veering away from Florida as it had been doing during its normal Northwest bearings. Owens told Kapusin that he was planning to erect a "wall" in front of the hurricane and make it turn towards the east, right into Florida.

The very afternoon of Owens' visit to Kapusin, Gladys came to a complete stop, began changing direction and proceeded to head directly for Florida. This was quite a surprise to weathermen, who had already announced that Florida was out of danger from the storm's wrath. The reason for Gladys's abrupt about-face, according to the National Hurricane Center, was the formation of a high-pressure area that had developed west of the hurricane. This, itself, might sound reasonable, but Gladys was behaving in a peculiar fashion by hurricane standards. An October 18 story about the storm, printed in the *New York Times*, especially noted that the hurricane "veered—suddenly" and had "caught many of the city's [St. Petersburg's] more than a million residents by surprise." The story further related that, because of its prior due north course, Florida residents had already relaxed their guard, and even weathermen were taken by surprise.

Owens gave up steady employment in 1969, even though he had a family to support, so that he could devote himself solely to his psychic work.

"I had to decide whether I would work in an office eight hours a day while trying to do what I'm doing for the Space Intelligences," he explained. "Immediately I knew I couldn't. You only have so much energy, and to do what I would have to do for the SIs, I need all my energy. It's turned out that's been right. So that was the best decision I've made in my life."

CHAPTER 4

THE SPACE INTELLIGENCES

The world of our present consciousness is only one out of many worlds of consciousness that exist, and those other worlds must contain experiences which have a meaning for our life also.

William James

"They Had Been Trying to Reach Me Since I Was a Child"

"The device emitted red, blue, green, and white colors that were vivid and very brilliant," Owens reported. "We watched the device approach our car. Suddenly, it vanished instantly as if a light had been turned off."

This is the story Owens told Warren Smith, a veteran author of several UFO books, in 1975 while explaining how he first found himself in contact with the Space Intelligences or other dimensional entities with whom he works. It was either January or February of 1955, and he was living in Fort Worth, Texas. He had been driving out in the country with his daughter when the UFO appeared over a field at the side of the road on which he was traveling. The object was cigar-shaped, a common form that UFOs took. But it was only years later, after Owens discovered that his innate psychic abilities had been remarkably enhanced, that he realized the significance of the sighting.

"They had been trying to reach me since I was a child," Owens reminisced as he explained how, after his sighting, he gradually found himself in contact with an alien intelligence. "But the SIs just didn't get through to me until after the UFO approached over my car in Texas. It appears somehow to be a combination of that UFO sighting plus my work in hypnosis and other paranormal fields and my natural psychic ability."

In 1965, when Owens drove to Washington, DC, he claims that he met with a CIA agent he referred to as George Clark, who appeared interested in his claims. As a result of their conversation, Owens began sending Clark copies of his predictions and intentions to cause weather changes. Validation as to their outcomes was also religiously provided, but to Owens' disappointment no action was ever taken by the CIA with regard to his requests for financial support. Nevertheless, Washington was not to be a total disappointment for the psychic. It was there that he had a second revelation, this time about how the UFOs were guiding his abilities. One day, while living in a little rented house, Owens had the sudden impulse to write Clark to inform him of an upcoming polar shift. The communication was dated March 9, 1965. The message entered his mind without warning, and Owens was confused by it.

"Frankly, this [message] made no sense whatsoever to me at the time," Owens recorded in a diary he was keeping. "And I even disliked having to forward the information to George [Clark] because it seemed ridiculous."

Several weeks later, when he read in the paper that UFOs had been reported over Antarctica, Owens decided that a UFO intelligence had been telepathically communicating with him. "It [the message] turned out to be the most exciting and thrilling happening of my whole life to date," Owens recorded.

After his Washington, DC, contact, he found himself constantly bombarded by what he took to be telepathic messages from the Space Intelligences. He had not yet learned how to initiate contact with them from his end, and he did not feel the need to commence with his own contact. Almost daily, it seemed, he received signals from the Space Intelligences—lengthy communications, in fact— almost instantaneously. Some of these messages instructed him on what demonstrations he was to carry out, while others pertained to the role he was playing for the Space Intelligences.

It was only some weeks later, on July 19, 1965, that the Space Intelligences explained to Owens why they had chosen him to be their prophet. Owens recorded in his diary:

> Tonight they told me that they could give me only so much power, so much knowledge, at a time. It is all my human brain can stand. Matter of fact, they said I'm an experiment with them—to find out just how much of the PK power a human being can absorb and stand. It took them literally ages to find a human being, myself, with whom they could communicate back and forth and obtain concrete proof for other humans in their own way.

This is the insight, I believe, that later led Owens to compare himself to the biblical Moses. Perhaps it was a comparison that merits further consideration. However, in at least one regard, it engendered a belief in Owens that, whatever harmful consequences resulted from his demonstrations, they served a higher purpose. Like Moses, Owens felt himself unconstrained by the rules of the prevailing authorities. He was answerable only to the mysterious Space Intelligences.

After this and similar revelations, Owens began making public even more predictions and announcements about upcoming events. The Space Intelligences would either communicate this information to Owens or instruct him as to what PK exhibitions they wished him to perform.

Perhaps the most astounding information the Space Intelligences provided for Owens was when, after first contacting him, they revealed that they had been abducting him periodically over the years during which time they had been altering his brain in order to render it half alien. This claim, of course, seems absurd at face value. But when studying psychic phenomena and UFOs, everything is absurd. So Owens' abduction story cannot be rejected merely because of its uniqueness. After talking personally to Owens about this matter, parapsychologist D. Scott Rogo and I have come to accept the fact that Owens really did believe this operation took place. He even had an odd indentation running along the base of his skull that he claimed was a remnant of this operation; but whether this was a result of a bone deformation, accident, or whatever, we were in no position to say. It was such a curious indentation, though, that Owens liked to show it to people, claiming it was physical proof that he had been abducted and operated upon. In 1982, Owens subjected himself to a CAT scan. No brain abnormalities were discovered at that time. Subsequently, many reports of alien surgical procedures have been documented. The most thorough account of these is presented in Dr. Roger K. Leir's book, *The Aliens and the Scalpel*.

On July 21, 1965, Owens again wrote to Clark, stating that UFOs would be seen over "one of our major cities." UFOs were seen over Washington, DC, before the end of the month.

A similar coincidence was realized on October 31, 1966. On October 15, Owens, who was living in Philadelphia, wrote to one of his correspondents to say that he had asked the UFOs to publicly appear by Halloween. On October 31, UFOs sightings were reported by several witnesses in the Philadelphia area. One might easily dismiss such events. However, in retrospect, we can now see that they marked the beginning of a most unusual career, one that was to continue for over two decades until Owens' death.

While Ted Owens could not recall ever meeting the Space Intelligences face to face, he developed several ways of communicating with them. Some of these contacts were instantaneous. The commands from the SIs would be complete and transmitted instantaneously. "One moment you are working at something," he claimed, "and the next moment you have received all the SIs' information."

"Two Small Creatures Resembling Grasshoppers"

Another way Owens initiated contact with the Space Intelligences is through a visualization technique that he claimed he learned from the entities themselves. Owens wrote in his 1969 book, *How to Contact Space People* (now out of print):

> They showed me, in my mind's eye, a small chamber. Inside the chamber were two small creatures resembling grasshoppers and insect-like but standing on two legs. These creatures looked down into a large, round, oval machine. In it they could see me. If I talked, they heard the sound, but the machine quickly turned the sound into symbols, then the symbols into very high-frequency sound, which they could understand. Thus, I would talk to them in English, which would jump around into odd symbols on the screen, then result in a high whistling sound, which they understood. After talking with them for months in

this manner, they suddenly, one day, pointed to a wall upon which was a screen. They made me know that their "boss," or Higher Intelligence, would appear on this screen. And for very important communications, I was to appear on the round screen and ask for "Control," and their Higher Intelligence would appear and listen to me. And this is what happened.

It wasn't a face that appeared on the screen on the wall but a shadow which had the form of a face. The only thing to be seen clearly were two green eyes, shining from the screen. They made me know that their Higher Intelligence is made up of what we call light. No form at all. But it had made a "face" out of shadow on the screen to converse with me because that's what I am used to talking to—a human face.

Owens has intimated that these grasshopper-like creatures were only forms used by the Space Intelligences when they decided to take physical shape, as they were actually comprised of light and energy.

UFO Researchers Open to Receiving Documentation from Owens

Up until the mid-1960s, Owens was mostly a voice in the wilderness, crying out his prophecies; but, like Homer's Cassandra, he was doomed by the curse of rejection. Things finally began to change about 1968, when a few insightful ufologists began keeping an at least partially open eye on Owens and started keeping files on his predictions and demonstrations. Two of these scientists, Drs. Leo Sprinkle and J. Allen Hynek, were originally contacted by Owens himself and agreed to try documenting his claims or at least filing his predictions and other communications to them. Leo Sprinkle, who at one time kept the most systematic files on Owens, was a clinical psychologist at the University of Wyoming. He held a long-lived interest in the Owens matter dating back to the 1960s but stopped corresponding when Owens began a hard-sell approach during his constant endeavors at self-promotion.

However, as of 1970, Sprinkle was intrigued enough to urge J. Allen Hynek, then an astronomer at Northwestern University in Evanston, Illinois, to work with the psychic. Owens first contacted Hynek in May, 1970, and the astronomer was initially open to his claims. This was perhaps due to the fact that Hynek was developing an interest in psychic phenomena at the time. But he, too, eventually broke with Owens because of the psychic's often capricious behavior.

Two other researchers kept tabs on Owens during the late 1960s and early 1970s—Berthold Schwarz, M.D., a New Jersey psychiatrist and parapsychologist, and Otto Binder, a writer of popular UFO books who eventually became Owens' greatest propagandist. Binder had planned to write a book on Owens; but, after arduously cataloging Owens' files, he died in 1974 before he could begin work on the project.

These ufologists and researchers collected fairly complete files that documented at least some of Owens' claims up to 1971 or 1972. Some of these documents are extremely interesting and pertain to both his predictions and alleged PK demonstrations. Highlights are presented in chapter 5.

Producing UFO Appearances and Related Phenomena

Owens produced UFO appearances that do not seem to be subject to interpretation as the result of precognition. In January, 1972, he visited Puerto Rico where he was hosted by a local physician, Dr. J. J. Arenas.

On the night of January 28, Owens was with the doctor and his son, Kevin, when Arenas asked him to make a UFO appear over the house. They were sitting out on a veranda facing the mountains at the time. Arenas later wrote the following statement regarding this event:

> He said that he could communicate with [the] UFOs and [would] try to bring one to our home. For quite a long while we waited. The sky was absolutely clear. Then peculiar clouds began to fill the sky directly in front of us, until our immediate field of vision was obscured. I went in to bed. Shortly thereafter my son, Kevin, rushed in to tell me that a UFO had in fact appeared. I went out to the veranda, with binoculars, and observed the UFO carefully.
>
> It appeared like a brilliant star, but not as bright. It kept perpetually changing color—from red, to gold, to blue, to red—and kept zigzagging about as well.
>
> It kept moving slowly, in an erratic manner and in a slight zigzag direction. It rose upwards, slowly, and then moved horizontally across the sky to another point some distance away, where it stayed, but still moving about erratically.

Arenas watched the object for quite a while, then decided to retire for the night.

The skeptic will probably argue that Arenas saw a star and mistook it for a UFO because he expected to see one and that the odd movements it made were the result of an autokinetic effect. It is well known that a bright light viewed against a black background will seem to move as it is watched. It often seems to dart about in an erratic way. This phenomenon has been dubbed the "autokinetic effect" by psychologists. "Hand jiggle," which may have resulted from his trying to hold his binoculars level, could have led the doctor to misinterpret the star's behavior as well.

However, the above explanations cannot account for all the particulars in the Arenas report. He saw the object stop and move slowly. Autokinetic and hand jiggle effects are always rapid and perpetual. It is also significant that the UFO manifested after the appearance of an odd cloud formation. Many UFO witnesses have made note of this same peculiar phenomenon.

F. W. Holiday, a British writer, reported in his book, *The Dragon and the Disc* (1973), that he also saw a UFO created out of a cloud that had suddenly appeared in the sky. He was out fishing at the time, and the sky was totally clear. Suddenly, he noticed that a single, small silver cloud had formed. Ten minutes later, a UFO, complete with hull and beacon lights, appeared right out of it. These effects were reported years before the concept was popularized in Steven Spielberg's 1977 film, *Close Encounters of the Third Kind*.

Nor is the Arenas case unique. Owens gave a similar demonstration to an acquaintance of his, Janice Leslie, in August, 1978, during a visit she and a friend were making to the psychic's home in Silverton, Oregon. Here's what she told me:

On Sunday, August 27, 1978, we, Janice Leslie and Jade Swan, each a mother of three children, were visiting Ted Owens, known as PK Man over the world, at his home in Silverton, Oregon. He is a famous psychic. He stated that it was *within his power* to bring forth UFOs to be seen and witnessed. He offered to prove it to us. So we put Ted Owens and his two sons, Beau, age 15, and Teddy, age 7, in our car and drove them to a certain isolated location in Silver Falls State Park.

Owens demonstrated and explained how he would telepath to UFOs overhead to bring them into view. Time and time again he extended his hand toward to sky and explained to us what he was doing mentally to make telepathic contact with UFOs. In the time that followed, in the night sky, six UFOs appeared overhead while we watched carefully. Yellow glowing lights moved across the sky. One UFO hung just behind a line of trees over us. It must have been the size of a football field, and it remained stationary for quite a long while before moving to the right. It had four pulsating lights around its framework in the same geometric pattern as a baseball diamond, that is, three lights at "first, second and third base" and the fourth pulsating light at "home plate." It was from this giant UFO that several glowing, yellow UFOs emerged and traveled across the sky overhead.

Owens had a long, powerful flashlight, which he turned on and flashed onto the giant UFO overhead. He switched the light back and forth over the UFO, and its pulsating lights seemed to blink back at Owens in patterns as he flashed light patterns at it. Also, the light reflected off the UFO back at us, seeming to indicate its closeness and solidity.

Both of us, Owens, and his children were satisfied that we had witnessed genuine UFOs. They could have been nothing else whatsoever.

These UFO appearances resulted from an intentional desire on Owens' part, rather than a prediction, since the first one was also made at the specific request of Arenas. Such a demonstration does not seem to have been the result of precognition. Somehow, a causal relationship must have existed between Owens' attempt to make the UFO appear and its subsequent manifestation. In fact, Owens eventually trained Janice Leslie to produce UFO sightings on her own. This is described in greater detail in chapter 9.

But were these UFOs produced by the Space Intelligences, as Owens believes, or could the psychic actually have created the objects through his psychokinetic abilities? One might argue that the witnesses themselves were duped or hypnotized but for the fact that Owens actually produced a sighting at my request, one that was videotaped and photographed as described in chapter 2.

The major issue ultimately confronting anyone trying to honestly solve the Owens mystery is this: what was the relationship between Owens and the Space Intelligences? If we can understand that, perhaps we can understand Owens himself. Was Ted Owens really in touch with extradimensional beings existing in some hyperspace dimension just beyond the reach of our all-too-limited sensory perceptions? Or were they a delusion that Owens had built up in his mind in a desperate attempt at self-understanding? But if the Space Intelligences were a delusion and Ted's psychic accomplishments were due solely to his innate psychic abilities, how can we explain his UFO contacts? Or were these contacts something totally separate from his psychic abilities? Or still yet, were the UFOs that Owens and his acquaintances saw so often actually only materializations brought into existence by Ted himself? This possibility, I believe, is the one that must be taken seriously. And it is potentially more awesome than the simple physical presence of alien spacecraft.

The world of Ted Owens can easily tangle one in a web of speculation. When talking with Ted, it often appeared to me that the psychic was himself confused over these issues. Sometimes he would swear that the Space Intelligences had produced a specific effect, such as a freak rainstorm, while at other times he would maintain that he had produced a similar effect through the agency of his own mind. On occasion, he even amended his claims by assuring me that he had produced an effect through his own psychic ability but with the permission of the Space Intelligences who had aided him in implementing his plan.

When researcher D. Scott Rogo first met Ted at his 1978 home in Vancouver, Washington, it was his intention to force the psychic to define this matter. So Rogo asked him simply, "Why do the Space Intelligences—with all their power—have to work through a human agency at all?" Owens' answer was most enlightening:

> They have to have human choice. The law is that they can't make a move on their own unless they have human choice tied up or involved in it. So it becomes my choice. Now that they have a human, luckily for them, they can. That's why I'm so priceless to them. They can have my choices to work with.

Far from this being an egocentric or megalomaniacal remark, Ted said something very important here. By claiming that he was Earth's sole ambassador to the Space Intelligences, he was admitting that he and the Space Intelligences were more deeply connected, on a psychic level, than one might assume. Did the Space Intelligences represent an actual part of Ted's own mind that he, through years of misinterpretation, had come to believe was some independent agency working through him? This is a possibility that can be explored in some depth. On the other hand, Owens might have been telling us that the Space Intelligences were really not an independent agency at all but are somehow inherently connected to life on this planet. This also is a viable possibility. I believe, ultimately, that Ted Owens and his Space Intelligences are a mirror reflecting back to us our own undiscovered human possibilities.

In evaluating the case of Ted Owens, it is useful to have some larger context. Owens was neither the first nor the last person to claim paranormal powers received as a result of a UFO-type encounter.

The Parallel Case of Uri Geller

Uri Geller, the famous Israeli psychic, stunned the world in 1972 with his demonstrations of everything from telepathy to psychic metal-bending. Geller achieved even more credibility when two physicists, my friends Hal Puthoff and Russell Targ at the Stanford Research Institute, published a favorable report about him in the October 18, 1974, issue of *Nature*, the prestigious British science journal. (See chapter 1 for my thoughts on the debate concerning the legitimacy of skeptical criticism regarding Geller.) The similarity between Owens and Geller is twofold. They both demonstrate ostensible psychic powers, and they both attribute their abilities to extraterrestrial intelligences. In addition, there is considerable evidence that both men possessed psychic abilities long before they wove the UFO angle into their lives and thinking-systems. These parallels may be more than just coincidental; they indicate that, perhaps, both psychics are of similar stock.

Before Geller came to public attention under the aegis of Dr. Andrija Puharich, an American physician who has long been interested in psychic phenomena, there is no evidence that he ever claimed UFO contacts. There is certainly no evidence that he made any such claims while a performer in Israel. Puharich, on the other hand, had nurtured a long-lived interest in the UFO mystery that predated by some years his first contacts with Geller in 1971 in Israel. Puharich hypnotized Geller while preparing to unleash him on the parapsychological world. The youthful Israeli psychic appeared on the U.S. psychic scene equipped with the assertion that he was being guided by an intelligence from space. Parapsychology researchers—uncomfortable with the idea of UFOs in the first place—suspected that Geller either borrowed this idea from Puharich, developed it as a result of his contact with the doctor or was simply hypnotized by him into promoting it. If Geller really believed this claim, it was possibly a self-delusion. Since divorcing himself from Puharich, Geller made fewer and fewer extraterrestrial claims in his public statements.

Nonetheless, Geller still maintains that the reports by Puharich, in his book *Uri*, of a distinct UFO connection with Geller's abilities are all factual. I have interviewed Wisconsin psychologist Ila Ziebel, another independent witness to UFO-related events with Geller and Puharich in Israel. She asserted that the UFO appearances described in Puharich's book—when she was with Uri and Puharich in Israel—did occur as presented. In short, there is evidence that Geller's abilities have something to do with UFOs or alien intelligences.

On the other hand, the idea that both Geller's and Owens' abilities stem solely from their own minds can be tentatively supported from several standpoints. For instance, some parapsychologists have argued that PK is an "ego-alien" ability. In other words, PK is so unusual, extraordinary and frightening that our natural reaction is to deny any responsibility for it when it occurs. In this respect, we may all be like the schizophrenic who is hearing only his own thoughts when he complains that the voices in his head are coming from his enemies or supernatural beings. One way to convince ourselves that we cannot affect the material world with our minds is to conjure up a scapegoat and then blame him whenever something supernormal occurs. There is abundant experimental evidence that we all possess minute amounts of PK ability, but all through history humans have been trying to ignore the fact.

The spiritualists and mediums of the nineteenth and early twentieth centuries had their spirit guides, the occultists had their "elementals" and now Geller and Owens have extraterrestrials. All these entities have been blamed over the years for everything from table levitation and spoon bending to poltergeist antics. This is not to say that these agencies don't exist in the universe and couldn't be genuinely responsible for *some* PK effects. However, when a psychic event takes place, such as a poltergeist outbreak, we often automatically blame it on some outside agency instead of realizing our own complicity.

Owens falls somewhat short of this extreme since he claimed some psychic abilities for himself while blaming other feats on the Space Intelligences—or at least as due to his involvement with them. But these conflicting allegations may result from the psychic's own unconscious desire to alienate himself from taking full responsibility for his predictions and demonstrations while attempting to absorb them within the framework of his own megalomania. When one examines Owens' life from an ethical and spiritual perspective, it is tempting to suggest that the Space Intelligences afforded him a convenient opportunity to lose himself in a glamorous fantasy, thus avoiding the more difficult path of self-awareness and real understanding. However, we would be well advised not to judge the PK Man too hastily.

Are the Space Intelligences a Psychological Crutch?

Perhaps Owens suffered from an exaggerated version of what might be called the "Padfield Complex." Susan Padfield, wife of noted British physicist Ted Bastin, is a psychic who had demonstrated PK abilities for several British scientists in the 1960s and 1970s, ranging from psychically interfering with light beams to moving pendulums in sealed containers. When Miss Padfield first discovered her abilities, she had to divorce herself from responsibility for them before she could demonstrate them. She therefore developed the belief that an extraterrestrial intelligence was working through her. Only later was she able to take full responsibility for her abilities and exorcize the extraterrestrials from her belief system.

This idea might make more sense if couched in terms of at least one psychiatric theory about the structure of the mind. Such a theory was first proposed by Dr. Pierre Janet (1859-1941), a pioneering French psychiatrist who developed it in order to explain many forms of unconsciously mediated behavior. Called "polypsychism," Janet's theory is that the unconscious mind is not a unified structure but is composed of one or more subpersonalities that exist independently from our conscious selves and even from one another. They are, however, capable of subtly and surreptitiously influencing our waking behavior and thinking. These subpersonalities, according to Janet, can even undergo development and lead "simultaneous or successive psychological existences" to the point of becoming psychic realities. Through such practices as automatic writing and crystal gazing, Janet believed one could enter into communication with them.

It shouldn't be difficult to believe that the Space Intelligences were perhaps some sort of subsystem working within Owens' mind that had gradually taken on an independent psychological existence and that regularly imparted psychic information to Owens' waking self. It is interesting that he communicated with the Space Intelligences through a form of visualization, one method through which Janet thought subpersonalities might be reached.

If we adopt this interpretation of Ted Owens and his powers, though, we still leave unexplained the ostensible fact that he did see UFOs, that he had contact with them and that many of his acquaintances have either witnessed or shared in these adventures. The theory that I've outlined above—that the Space Intelligences are merely a polypsychic extrusion from Owens' own psyche—would have to be extended to explain the appearances of these mysterious lights, apparitions, and crafts.

But is it not also possible that these subpersonalities can take on an independent existence as well? This is an idea that never occurred to Janet, despite the fact that he was interested in psychic phenomena. Could it be that these subsystems can divorce themselves from the physical body and live separate and apart from our conscious minds and bodies, though remaining weakly connected to us? These subpersonalities may also have access to PK powers and may use them to a degree beyond that which even those of us who accept the reality of psychokinesis normally imagine possible—even causing UFOs to appear in the sky and alien beings to walk the Earth who all too often just vanish into thin air as though they were partially immaterial to begin with. Perhaps Owens had either created a subpersonality that developed to monstrous proportions or was somehow participating in a subpersonality created jointly by several minds or by some sort of universal mind.

One way we might enlarge this theory would be to postulate that this hypothetical element of Owens' mind was endowed with such formidable psychic powers that it could literally create UFOs and project them into physical space through a process of psychic materialization. This theory isn't as bizarre as it may sound since Owens himself often maintained that UFOs, while real objects, lacked total physical objectivity. He even compared them, during a late-night talk session he once had with D. Scott Rogo, to optical illusions or holographic projections. UFOs, according to Ted, were therefore only partially physical. Supposing that Owens possessed extraordinary psychic abilities, could it be that the UFOs he and his acquaintances saw were actually creations generated by Owens' unconscious mind? In this respect, the UFOs may have been super-thought-forms created and engendered into a temporary physical existence by Owens himself. This idea was originally explored in the classic science fiction film, *Forbidden Planet* (1956).

This idea is distinctly possible, and, although it may seem far-fetched, there is considerable evidence that UFOs are linked to the human mind and might therefore be created by it. The possibility that we are producing the UFOs which occasionally haunt our skies can explain many mysteries about the phenomenon that the extraterrestrial hypothesis cannot. It can explain, for instance, why UFOs have periodically changed shape over the years in order to conform to cultural beliefs and technology, why UFOs suddenly disappear or change shape as though they are only partially material, and why some close-encounter witnesses seem to possess PK abilities either before or after their experiences.

In light of this evidence, many ufologists—including J. Allen Hynek, Jacques Vallee, Ann Druffel, Jerome Clark, John Keel, and other luminaries of the field—have maintained that the UFO phenomenon is basically a psychic one brought into being through our own psychic talents. This thought brings us back to a point that was made before: the UFO phenomenon cannot be isolated as something distinct from the minds that perceive it. Of course, each of the aforementioned researchers has a different approach and theory as to how all this occurs. Some believe that UFOs are created directly by our own minds, while others believe that they are created by a supermind that reflects our wishes and unconscious archetypal symbolism back to us. Yet others believe the phenomenon to be extradimensional, entering into this world through a psychic process set up by the mind. Now, if this general theory is correct—and I believe that at least part of it is—there is no reason to reject the possibility that a UFO could be brought into existence by the creative process of *one individual mind*.

Owens apparently had possessed remarkable PK capabilities long before his UFO experiences. So he himself may have been responsible for the UFOs—and not vice-versa!

Plagued by Poltergeists: "It Will Happen No Matter Where We Move"

This idea is further supported by the fact that Owens was not only plagued by UFOs but by monster visitations and polter-geist-like activity as well. In other words, his physical presence in any given location would often give rise to a wide range of paranormal effects in that area. This activity would often focus directly on the house in which he was living. All this indicates that somehow Owens' mind might have been solely responsible for these diverse phenomena.

One such display was reported in 1968 by a Maine real estate agent, Edward Ames, who later sent all the details to Berthold Schwarz, a New Jersey psychiatrist who had been collecting material on the Owens case since 1968. Ames had become interested in the commercial value that could result if Owens could make good on his claims; so, along with several other local businessmen, he invited the psychic to Brewer, Maine, in July 1968. Owens stayed at Ames' lakeside lodge outside the town, where he was supposed to make UFOs appear in the general area. In his statement, Ames explained that Owens had made good on his promise to produce UFOs and had even predicted some of their appearances accurately. But this was only part of the story resulting from Owens' visit.

While at Ames' lakeside lodge, Owens also became the victim of a recurrent "monster invasion" that seemed to manifest around and even in the lodge. The following events were witnessed not only by Owens but by his wife, Martha, and their son, Beau. (The ellipses below [. . .] do not indicate deleted text but were Owens' usage.)

We were installed in Mr. Ames' fine lodge, just on the very edge of Eddington Pond (no pond, it's a giant lake). On Tuesday morning, Martha told me that during the night she had heard something coming up the stairs (to our bedroom in the top of the lodge), but it had stopped where I had blocked the stairs with a chair, and then gone away. I had also heard it. Both Beau and Martha became badly frightened of the upstairs of the lodge, (Beau) claiming a "monster" was up there. Thursday I caught an explosive type of flu . . . and sneezed and coughed continually, without let-up. Also, during the day, there was a *tremendous* explosion at the side of the lodge . . . and Beau screamed (he was outside the lodge at that location, playing . . . we were both inside). We ran outside and Beau was hysterical with fear, crying and wringing his hands, his eyes as big as saucers . . . and he told us that a "giant with black eyes, black legs, black arms and black nose, and extremely tall" . . . had tried to pick him up with its foot.

. . . Also on Thursday night, July 25 . . . Martha and I both heard something two-legged walking on the roof, over our heads, on top of the lodge. Friday, something stole all our drinking water, kept in gallon jugs, out of our tightly locked-up kitchen!

Friday, July 26 . . . we had a party at the lodge for Ed Ames and his wife, Agnes; Jack Littlefield and his wife, Kay; and Bud Stratton and his wife, Gwen. During the evening Jack was sitting outside the front door, watching for UFOs, and called us out excitedly . . . a UFO was slowly inching across the sky! The same size and color of a star, with a constant glow (not blinking), it moved in a sort of slow motion, so that we couldn't possibly miss seeing it. We watched it through binoculars for about five minutes . . . and while in full view, it vanished completely. That is, it did not fade out in the distance . . . it was up over us in full sight, and just turned off. Ed Ames, a short while later, spotted the second UFO . . . in a straight line up overhead, and this was completely different than the other one. This was a gold color, with alternating red, blue and green lights flashing across its body. It hung in the same spot for an hour or more . . . then moved across the sky to another position for a while . . . then went off away from us until it went out of sight.

On Saturday, July 27 . . . I was semiconscious all day, weak, with just enough strength to stagger out onto the front porch and lie down in the hammock there . . .

It is very likely that these haunting-like disturbances were actually fall-out or secondary manifestations that resulted from

Owens' PK attempts to bring, or create, UFOs in the area. The above events, however, constitute only the beginning of the disturbances. Again, to quote from Owens' own description of his Maine demonstration:

> The next Monday night I saw a remarkable sight—two UFOs, both half-moon shaped, glowing ruby-red color, one over the other, fluttering across the sky over our lodge faster than any plane ever could. But what was remarkable was that they changed positions as they flew. I mean, first one would be on top, and the other on the bottom, then they would reverse positions—this done with indescribable speed. Their forward movement traversed a wide expanse of sky in only a few seconds, at which time they "turned off," or vanished, while still in full sight in the binoculars.
>
> At 10:42 P.M. I went into the lodge, and Martha and I heard a loud metallic *whack* a few feet from us. There was absolutely nothing that could have produced the noise.
>
> I went back outside the lodge at 11:30 to look at the sky again. It was utterly quiet, except for a fish jumping here or there. Suddenly a loud metallic "bong" noise sounded from about five feet away.
>
> On Wednesday, July 31, again, just after lunch I pointed out to Martha two identical clouds over the lake, which I was certain contained two hidden UFOs. At 3:53 all our power went off . . . lights, radio, everything, for two minutes. Then it came on again. At 4:40 the power went off again completely . . . and during this time I could hear quite plainly the noise in the lodge, the deep animal gasping sound. Beau said he heard "the giant." At 4:48 the power came back on

again, and I sneezed steadily for quite a long while, although my flu was over.

That evening, Wednesday evening, Ed Ames and his wife, Agnes, came over . . . and Ed Ames was the first to spot another "star" UFO, moving across the sky quite rapidly. Then we saw a second UFO . . . the gold one, with the flashing red, blue and green lights across its body, stationary in the sky. It stayed there until the Ameses left . . . then it moved to a new location at the edge of an airfield on the far side of the lake, then moved on a straight line away, until it vanished.

Thursday, August 1, no UFOs. I went to bed in the evening, heard a noise, sat up in bed, and saw an orange ball of light flare up at the front of the lodge illuminating the entire front of the lodge. I was horrified, for it looked as if the lodge had caught fire downstairs. I leaped out of bed and flicked on my flashlight and the orange ball of light vanished instantly! There was no fire in the fireplace, as it had been a hot night . . . absolutely nothing to cause the orange ball of light in the otherwise pitch-dark lodge. At the same time of the orange ball of light I heard a strange tapping noise.

All of these events—the UFOs, the unseen monster, and the poltergeist antics—are most economically explained by the theory that they all represent *the results of a single psychic process*, a process that eventually branched off into several different directions, thus giving rise to seemingly separate manifestations. This idea is further supported by the fact that similar psychic epidemics followed Owens no matter where he lived.

Similar weird, monsterish sounds and noises plagued Owens until the end of his life. Although he himself believed that they were created by the Space Intelligences, it is hard to fathom why or for what purpose the Space Intelligences, if they existed, would have had for creating these disturbances. The Space Intelligences, Owens claimed, could contact him instantaneously at any time, so why would they resort to grunting, groaning, and stomping about his residence? Far from displaying any purpose, these disturbances seem to have been random or germinal poltergeist effects sparked by Owens' mind as it tried to work up a UFO sighting or similar display. Even Owens seemed to be dimly aware of this possibility. In a letter he sent to me on November 29, 1977, he reported that similar monster-like disturbances were plaguing his home in Vancouver, Washington, and were terrifying his children:

> Two weeks ago, after I had put Teddy to bed in his own bedroom, I heard loud, savage, leopard-like growls coming from his room. I thought that somehow he was making the noises and told Beau about it the next day. But last week, one night about four in the morning, I was awakened in my own bedroom by loud, savage animal growls at the foot of my own bed. I got up, checked the room with a flashlight, but nothing was there. The next morning when I got Teddy up, the first thing he said was, "Daddy, something was growling real loud in my room last night." He and I had both heard the loud, horrible growls that would raise the hair on your head. Also at night we hear constantly, and night by night, a huge animal running through our mobile home, dragging claws, footsteps, and other weird noises like mysterious knocks on the walls. The kids are scared witless and Teddy has asked me to move out of here. What he does not understand is that it will happen no matter where we move.

Owens was correct in explaining that these manifestations would probably follow him wherever he went; but perhaps not for the reason he thought.

A Paranoid Schizophrenic

In this regard, the Owens case is very similar to that of Stella Lansing of Palmer, Massachusetts. She first came to ufology's attention through New Jersey psychiatrist Dr. Berthold Schwarz, who first met her in 1971 and has since written several papers about her that have appeared primarily in the *Flying Saucer Review*. Lansing, like Owens, claimed that she was in constant contact with UFO intelligences and that she had had many encounters with their craft. Her claim was supported by the fact that, on several occasions, she gave demonstrations of her abilities by producing UFOs on demand, similar to the way Owens and Janice Leslie have. Oftentimes she would drive out into the Massachusetts countryside on spur-of-the-moment UFO hunts, and many of the people who have accompanied her, including Schwarz himself, have seen UFOs while out on these expeditions. Also like Owens, there can be little doubt that Lansing possessed psychokinetic ability. She would sometimes produce photographs of apparent UFOs, even when none could be seen by observers with her at the time. To date, at least two parapsychologists have witnessed apparent PK phenomena in her presence.

The critical issue at stake in the Lansing case, though, is more complex than merely substantiating that she seems to have some sort of psychic link with the UFOs. A more central issue is how her UFO contacts related to her own psyche. Apart from her UFO contacts, Lansing had a long history of mental illness and had been hospitalized on one occasion with a diagnosis of paranoid schizophrenia. It may be more than coincidental that her psychic claims—that she was in contact with beings from another world and could manipulate matter with her mind—

parallel typical psychotic delusions. We still have much to learn about the interface between mental illness and the paranormal.

This may be a clue to understanding Stella's abilities and perhaps Owens' as well. It is quite possible that Lansing was suffering from a psychiatric disturbance but that through her psychic powers she has been able to bring her delusions to life. In other words, to prevent a total descent into insanity, she used her psychic powers to physically create the very objects of her delusions. By making her delusions real, i.e., by materializing UFOs and their occupants, Lansing's mind perhaps found a safety valve with which it could express itself without causing enormous emotional damage to the psyche.

Now, this is not to say or imply that Ted Owens was or was not a psychotic, or even a borderline personality. It is simply possible that he might have been using his psychic capabilities in order to reinforce his own beliefs—and doing so by materializing the UFOs with which he felt he was in contact. The implications of this hypothesis are astounding and also suggest a new interpretation for the miraculous origins of dozens of religious movements.

CHAPTER 5

THE PK MAN'S GREATEST HITS

*I teach you the superman. Man is something that
shall be overcome. What have you done to
overcome him?*

Friedrich Nietzsche

By early 1977, after the UFO appearance during my San
Francisco experiment, I had good reason to take Owens' claims
seriously. He had clearly given Puthoff and Targ advance notice
that he was going to end the drought in California. The events
occurred as he had specified. Then he was invited to England to
help end the drought there. The rains began the day he set foot
on British soil. I had clear knowledge of these events. When it
came to the letter written by Dr. Max Fogel regarding the Chase
City UFO sighting, I was suspicious that Owens had made the
whole thing up. I did not know Max Fogel. For all I knew, he

was Owens' confederate—or, perhaps, Owens had simply managed to fake the letter on Mensa letterhead. These suspicions were greatly alleviated, however, when we obtained a much better UFO sighting in the San Francisco experiment.

So, I set about reviewing the thick file folders that had been given to me by Puthoff and Targ. Another of Owens' scientists, Dr. Leo Sprinkle, psychologist and UFO researcher from the University of Wyoming, had been happy to send me his files. I was interested in two types of events, those that provided good factual proof of Owens' talents, and those that offered some insights into the mechanisms or processes by which the various events associated with Owens manifested. In order to provide you, the reader, with a representative picture, this chapter will enumerate the evidential highlights from Owens' career that demonstrate his Space Intelligences at work.

Let me state at the outset that Owens was probably a better psychic practitioner than was Babe Ruth a baseball player. Babe Ruth struck out more often than he hit home runs, yet that did not negate his greatness as a ballplayer. What follows in this chapter are some of Ted Owens' home runs. But it would be a big mistake to think that either Owens or Uri Geller or any other psychic practitioner will be miraculously accurate each time they attempt to perform a miracle. Miracles occur at about the same frequency in parapsychology research as home runs occur in baseball. A good baseball player will either get a base hit or a walk approximately one third of his times at bat over the course of an entire season. Home runs are more rare. I think it is an apt analogy. When I reviewed over 150 different demonstrations from the files, it seemed to me that, in about half of them, Owens was successful in producing, or predicting, effects that had a probability of less than one percent.

Let me also state at the outset that many of Owens' so-called demonstrations had an unsavory aspect to them. There is a clear sense that he went about with a chip on his shoulder—challenging the world to believe in his miracles and then lashing out when people reacted with sarcastic ridicule. While I, personally, found it natural to treat Owens with courtesy and respect—in spite of our various disagreements—others were often not so kind. Honest skepticism demanded from virtually all witnesses that Owens' claims be met with a reluctance to believe in them. However, many went beyond that reluctance to believe and treated Owens with outright hostility, contempt, and ridicule. Such an attitude goes far beyond skepticism and enters the realm of debunking. Intellectual honesty is often sacrificed in the process. These emotions seemed to trigger Owens' anger and often colored his demonstrations in a negative manner. Further discussion of this dynamic is reserved for chapter 10.

"There Was No Other Lightning Either Before or After the Experiment"

There is a traditional Native American belief that a skilled shaman can cause lightning to strike any place he wishes it to. Doug Boyd writes in detail about this phenomenon in his book, *Rolling Thunder*. The phenomenon is also described in the book by Lee Grandee called *Strange Experience: The Autobiography of a Hexenmeister*. Testimonies that Ted Owens could produce this same feat abound. For instance, consider the following notarized statement from a Philadelphia lawyer, Sidney Margulies:

> I certify this to be a true and correct statement:
> On the night of May 8, 1967, while watching a rainstorm in the company of H. Owens (Ted) from the top of a tall building in downtown Philadelphia . . . Mr. Owens offered to make lightning strike in any area that I might point out, as a demonstration of a new weather principle he had discovered. So I took him up on it and pointed to an area squarely in front of our window—the bridge leading to Camden.

In a few moments after Mr. Owens concentrated on making lightning strike the aforementioned bridge, a lightning bolt did in fact strike that area, just to the right of the bridge.

Since we were standing at the top of a tall building, our field of view was very wide and expansive. Therefore, the lightning bolt striking the pinpointed area, which I had designated, was interesting.

According to Margulies, whom I personally interviewed in 1976 and again in 1998, "There was no other lightning either before or after the experiment." It is interesting to note that, according to an SRI International report, the probability of accurately predicting when and where lightning will strike is less than one in a million.

Two months later, two of Owens' acquaintances—Kenneth Batch and Charles Jay, both of Merton, Pennsylvania—were determined to see whether he could make good on his energy claims. Charles Jay later provided the following affidavit for Owens. I recently interviewed Charles Jay who affirmed that the events did, in fact, transpire thirty years ago as described:

It was a rainy day, and we had heard of Ted Owens' ability to make lightning strike by his signaling UFO intelligences to do it. So we asked Ted Owens to give us a demonstration of his so-called power to communicate with UFO intelligences by having them make lightning strike in a given area we would designate. The three of us went out onto a balcony outside Ted Owens' apartment, and my friend and I asked Ted Owens to have lightning strike at or near the top of City Hall. In the ensuing period of time, there were three massive strokes of lightning which struck at intervals in that exact direction. And those were the only three bolts that struck in the entire day just where

Ted Owens pointed his hand. To test this, we then asked Ted Owens to make lightning strike in an entirely different portion of the sky. He pointed his hand, and the lightning appeared in that different area, exactly where we had asked it to appear. No other bolts appeared anywhere in the sky at any time during our experiments, except exactly where Ted Owens pointed his hand. My friend and I were in complete agreement that the experiment was a complete success.

"President Nixon . . . Will Resign or Be Forced out of Office"

In 1970, Owens told Warren Smith that "President Nixon will not end in office. Something most unusual will occur, and he will resign or be forced out of office." This statement appeared in Smith's *What the Seers Predict for 1971*, and was also registered in an issue of *Saga* magazine published in January 1971. Although this prognostication was not realized until three years later, Owens' statement is nonetheless impressive for two reasons. First, the Watergate scandal had not then emerged and, second, no American president had ever resigned or been forced out of office before.

"Streets Buckled and Manhole Covers Popped"

One of Owens' tests was directed towards the Cleveland-Akron area in May 1972. He had visited the city as part of a self-promotion tour earlier that month and had not been pleased by his reception. He reported:

> I was broke in Cape Charles, Virginia, and the SIs suggested I go to Cleveland, give some lectures and make some money. So I called up a friend I had in Chicago and asked him if he could scrounge up some money to organize a tour. He agreed and met me in

Cleveland. I guess we were there a couple of weeks, and, as a matter of fact, we lost everything. We rented two difference places, and I think only about six people showed up. It was the weirdest thing. Nobody had come to the lectures; they didn't believe that I'm for real.

Owens made a radio talk-show appearance, but found the interviewer insulting. There was a quality in Owens somewhat akin to that displayed in Sylvester Stallone's movies about a fictional boxer called Rocky. It seemed as if Rocky never gave his best performances in the ring until he had been sufficiently angered by his opponent's attacks. In more than one movie, he even taunts his opponents to hit him harder. Similarly, Owens seemed to set himself up for such attacks in order that he could work up enough psychic energy to somehow produce a demonstration that would teach his critics a lesson. Later, we will see that Owens attributed the "setup" to the Space Intelligences.

So on May 30, he wrote a letter to several of his contacts announcing that he was about to wreak destruction on Cleveland. In a communication to science writer Otto Binder, he claimed that he was going to contact four huge UFOs, then circling the Earth, and have them deflect heat towards the Earth and at Cleveland in particular so that the city would be hit by heat waves and drought. He also stated that this attack would cause Cleveland residents to "do odd things." Owens also informed George Delavan, a computer analyst living in Illinois and a personal friend of his, of his intentions and predicted electrical disturbances, lightning storms, plane and shipping accidents, and a blazing hot drought. Later he added odd animal behavior, sixty- to ninety-mile-per-hour winds, and blackouts as part of his revenge.

This was varied fare, and by chance one might expect at least some of it to have occurred by simple coincidence. Certainly heat would have been expected in the Midwest during the summer months. But in local newspapers during this time, there is suggestive evidence that something strange had happened to Cleveland and its surrounding areas that summer.

Let's begin with Owens' claim that he would hit Cleveland with lightning attacks. That July, there were three spectacular lightning accidents noteworthy enough to receive newspaper coverage. On July 23, no less than three people were killed and two more injured when lightning struck them as they were fishing. The *Cleveland Plain Dealer* reported the story and also noted the large amount of damage that lightning had caused during the past days. On July 29, the paper ran an even more spectacular story headlined, "Lightning Strikes CTS Car, Starts Fire With 12 Aboard."

"Lightning struck a CTS [Cleveland Transit Service] rapid car," the story stated, "and set it on fire last night as high winds and heavy rain swept across Greater Cleveland to cool the year's warmest day." Although no one was injured by the mishap, "the rapid [trolley car] burst into flames but firemen extinguished the blaze." "The car's interior was completely destroyed," according to the local assistant fire chief.

Two bolts of lightning struck a transformer in the West Park district of the city that same day, leading to a blackout and thus fulfilling another of Owens' predictions. The storms that struck Cleveland that week also brought winds of sixty-five miles per hour, confirming Owens' warning. According to the story cited above:

> What began as a mild day turned into the warmest of the summer. Temperatures climbed to a high of 97 degrees. In the late afternoon and evening, a chain of thunderstorms moved through the Cleveland area.
>
> The National Weather Service reported wind gusts up to 65 miles per hour at Cleveland Hopkins International Airport as one storm dropped 5.9 inches of rain in about 5 minutes.
>
> The weather service also said that 1.5 inches of rain fell at Hopkins in five hours last night.

Despite the storm activity, the heat wave Owens predicted struck as well. And it was a spectacular one. The *Plain Dealer* ran headlines on July 21 reading, "The Heat Wave Is On—And How," and reported that "streets buckled and manhole covers popped as the temperature climbed above 90 degrees in Greater Cleveland." The paper went on to relate that the police reported a number of calls about rippling streets and exploding manhole covers within an hour after the temperature had gone into the nineties. This almost broke a record: the previous high for the day was set in 1930 when it hit 98 degrees. At least two sections of one of Cleveland's major interstate highways were damaged by buckling, and the Cleveland Electric Illuminating Company reported that, due to the massive reliance on air-conditioning in the city, a new record for power consumption had been set.

The heat wave became even worse when it combined with local pollution. This unfortunate situation produced a rotten smelling blanket of air that engulfed the city for days. The pollution got so bad that a spokesman for the local air control board called it "the worst it has ever been" and warned that, should the problem continue, several industries would have to suspend operations.

Owens' statement that Cleveland residents would "act peculiar" may seem vague, but even this odd prognostication came to pass. The *Plain Dealer* reported on July 23 that the heat wave was causing "crackpots" to swarm city hall. The story went on to relate that "The flow of those claiming to hear the voice of God, receive messages from outer space, or be secret agents on secret missions started to climb last Monday and remained at a high level all week." One man even called city hall claiming to be a representative of Howard Hughes!

By July 23, the *Plain Dealer* was still reporting the heat wave, now in its sixth day. Since the average temperature for Cleveland in July was in the low to mid-80s, this was unusual enough to serve as support for Owens' prediction.

It was Otto Binder, however, who made another discovery that tied in with Owens' Cleveland demonstration. Owens had originally informed Binder that the heat he was projecting at Cleveland was caused by "deflections from the sun." By following meteorological reports, Binder discovered that, during the approximate time of the Cleveland demonstration, there were considerable solar disturbances. In fact, shortly after the demonstration, tremendous storms raged on the sun of an intensity puzzling to scientists. This situation was capped when a huge sunspot manifested in August so out of cycle, as sunspots are cyclical in nature, that one scientist said that its appearance was "like snow falling in July."

Since solar conditions, especially sun spots, can affect our weather by changing the disposition of low and high pressure areas over the globe, perhaps the heat wave that struck Cleveland did have something to do with solar conditions— conveniently deflected to the Cleveland area and monitored by Owens. This is only a conjecture, though, since the possible relationships between solar activity, sunspots, and our own weather have not been unequivocally defined.

One other thing: the radio announcer who gave Owens such a hard time lost his job that summer, too.

It was only in retrospect that Owens realized that the Space Intelligences had deliberately set him up. Owens told researcher D. Scott Rogo, who had joined me in the Owens investigation:

> Only after the demonstration was over did the UFOs get to me and communicate to me that they had led me to Cleveland just so I'd get insulted, come back to Virginia, get mad and give a demonstration to demonstrate powers that I had and to prove their reality. This is the way they do things.

The dynamic that Owens here attributes to the Space Intelligences is, ironically, not dissimilar to the portrayal of God in the Book of Exodus, who hardened pharaoh's heart in order that he could then demonstrate his powers in the form of the ten plagues that consumed Egypt.

If we allow the traditional theological claim that God's behavior here is the epitome of goodness (after all, God and good come from the same Old English root), then I think we must grant the possibility that Ted Owens is acting in this tradition—as he claims. Personally, however, I believe that both God and Owens deserve our moral scrutiny—and are not necessarily morally blameless.

"Where Did Winter Go?"

On October 25, 1972, Owens wrote letters to Leo Sprinkle, Max Fogel, and others announcing a new demonstration. This one was aimed at his hometown of Norfolk, Virginia:

> I propose to create summer-like weather this winter—warm, pleasant weather, little or no snow or cold. In this manner the fuel shortage need not happen, and people in the U.S. will not suffer.
>
> To do this I am going to communicate with my four giant UFOs and arrange for one (or two) on the far side of the Earth to reflect the sun's rays onto this side of the Earth, these rays to then be reflected downward onto our side of the Earth by the one or two huge UFOs on this side.
>
> Whether my understanding of the sun is correct or not, I am going to use the four huge UFOs positioned around this Earth to furnish heat to the U.S. this winter! So that the U.S. can have one of the warmest winters in history.

Owens really went out on a limb with this one, even though his predictions were eventually proven correct. News clippings from Virginia that winter (1972-73) often commented on the unseasonably warm weather. One story appearing in the *Virginian Pilot* (December 20, 1972) was titled, "Where Did Winter Go?" Virginia had extremely mild weather all winter. This does seem odd since, the day before Owens made his announcement, officials in Washington, DC, warned that the U.S. public would face dire fuel shortages should a severe winter set in. So government agencies certainly weren't expecting it to be a sunshiny season. Because of the warm weather, the fuel shortage never materialized and the East Coast found itself basking in springlike conditions. Norfolk even found itself in what might be called a winter heat wave. On December 5, 1972, the temperature reached 73 degrees, the warmest for that day in forty-seven years.

An AP release, dated January 21, 1973, reported that New York City had set a new record high for the day of January 18 with a temperature of 66 degrees. Washington, DC and Philadelphia also set records that winter and went completely without snow for the entire season. Yet these enviable conditions were somewhat localized since the weather in the South was typically miserable all winter long, and it snowed in some areas where they hadn't had any flurries in over ten years.

An Earthquake Rocks the Panhandle

The Texas demonstration, which Owens gave in 1974, exemplified the odd coincidences between the timing of his announcements and the odd weather conditions that all too often seemed to follow them with a vengeance.

The Texas challenge came on February 12, 1974, when Owens wrote to Ed Busch, a programmer for radio station WFAF in Dallas, about his intentions. He had been on the air with Busch and a co-host the week before, and the two broadcasters had badgered Owens about giving them a demonstration of his powers. In his letter to Busch, a peeved Owens announced that he had opened contact with a group of UFO intelligences and that they had agreed to a test. He claimed that he would "cause freakish weather and, of course, heat." Owens also intimated that the upcoming summer would bring record-breaking heat waves, and he warned people to expect "great storms, lightning attacks, etc." However, the psychic pledged that the havoc would not claim the lives of any Texans, as it was only a demonstration to show how he and the Space Intelligences could control weather any place in the world.

Four days later, a shattering earthquake rocked the Texas Panhandle. By the end of March, a storm raged violently, producing winds so intense that a meteorologist with the National Weather Service said that they constituted "the strongest winds I've ever seen in the continental United States." Tornadoes touched down on two occasions during the storm, followed by freezing rain and, later, destructive hot winds.

Owens made three "hits" in his original letter to Busch. His warning about freak weather conditions could indeed have referred to the earthquake and the colossal winds that struck six weeks later. The reference to the heat waves seemed to prognosticate the hot blasts of wind that destroyed a good portion of the Texas wheat crop that year. A "great storm" certainly manifested as well. Owens did make one miscalculation. He promised that no one would be killed by the freak weather. Although no one was killed by the two tornados that touched down during the March ordeal, the freezing rainstorm that bombarded parts of Texas resulted in several fatal automobile accidents. Owens' trademark UFOs were also sighted over the Dallas-Fort Worth Airport.

Busch himself did not hesitate to provide Owens with an account verifying the accuracy of his February prediction. This he dictated on May 7, 1974, but would not state that Owens caused the havoc. He only admitted to the many strange coincidences that seemed to link the proposed demonstration and the actual freak weather conditions that followed.

One could, along with Busch, place this series of events under the convenient heading of coincidence. This demonstration was similar to many of Owens' weather predictions or productions in that it was general in content, did not specify dates or specific incidents, and resulted in a curious mixture of accuracy and error, so it is more a case of a general prediction—upcoming freak weather—that was then borne out.

From a moral perspective, how do we evaluate Owens' behavior? Should we hold him accountable for the damage to the Texas wheat crop or for the highway deaths during the freezing rainstorm? Psychokinesis and telepathy have little or no status as causal factors in either our scientific or legal systems. But, if we are to take Owens' claims seriously, shouldn't we then also hold him accountable for his actions and responsible for reparations to his victims and to society? I would argue in favor of this, and I suspect that Owens would not necessarily disagree. In his defense, however, he would claim that his actions, however harmful, were in the service of a higher purpose—that of awakening humanity to our connection with the larger universe and our own deeper potentials.

"The Wildest 90 Days in the History of Chicago"

Owens decided to embark on a more destructive demonstration in October of 1975. This time he directed his PK at Chicago. The psychic energy practitioner made his announcement on October 8 in a letter to Doug Dahlgren, an announcer on radio station WCFL in Chicago. As he told Dahlgren:

> You have requested that I give a UFO demonstration over Chicago. I can do much better than that . . . and have cleared it with the SIs by direct communication

today. I will spell out what I am going to do, and then notify my scientists, so that they can observe.

UFO appearance . . . will ask the SIs to appear outstandingly in and around the Chicago area, and possibly do some very strange things to accompany the appearances.

EM phenomena . . . I will cause electromagnetic changes in the Chicago area. This will cause power blackouts and various forms of magnetic and electro-magnetic anomalies. It should also cause many light-ning strikes, violent storms, and high winds.

Poltergeist phenomena . . . I will send hundreds of poltergeist entities into the area . . . to cause all sorts of mischievous, prankish, freak happenings. This will cover, of course, the O'Hare Airport and the stadium in which the Chicago Bears play football. I will especially request that the poltergeists not harm anyone, or make any planes crash. But the football games of the Bears in that stadium in the months ahead . . . should be wild, freakish, and quite funny. And all sorts of strange things should happen at O'Hare Airport. Instruments going crazy; tires blowing out; etc. Not to mention human error by the bushels full.

The Grid . . . I will set up an other-dimensional grid over the Chicago area. Won't tell you what it will do . . . but you'll see the results.

Now . . . I have never yet failed in a demonstration on this huge scale. Never. But the difficulty here is . . . to try and minimize the effects so that no one gets hurt. In short, I have far too much power for such an exper-iment. Sort of like using a shotgun to shoot a fish in a barrel. This will not make too much sense to you, but believe me I know what I am talking about. . . .

P.S. The time element on this: will set all up today.

Things should start popping within days or weeks.
The entire demonstration should cap and climax
within 90 days. It could well be the wildest 90 days in
the history of Chicago!

The files I have on this demonstration include an extensive
assortment of magazine and newspaper clippings, some of
which serve as tentative confirmation of Owens' success. For
example, the *Chicago Tribune* for October 14, 1975, reported
that "A mysterious radio signal apparently coming from the
Michigan Avenue Bridge has caused occasional brake failure on
new buses operated by the Chicago Transit Authority and the
United Motor Coach Co . . . " [Note paragraph five in Owens'
letter about strange electromagnetic phenomena.]

On October 15, the *Tribune* reported, "Police are investigating the possibility that the recent slaughter of two calves and
the beheading of a rabbit in an area fifty miles northwest of
Chicago may have been the work of a mysterious UFO group
reportedly traveling across the country from Oregon." [See
paragraph four in Owens' letter regarding bizarre phenomena
associated with UFOs.]

A December 22 *Newsweek* article reported an epidemic of
unusual traffic jams that had recently been occurring at O'Hare
Airport, while a *Tribune* story of December 13 noted that there
had been four near-collisions between commercial jets flying to
or from O'Hare Airport in less than two weeks. [See paragraph
five of Owens' letter on poltergeist phenomena.]

As if all this were not enough, Chicago's weather went
haywire, jockeying between unusual warm spells and typical
winter winds and storms. On October 14, the temperature hit
88 degrees, setting a new record for the last quarter of a century.
Yet this heat struck the city after a month of below average
temperatures. In November, seventy-five-mile-per-hour winds
pounded the city, and several tornadoes struck northern Illinois.

It was the warmest November in Chicago history, even though a snowstorm struck on Thanksgiving Eve.

Owens' most amusing success during Chicago's tribulations related to his warning that he was going to send poltergeists to plague the football team, the Chicago Bears. The team ended up with a disastrous season. Mishaps abounded, clobbering came fast and furious, and sometimes the team played so ineptly that die-hard fans often became disgusted. The Bear's coach, Jack Pardue, had to admit to a reporter from the *Tribune* that his team was functioning so poorly that he was embarrassed by it. "This is the first team I've ever been associated with where we were so bad the opposition laughed at us in the field," he admitted. This statement came after a memorable game with the Pittsburgh Steelers. It had been a close game, and at a critical moment, a play had been initiated when the Bears didn't even have all their players on the field! The Steelers scored a touchdown and eventually won the game. (More about Owens' penchant for influencing athletic events will be presented in chapter 8.)

One could go on and on. Indeed it does seem as though, to quote Owens, it was "the wildest 90 days in the history of Chicago." But despite all the hilarity, there were sinister aspects to this demonstration. (A further examination of the dark side of Ted Owens' demonstrations appears in chapter 10.) Perhaps the most disturbing aspect of Owens' Chicago performance was the odd influence it presumably exerted over the Bears. Owens long maintained that when he focused on an area, his concentration somehow caused people to act oddly. Scattered throughout his files are tentative confirmations testifying to this.

"Get in Your Car and Drive Away from Here"

Owens engaged in storm-raising until the end of his life, and a demonstration he staged in Virginia during June 1977 was one of his greatest successes.

On June 1, Owens telephoned Charles Powell, the police chief of Cape Charles, Virginia, and warned him "to get into his police car and drive away from here" because he, Owens, was about to bring a hurricane to the area. Powell naturally demurred from acting on Owens' advice. Yet on June 6, a freak storm—totally unexpected by weathermen—struck the Virginia coast. Boats were sunk in the Chesapeake Bay, radar screens were blanked out, TV broadcasts were interrupted, and even airplanes parked on airstrips were blown over. Hailstones the size of golf balls pelted the ground, while ninety-eight-mile-per-hour winds whirled over the Bay and ripped into Virginia. The storm, which struck without warning, was so severe that it left five dead in its wake.

"I was out at 3 P.M. and it was sunshiny," one eyewitness told a reporter from the *Virginian Pilot*, "and all of a sudden it got dark and you could hear the wind and you could see the hail. You can't describe it. It's such an eerie feeling to see it light one minute and dark the next."

During a phone conversation with me, Police Chief Powell confirmed this event and verified the content and timing of Owens' advance warning.

"I Never Believed in UFOs Before"

The Australia case is interesting and emblematic of Owens' best work. On April 9, 1980, Owens received a letter from a Mr. B. K. (who wishes to remain anonymous) from Sydney, Australia, who had obviously read somewhere about Owens' accomplishments. B. K. wrote:

> You have been given the mind of "future man" to help the human race, if possible. The SIs have made you their only link with the human race so that the SIs can step in and help the human race with your human choice and permission.

Would you please consider helping to relieve the drought in Australia? If the size of Australia is too big to contemplate, please consider relieving the drought for, say, a tenth of the area for a start.

How about starting on the northern tablelands and north coast of the state of New South Wales? Would you please consider helping to relieve the drought in those areas? Thank you.

At the time B. K. wrote this letter, the drought was reaching staggering proportions. A United Press International (UPI) story on April 7 stated:

Australia is reported to be on the verge of a crippling drought that could turn the southern half of the continent into a giant dust bowl in a month. Thousands of kangaroos have already perished in the Outback areas of Queensland and New South Wales, and agricultural experts said millions more will die of thirst and starvation unless rain comes soon.

The *Daily Telegraph*, an Australian newspaper, reported in a headline on April 9, "Drought set to linger for six months." An AP story on April 10 reported that, "Authorities have declared a drought over an area of 656,000 square miles, almost the size of Western Europe."

The final result of Owens' efforts to end the 1980 Australian drought were strikingly similar to the pattern I have reported for him in California in 1976, and then later that year in London. In Australia, sudden storms brought flooding rains, starting with the areas specified by B. K. in his April 9 letter. By May 30, the *Sydney Morning Herald* declared that the drought was over. B. K. monitored the situation carefully, and regularly sent Owens newspaper clippings and official weather reports, all of which are now in my files. But most interesting to me is that a rash of UFO sightings were reported over Australia at the same time. Hundreds of corroborating reports were filed with authorities and with the media during this time.

In one instance, a UFO apparently landed in a barley field, leaving four circular indentations 4.25 feet in diameter by 4 inches deep and evenly spaced at 28.5 feet apart. Although the soil was soft, the four "pads" under these indentations were described as "rock hard," suggesting they had been compressed by a weight much heavier than the farmer's seven-ton tractor. The farmer, a Mr. Parker, stated, "Whatever it is, it couldn't be man-made. I never believed in UFOs before, but now I'm just about a strong believer." On June 20, 1980, the *Geraldton Guardian*, a local newspaper, interviewed a neighbor who had seen a strange light rising from the ground on Parker's property. He said, "You sometimes see lights coming down, but I definitely saw a light going up."

Owens sent me the clippings of these sightings, along with a handwritten note stating, "My UFOs put their 'signature' on working with me to end the Australian drought." All of this, however, was taking an unfortunate toll on Owens' faithful colleague in Australia, B. K., who had documented the entire affair from beginning to end. On July 7, 1980, Owens received this sad letter from B. K.:

> Please remove my photo from your Healing Wall. Please sever all connections with me, viz.: no postal or telephonic communications whatsoever.
>
> Thank you but please do not use my name and address in any articles or publications. It should be sufficient to use initials such as: "Mr. B. K. of Sydney, Australia." Thank you.
>
> Please do not contact me in any way, shape, or form whatsoever, and I shall hope you accept my sincere regrets.

And now I think we should dissolve all ties that have been so carefully nurtured by respect and gratitude and good will.

For my part, my Repatriation (Veterans') Department medical doctor-psychiatrist insists that I drop all contact and that I withdraw completely and immediately for my own state of health.

Therefore under medical direction I am bound in honour to conform to orders of withdrawal or else I lose the honours of war. Let there be no recriminations but let good will remain for your special endeavors on behalf of suffering humanity.

Regretfully on my part, I advise that the old signs and symptoms are reappearing and these are danger signals to the trained medical practitioners. So "Thank you" but that's the finish or I am finished. . . .

Unfortunately, I have not been able to ascertain further details on B. K.'s medical or psychiatric condition. He must have been an unusual man to have seriously considered that an American psychic energy practitioner would be able to end the drought in Australia. The fact that he was able to contact Owens at all suggests that he obtained Owens' address from an advertisement Owens ran in *Fate* magazine. For about three months, he wrote to Owens regularly regarding the situation with the Australian drought. With almost every letter, he made a small cash contribution. Apparently, however, his involvement with Owens coincided with the reappearance of psychiatric symptoms.

Apparently, early in their interaction, Owens and B. K. communicated about some medical problem B. K. was having. In a letter to Owens, dated April 30, 1980, B. K. wrote:

I am aware that help is needed for your work and research, and I am aware that, should you place my photo on your Healing Wall, any healing would be maximized.

However, my first thought and object in contacting you was to ask assistance and intercession to bring rain to the parched continent of Australia. I doubt if you would respect me very much if I now choose to dump Australia and concentrate on my own personal needs.

It is impossible, however, for me to imagine a medical condition that would have necessitated that B. K. sever all of his contacts with Ted Owens. More likely, as the July 7 letter implies, the matter was psychiatric. Apparently B. K.'s psychiatrist felt no need whatsoever to examine the actual evidence regarding B. K.'s interactions with Ted Owens before urging B. K. to sever all relationships and then actually issuing threats as to what might befall B. K. if he did not follow the doctor's orders. This would not have been unusual, since claims of paranormal knowledge are often regarded, *a priori*, as symptomatic of psychotic disorders. The psychiatrist must have felt, rightly or wrongly, that B. K.'s involvement with Owens was contributing to a mental condition that he found pathological. However, given Owens' actual track record in working with B. K. to end the Australian drought, perhaps it is psychiatry itself here that should be called into question.

CHAPTER 6

DANCING WITH HURRICANE DAVID

Over a more-than-five-year period, Owens phoned me several times a week, usually after midnight, and predicted dire events about to happen, including earthquakes, hurricanes, tornados, and violent events worldwide. Within two days or so, I always received the same prediction via letter, often accompanied with some strange drawing of unknown symbols and signed "PK Man." The predictions usually were about five-to-ten days before actual events took place. When the event took place, he copied the news stories and sent me copies. At one time, I estimated that—with some flexibility on the matter of timing—Owens' predictions were about 80 percent accurate.

Wayne Grover, *National Enquirer* journalist

"It's the Worst Storm to Hit Dade County since 1965"

The Florida experiment that began in March of 1979 is a complex one, a two-part demonstration, divided by a macabre interlude, that can be broken down into more specific phases: ending a drought, reinstating the drought and, finally, controlling a hurricane.

Ending the Florida Drought

One of the bases for this demonstration, as with Owens' earlier 1976 California performance, was a severe drought then plaguing southern Florida. It was the worst in years. Not only was it menacing Florida's agriculture, but accumulations of dust aggravated by the dryness were interfering with local power transmission. Firefighters were busy protecting residential areas from the huge number of brush fires that were multiplying like deranged rabbits as the dryness continued to turn the Florida countryside brittle. Emergency conservation methods were the order of the day, and by mid-April, residents in some parts of the state would be fined for overusing their sprinkler systems. According to a *Miami Herald* story:

> Miami firefighters no longer are worrying much about grass fires this dry spring. Few brushy areas remain in the city that have not already burned, they say.
>
> That is not the case in unincorporated Dade.
>
> Thousands of wild acres are out there, and they're burning with regularity. Last month, Metro firefighters took 972 brush-fire calls, a record. This month, the calls have been averaging 44 a day.
>
> "We sure could use a good dousing rain," said Metro Fire Captain, Ed Nefey.
>
> None is forthcoming.

"There may be some widely scattered showers this weekend," said National Weather Service forecaster Vaughn Carmichael, "But we don't really see any good general rains in sight at the moment."

"April showers," said Nefey. "There are going to be more fires than flowers."

March and April are generally dry months. But they are not generally this dry. It is the fourth driest spring in four decades. Less than an inch of rain has fallen since late January.

So far this month, there hasn't been enough rain to measure. Tuesday didn't see a sprinkle. The afternoon high temperature was 88 degrees—by no means a record, but 14 degrees above the norm for the date.

This year's total rainfall is 2.15 inches. That's a 5.01-inch deficit.

Things only got worse after this report. A story about the drought printed in the *Herald* soon after noted that only three times in the previous forty years had southern Florida gone so long without rain. But this one topped the record. It was the worse dry spell since 1940.

Wayne Grover, a freelance writer with connections to the *National Enquirer*, had been studying the Owens case during this time and felt that here would be a good opportunity to cajole the psychic into a new demonstration. Being a reporter by profession, Grover also realized that a successful demonstration would help him successfully market a profile on the psychic for the tabloid. Grover wrote the following as part of an affidavit describing his plan for a Florida experiment:

> I began working with Ted Owens via telephone in February of this year [1979]. I studied his past work in depth, I contacted many of the people who have

been involved with him in past PK experiments, and I was commissioned by the *National Enquirer* to write a story about the entire event.

I asked Ted to set up a PK demonstration for further study. He agreed to do so even after having had to prove to so many other people that he was what he purported to be. This demonstration was to last for a year and would be a control of the weather over the state of Florida. It was to begin 1 March, 1979.

Mr. Owens said he and the SIs (Space Intelligences) would produce several kinds of weather phenomena characteristically out of chronological sequence for normal meteorological conditions.

As this statement implies, the Florida demonstration was not originally designed solely as a drought-relief plan. In one of his annoyingly typical and vague pronouncements, Owens originally wrote to Grover, on March 7, 1979, to say that he would create a host of effects over the state including electromagnetic oddities, freakish violent storms accented by lightning attacks, blackouts, tremendous heat, hurricanes, and UFO appearances. Of course with such varied fare, the Florida experiment would have been impossible to evaluate no matter how many of these phenomena came to pass. But the real importance of this demonstration is that, during the course of its implementation and as it entered into various successive phases, Owens began to refine his predictions and make them more specific.

The first phase of the Florida demonstration was inaugurated in April, during the severe drought. On Easter Sunday, April 15, Grover phoned Owens in Vancouver, Washington, where the psychic was then making his home. Grover wrote in a notarized statement dated May 15, 1979:

At that time, Florida was in the midst of a terrible drought, so I asked Owens if he could bring rain to

Florida in order to alleviate the drought. Owens agreed to do so. He sent a written confirmation of his agreement to me and to [the] *Enquirer* on April 15, 1979. He promised, via my phone call to him, to deliver rain "in a few weeks."

Just as with so many of Owens' promises, it didn't take a "few weeks" for the rains to come. They struck Florida in ten days. A storm of tremendous magnitude hit on Wednesday, April 25, and its spectacular torrential rains ended the drought in no uncertain terms. In one respect, it was a typical Owens' storm, since weather experts, though aware that a storm was brewing, had not expected it to be as intense as it turned out to be. An April 26 news item appearing in the *Miami Herald* headlined its story, "Even the Weathermen Caught Napping," and reported that "Forecasters at the National Weather Service in Miami were as surprised as anyone else at Wednesday's record-breaking rainfall."

The storm was indeed a record-breaking one. It dropped in excess of sixteen inches of rain in Miami alone. The storm had been drifting northeast through the Gulf of Mexico, and had been tracked by satellite for three days before striking Florida. The storm itself, therefore, was no surprise to water-hungry Florida residents, but its freak intensity was. Although weather monitors had announced on the previous Tuesday that heavy rain was due, "None of the weather services meteorologists expected the storm to inundate a wide area of the coast and wash away a 54-year rainfall record for the city of Miami," wrote the *Miami Herald*.

The severity of the storm was not only unpredicted, but the storm itself was statistically unusual in other regards as well.

"Predicting that a 90-day drought would be ended by a record-breaking rainfall a month before the dry season normally ends," reported Bob Cole, a spokesman for Florida's National Hurricane Center using a poker metaphor, "would have been like drawing to an inside straight." Even as of late Tuesday, the Herald reported, Cole and his associates were only expecting half the amount of rain that actually fell.

Cole also told the paper that the storm, an improbable one to start with since it was out of season, had been complicated by several factors. The cloud mass that produced the rain had formed during the previous weekend just north of the Yucatan Peninsula in the Gulf of Mexico. Because it had formed over water, its rainfall rate could not be measured even though it was being tracked by satellite. So, while the weather experts knew the extent of the cloudiness and the temperature of the cloud mass, they could not measure its rainfall potential. In addition, Cole added, the rain brought by the storm was scattered. Some areas of Florida were drenched while other localities had only sparse precipitation.

Whatever the case, the storm did fulfill Owens' promise. It struck Florida within the time allotted, was unseasonable, produced record-breaking rain, and ended southern Florida's drought. An AP bulletin issued from Miami on April 27 noted the end of the drought, and the *Herald* quoted a local Dade County civil defense director as saying that "it's the worst storm to hit the county since 1965." It was so intense, in fact, that it dropped more rain than in any previous twenty-four-hour period in Miami's recorded history—more than any hurricane had dropped since 1942.

It would have been gratifying had the Florida affair ended here, with everyone happy about the end of the drought. Unfortunately it did not. Owens had promised the *Enquirer*, through Wayne Grover, a year of weather control, and that's just what they were about to get.

The Florida demonstration might have had a happy ending, but things rarely go smoothly when Owens is involved. And when the psychic decided that the *Enquirer* had double-crossed him, he became enraged. The weather changed accordingly.

"The Group Seemed to Have No Real Interest"

The key factors that led to Owens' change of attitude towards Florida and the *Enquirer* came when the tabloid began to stall publication of Grover's story on the demonstration. Owens had been under the impression that his performance had been put on as a test for the *Enquirer* in order to serve as a background for Grover's profile. Then the paper threw Owens for a loop. A high ranking editor phoned him and explained that they also wanted him to put on a UFO show for them! Aside from the Florida demonstration, *Enquirer* officials expected to send a team to the Pacific Northwest, meet with Owens and film a UFO conjured forth by him through his contact with the Space Intelligences. Owens was nonplussed and for good reason. His time, he explained to the *Enquirer*, is as valuable as anyone else's, so he expected to be paid for his time and effort. This request caught the paper off-guard, and at first they refused, but then agreed to pay Owens an award if he could produce a significant UFO sighting for them.

At first Owens demurred but then agreed to the test. His feeling was that the publicity arising from the sighting might be worth the effort. The experiment was to take place in Northern California, so Owens drove with his son, Beau, to Willow Creek, a bucolic area south of the Oregon border, where he met with Professor James Harder, a noted UFO researcher (and a member of my doctoral dissertation committee at U.C., Berkeley), and a crew from the *Enquirer*. After surveying the area, Owens chose a particular spot of sky near a cliff that he would "energize" to bring in the Space Intelligences. The cliff itself descended onto a small beach by the creek. Owens already had an inkling that neither Harder nor the *Enquirer* people were too keen about the demonstration, so it looked as though the whole plan was off to a bad start.

"The group seemed to have no real interest in the project," Owens wrote to me on May 14, 1979, shortly after the experiment had ended. "They just seemed to want to show up for the project, and that was the extent of it." Owens also sensed a remoteness on Harder's part that made him uncomfortable.

But Owens proceeded with the test anyway. While Harder and the film crew were left to enjoy the countryside, Owens and his son located an area out of their sight and by the cliff where they could begin to energize the area. Owens was not sure exactly how long the demonstration would take to consummate, so both he and the *Enquirer* team ended up playing a nerve-wracking waiting game.

Nothing happened during the first day of the UFO hunt. Owens, Harder, and the newsmen waited the entire day for a UFO to appear, but nothing happened. The second day was more eventful, though. Owens was now focusing his concentration on a particular area of the sky he was calling his "time window," an opening he was creating between this world and some other dimension through which the UFO would materialize. Most of the day's vigil had been as unsatisfactory as the previous one until late that night.

Then it happened. According to Owens:

> That night we went out. So that I could concentrate, Beau and I climbed down the forty- to fifty-foot-steep cliff to a spot out of sight from above onto the beach below, right on the edge of the river. The night then turned black again, as soon as I began to telepath . . . and for a while there was no visibility. Then the sky cleared and a gorgeous UFO appeared exactly in the time window, moving at a leisurely pace across the sky . . . making no sound . . . a yellowish ball . . . no blinking light, just one yellowing glowing ball. I blew my whistle twice for those on the cliff above, our signal, and pointed my flashlight up at the UFO. A bit later Beau, who was lying flat on his back, saw a UFO directly overhead.

Luckily, Owens and Beau were not the only ones who saw the UFO. On climbing back up the cliff, Owens learned that Harder had seen the UFO as well, although he did not interpret it as such. As the psychic wrote to me:

> We climbed back up the cliff to rejoin the others. I asked if they'd seen the pretty UFO. Harder said it could have been an airplane (we'd seen no planes at all). I pointed out that it made no sound and had no blinking lights, which would rule out a plane. Well, he said, it was a light in the sky. Ha ha. I pointed out to him that's what a UFO is . . . a light in the sky that cannot be identified. (Mrs. Harder later informed me that she, too, had seen the glowing ball.)

Under the circumstances, an even greater coolness developed between the *Enquirer* group and Owens, and the crisis finally hit during the third day of the experiment.

Grover had previously promised Owens that he would have four to five days to complete his project, while Owens himself had told the paper that he needed seven. Despite these negotiations, Harder, who was serving as the paper's resident UFO expert, was getting a little tired of the enterprise. The showdown came during a lunch break when he expressed his dissatisfaction with the way things were going. The Berkeley professor was particularly annoyed because he wanted Owens to change the location of the demonstration. Owens' response was that such a change of protocol would be unthinkable, since he had already sensitized the Willow Creek target so that UFOs would specifically manifest there. There would not be time, he assured Harder, to recharge a new area.

Harder wouldn't buy this answer, although, from a parapsychological perspective, it has some merit, so he and the *Enquirer* pulled out of the demonstration only three days after it had begun. This move violated the agreed-upon conditions Owens had negotiated with the tabloid; and it now seemed as though the *Enquirer* was disenchanted with the space prophet. The upshot was that, while Owens was paid his expenses, the *Enquirer* killed Grover's story on the psychic. It was another in a long list of setbacks for Owens. (Harder's final and more favorable opinion of Owens is presented in chapter 12.)

This wasn't the end of Owens' trouble with the *Enquirer*, though, and it didn't help matters any when a snide story appeared in the *Palm Beach Post* on May 28, commenting on Owens' Florida demonstration. The story related Owens' rainmaking attempts and their successful outcome. It also correctly reported that Owens was currently attempting to bring a renewed drought to Florida by having the Space Intelligences deflect rays from the sun into the state. Long before the Willow Creek incident, Owens had promised this dry spell as one phase of his overall demonstration. The story ended by saying that "the *Enquirer* had little to say about Owens or his predictions." What was worse, the paper ran a story along with the Owens' profile quoting a local meteorologist who not only rejected Owens' claims but also parodied the psychic and made several gratuitous cracks about him. This was precisely the sort of behavior guaranteed to trigger a "lesson" from Owens.

"Their Work in Bringing Rains . . . Was Not Recognized"

The whole matter had, by mid-May, become so infuriating that Owens could hardly contain himself. The result was that he immediately began renewed efforts to bring another drought to Florida. On May 15, Owens wrote to Wayne Grover:

> Yesterday my UFOs (the SIs) communicated with me and told me to write and send this letter.
> Since their work in bringing tremendous rains to Florida and ending the drought in Florida . . . was not

recognized nor appreciated . . . they will utilize one special UFO to beam HEAT down onto Florida . . . not just heat, but tremendous heat, unusual heat, freakish heat (see my Cleveland, Ohio, file where this was done before).

The effect will be to create another terrible Florida drought, only worse than the previous drought . . . amplified perhaps a hundred times.

And it would seem that he was successful. Despite the fact that the rainy season begins in Florida in mid-May, the 1979 summer turned out to be mysteriously devoid of precipitation. August saw hardly a drop of rain, as though Owens were somehow psychically extending the normal dry season. In one of his original announcements reported in the *Post*, the psychic claimed that he was about to make Florida's water table go dry "from the inside out." By August, that's just what seemed to be happening, as reported in the *Miami Herald*:

South Florida water managers are warily watching both Lake Okeechobee and the sky as the summer's traditionally wet season threatens to turn bone dry," reported the *Miami Herald*. (The lake is a good index of the water supply needed for many parts of Florida. Since it supplies a good percentage of water to southern Florida, any alteration in its depth is cause for concern.) The story went on to report that, though no one is crying drought, officials say the vastly important Lake Okeechobee basin has received only 38 percent of the seasonally normal rainfall thus far. And the lake itself, which should be awash with usually plentiful summer rains, has been dropping steadily since mid-May when the rainy season should have begun.

"We're halfway through the rainy season and we haven't had a rainy season yet," quipped Jack Malow, the executive director of the South Florida Water Management District, to the *Herald*. "If that trend isn't reversed," he added, "it should be obvious to everyone that we might be running into some problems in the dry season."

As this quote notes, Florida's dry spell should have ended in mid-May, yet it didn't. Since this was just about the time Owens went into action to cause a drought in Florida, the coincidental timing appears to be significant.

The *Herald* went on to report that Lake Okeechobee, so critical to southern Florida, had a water depth of only about 14 feet when it should be at a level of about 16.25 feet. This signified a water shortage of 1.5 million cubit feet—enough water to supply a city the size of Fort Lauderdale for twenty-four months. The paper described the situation as "particularly startling" since the lake had shown a 17.3 foot level during the previous January. Perhaps no one was shouting "drought," but Florida officials weren't taking any chances. As a result, water consumption was severely restricted in August. County commissioners in Key West made it a misdemeanor to use water for any purpose other than drinking or bathing, and the Florida Keys Aqueduct Authority asked the governor's office to erect roadblocks to advise tourists, who might make added demands on the water supply, to stay out of the area. While this plan was never put into effect, southern Florida officials did threaten to cut off water to any residents caught washing cars, watering lawns, or filling pools.

The Keys were the worst struck area of Florida, according to the *Herald*. While by August 16, all of southern Florida was in near despair over the drought, the Keys were on the brink of disaster. The situation was so critical that the *Herald* ran the following "scare" story about the situation. It read in part:

> State authorities, fearing the Keys will run out of water unless emergency measures are imposed in Monroe County, Wednesday ordered a drop in water pressures to half the minimum level established as safe for public health.
>
> To conserve water, the three state parks in the Keys were closed to overnight visitors. The County Commission also was requested to immediately institute mandatory water conservation measures to stop all "nonessential" water use. Philip Edwards, who heads the Department of Environmental Regulation's [DER] South Florida district issued his order after several hours of discussion with other state officials.
>
> He maintained public health won't be endangered by the sharply lowered water pressures, but added the DER will be monitoring for possible infiltration of disease-causing bacteria into the drinking-water system.
>
> "They're going to run out of water," Edwards said. "It's nothing I like to do but I have to. Obviously something has to be done, either by us or the governor or the FKAA [Florida Keys Aqueduct Authority]."
>
> State authorities also are considering using National Guard troops to bring water to the Keys if the shortage becomes more acute, he said.
>
> Meanwhile, rangers in the three packed Keys state parks began turning away hundreds of would-be campers Wednesday after the FKAA turned off water in all recreation areas.
>
> The parks will get water only between noon and 2 P.M. and 6 and 8 P.M., leaving them open only to day

visitors. City and county recreation facilities also will fall under the water-rationing plan. Local officials said they will stay open, but restrooms will be locked.

Earlier Wednesday, FKAA Manager Dennis Wardlow conceded that the water shortage is "serious," but maintained that pressures in the distribution lines are at the minimum 20 pounds per square inch, considered safe under state law.

The first two phases of the Florida demonstration were now complete. Owens had apparently ended the drought in April and had then reinstated it during the summer when the state should have been entering into its rainy season. These events seem like a soap opera echo of the biblical ten plagues. The media and government of the United States, or in this case Florida, were no more prepared to recognize Owens' SIs than was Egypt's pharaoh willing to recognize the God of Moses. Still, like Moses, Owens persisted. Now he was ready for the third phase of his Florida weather engineering.

"One of the Mightiest Storms of the Century"

As far back as February, Owens had promised Grover that he would raise a hurricane in the Atlantic and guide it directly into Florida. This prediction was also published as part of the *Palm Beach Post*'s May 28 story on the psychic, which reported that Owens would attempt to bring a hurricane to Florida but that it would be especially programmed so that it would not cause any "unnecessary" deaths among the Florida population. Now, since late summer initiates hurricane season in the Atlantic, Owens' forecast was a safe one. There would be nothing particularly impressive if it came off. Only if a hurricane of dramatic proportions were to develop in the Atlantic and were to crash into Florida could it be inferred that Owens had something to do with the catastrophe. On the other hand, no hurricane had struck Florida since 1966, so this was no mean order!

As you might be suspecting by now, just such a hurricane hit Florida during the 1979 season, and it was a category five—the most intense. Despite the fact that Owens had promised that the hurricane would avoid unnecessarily causing deaths, this hurricane soon became known as the "killer storm" because of the high fatality rate it left in its wake as it meandered northward from the Caribbean to the Florida coast. In fact, according to a report published in the September 17 issue of *U.S. News and World Report*, 1979 became one of the most active hurricane seasons of the century. But this is getting a little ahead of ourselves.

Although he had first announced his plan to bring a hurricane to Florida in February, Owens phoned Grover on August 22 from Washington warning him that the promised hurricane was now in the making. "Stand by for a ram, people of Florida," he jotted down in a quickly scrawled note he mailed to Grover the next day. "The real action begins during the next month or two." But as is so typically the case, it didn't take thirty to sixty days for the psychic's word to come true. On August 26, only four days after his prediction, a tropical depression formed about 1,500 miles east of the Windward Islands. The National Weather Service quickly announced that the storm could turn into a full-fledged hurricane.

It turned out that the National Weather Service was being a little conservative. By August 29, tropical storm David had become a hurricane of immense proportions. Headlining its story, "Monster Hurricane Menaces Caribbean," the *Miami Herald* was already noting that the storm was acting peculiarly:

> Hurricane David, a monster storm with 140 m.p.h.
> winds and 10-foot storm tides, struck a glancing blow
> early today at the resort island of Barbados and headed
> for Martinique and St. Lucia.

The eye of the hurricane passed within 50 miles of Barbados, bringing hurricane-strength winds of more than 75 miles per hour over the island, according to the National Hurricane Center.

A hurricane watch was issued at noon for Barbados as David, traveling at a steady 15 m.p.h., gathered strength 150 miles to the east. By midnight, its core was just 50 miles east-northeast of the island, with its strongest winds boring along 50 miles in front.

For reasons not immediately clear, pressure at the center increased between 6 P.M. and 9 P.M. from 942 to 954 millibars, and maximum wind strength dropped from 150 m.p.h. to 140 where it held steady.

"We don't have much of a handle on why it happened," said John Hope of the National Hurricane Center in Miami. The decrease should not be taken as too hopeful a sign, he added: we've seen these kinds of punctuation quite often. If it gets out in the Caribbean, it could very well intensify again."

The paper also quoted Neil Frank, speaking for the National Hurricane Center, who admitted that David was "the strongest storm to threaten this group of islands in this century." Already it was lashing out at the Texas coast, producing huge waves and intense wind currents. And as the storm grew in intensity, Florida went on alert, especially when the *Herald* reported on August 29 that David had become "one of the mightiest storms of the century" with winds blowing at 150 miles per hour. No other storm of such magnitude had struck the Caribbean since 1831 and 1891, according to the National Weather Service.

Owens eagerly took credit for producing Hurricane David. He certainly cannot be faulted for doing so since, admittedly, the storm had formed almost immediately after the psychic predicted its materialization. But Owens wasn't satisfied merely with producing the storm. On August 29, securely situated in his Washington home, he drew a map of the Caribbean and started attempting to guide the storm directly into Florida as he had vowed to do months before.

So far, Hurricane David had struck Barbados, Martinique, and Dominica as well as other islands of the Antilles with devastating force, and Florida weathermen were at a loss to predict just where it would go next. On August 30, for example, the *Herald* reported that the storm might strike the lower tip of Florida but added that it was "too early to know where the hurricane will go." Later that day, though, the hurricane started to bend northward from Barbados towards Puerto Rico. The National Hurricane Center had by this time designated David as a Class Five storm. This is the highest rating that a hurricane can achieve, and only two other such storms had formed in the Caribbean anytime during the twentieth century.

Florida residents began to feel even more uneasy when, by August 31, Hurricane David seemed to be moving towards Florida after passing Puerto Rico. Guided by steering currents in the Atlantic, the storm gradually made its way northward and then veered westward towards open ocean, but U.S. weather experts were still worried that it might touch Florida on the way. Their fears became more intense when, on September 1, it became apparent that the storm was behaving erratically. While following a northwest course, the hurricane startled weathermen by veering sharply north and thereby ramming directly into the Dominican Republic. Several people were killed by the storm as it thundered ashore, but even this did nothing to alter Hurricane David's course. Weathermen were not taking any chances and, on September 2, Florida was placed on alert. Even the Red Cross began publishing a list of shelter locations. A major disaster now seemed inevitable.

"We Were Expecting It to Intensify. . . . Instead It Has Weakened"

By this time, even Grover was getting concerned since he could not intellectually reject the idea that somehow the hurricane's erratic behavior was being caused by Owens. So, on the evening of September 2, the *Enquirer* reporter called Owens and advised the psychic that thousands of residents would be killed if the storm struck Florida. This information seemed to cool Owens' ire against Florida in general and towards the *National Enquirer* in particular. He brooded over what Grover had told him and then agreed to "let go" of the hurricane before it wreaked destruction on the state. Owens wrote to Grover the next day:

> After you phoned and told me that the [hurri]cane would kill 20,000 people if it came through Miami, I brooded and brooded about it all day long; worried about you and your wife and kids, then cooled the cane so that it wouldn't come through and kill a bunch. After all, that wasn't what I was after. I did get it onto "target" . . . I wanted to run it right over [the] *Enquirer*, but it wasn't worth killing people to do so.

That is pretty much what happened, too.

Hurricane David struck Florida on September 3, but suddenly just weakened! The *Herald* reported that the hurricane "baffled forecasters" after the "once fierce storm weakened as it passed meekly 50 miles off Miami." The paper went on to say that "Forecasters earlier had warned that the hurricane, around at the South Florida coast, would intensify as it entered the warm waters of the Gulf Stream. Instead, the storm's sustaining winds dropped from 115 m.p.h. to barely 100 m.p.h., and meteorologists say the hurricane might be downgraded to a tropical storm today."

Weathermen throughout the country were puzzled by the storm's sudden decrease in magnitude. "We were expecting it to intensify," reported Jim Gross of the National Hurricane Center. "Instead it has weakened, and the trend appears to be continuing. We have no reason why. Your guess is as good as mine." In the words of Neil Frank, at the National Hurricane Center, the hurricane "just died." The only possible explanation meteorologists could come up with was that perhaps the storm had lost power when it had struck Andros Island in the Caribbean earlier. The eye of the storm had hovered over the island for three hours, and since hurricanes are adversely affected when they travel over land, a few weathermen thought that this critical moment in the hurricane's life might hold a clue to the mystery.

But no one was taking bets as to what really happened, and on September 4, the *Herald* ran a story headlined, "Hurricane's Fizzle Still Bewilders the Forecasters." Noting that Florida residents had made extensive preparations for the beating they expected to take, the paper reported that no one had anticipated that the storm would just fade away.

Perhaps the most notable statement made during the ruckus was by Neil Frank. "This was one of the most dramatic changes in strength that I've seen in my 20 years of tracking hurricanes," he told a reporter for *U.S. News and World Report.*

During a telephone conversation, Grover described what had been happening to Florida's 1979 weather as the "weirdest in the state's history." It's hard to disagree. Here is Wayne Grover's own account of events:

> In September 1979, when Hurricane David was heading for West Palm Beach, I spoke to Owens about two A.M. the night of the approach. I told him thousands of people would be made homeless because the "manufactured" hurricane was bearing down on us. In an unusual softening, he said something like, "I

don't want to hurt you or your family or others needlessly. I'll ask my SIs to turn the cane away from you. Keep watching the TV to see what happens."

By five in the morning, the local TV weatherman had the National Hurricane Center on the air with new coordinates for the storm. It had suddenly stopped moving toward West Palm Beach and was veering northward away from us. We got fringe winds but nothing more. Owens called about seven and said, "That was for you, Wayne." I didn't believe it was possible, but the series of events went as Owens said they would.

The Florida Demonstration in Summary

In conclusion, then, the Florida demonstration stands out as one of Owens' most successful demonstrations. Although he originally gave only vaguely worded weather predictions regarding Florida's year of trial, he modified them in no uncertain terms during the period of March through August 1979. These revised predictions did, in fact, herald alterations in Florida's normal weather patterns. Perhaps a brief tabulation of these revisions might reiterate just how impressive the demonstration really was. A modified version of the Florida demonstration would shape up something like this:

During Phase One, Owens attempted to offset southern Florida's long-lived drought. He began on April 15, giving himself a few weeks to end it. The drought ended on April 25 when an unseasonable storm of immense proportions struck the state and dropped record rainfall.

Phase Two began after the *National Enquirer* fiasco. Owens had previously warned of oncoming drought conditions in May. That season's expected rainy season never materialized though it should have begun at about the time Owens began reinstating the drought. It was a severely critical dry spell, forcing the enactment of emergency conservation procedures.

Phase Three was initiated by Owens on August 22 when he told Grover that he was about to create a hurricane and bring it to Florida. Though giving himself over thirty days to succeed, the worst hurricane of the century developed only a few days later and threatened to become the first to strike Florida since 1966. Owens decided to abort the hurricane on September 2, and *it mysteriously petered out the next day.*

It should also be pointed out that none of these weather changes could have been inferred normally. No end to the ninety-day drought was foreseen in April. Owens successfully reinstated a drought during a time when Florida usually has abundant rainfall. Further, no hurricane had reached Florida in thirteen years.

Taking all factors into consideration—the normal weather expected during these critical times, coincidence, and natural inference—it certainly looks as though Florida's 1979 weather was somehow manipulated by Ted Owens. The coincidences between the psychic's pronouncements and the resultant changes in Florida's weather are too numerous and exact to be dismissed.

Some will suggest that this Florida sequence of events—if truly manipulated by Owens—reveals him to have been a monster. I understand that some people will feel this way and will think of his demonstrations as demonically inspired. Others will argue, as I myself believed for many years, that Owens was activating forces that are better left undisturbed, at least until the human race has achieved greater moral maturity. Now, however, I have come to view Owens, for all his flaws, in another way. I see him as a liberator, like Moses, struggling to free humanity from a slavish attitude toward serious misconceptions that we hold about our own nature and potentials. If Owens is a monster, in my view, he is no more of a monster than Nature herself. He, after all, did not invent hurricanes or droughts.

CHAPTER 7

IS IT REALLY PSYCHOKINESIS?

In science it often happens that scientists say, "You know, that's a really good argument; my position is mistaken," and then they would actually change their minds, and you never hear that old view from them again. They really do it. It doesn't happen as often as it should, because scientists are human and change is sometimes painful. But it happens every day.

Carl Sagan

"The Book Could Do You Professional Damage"

Unless Owens was a liar and his witnesses were confederates, including myself, some of his demonstrations were nothing less than startling. Therefore, it would be almost unhealthy for most readers, at this point, not to be harboring doubts about the authenticity of cases reported in the previous chapters. Perhaps you suspect that I allowed myself to be duped by Owens for all these years. And why not?

David Henry Hwang's successful Tony Award and Pulitzer Prize winning 1988 Broadway play, *M. Butterfly*, for example, tells the true story of a French diplomat in China who had sexual relations for many years with a man whom he believed to be a woman! None of us are above being fooled. Many people would rather assume that I had allowed myself to be duped than to engage in the difficult work of integrating all of this bizarre data. So, before attempting to develop a scientific context for the "Owens Effect" and related phenomena, it is incumbent upon me to put to rest issues relating to the validity of the material itself.

After casually reading a first draft of this manuscript, the skeptical sociologist Professor Marcello Truzzi of Eastern Michigan University, co-author of *The Blue Sense*—a man generally regarded by parapsychologists as an honest skeptic— urged me to rethink the entire project. Truzzi wrote:

> I think the book could do you professional damage . . . it . . . makes you look enormously credu-lous. Over and over, Owens relates facts that simply stand unchecked and doubtful. My general impres-sion from what you do tell me is that Owens was a prankster early on, worked as a psychic counselor, hypnotist, hustler and probably was familiar with the techniques of deception in this area.

This is a valid concern and needs to be addressed directly. There are various tricks a con artist can use. The most obvious one is that, after an event had occurred, Owens might have fabricated letters purporting to have announced in advance that he would cause such events. Another possible trick is that Owens might have been making multiple predictions all along to different individuals regarding various events, and then simply followed up with documentation for those individuals who received the correct predictions.

The problem with these skeptical hypotheses is that, from 1976 on, all of Owens' predictions and announcements were sent to me in advance of his demonstrations. Prior to that time, he sent them in advance to a group of scientists, including Dr. Leo Sprinkle, a psychologist and ufologist at the University of Wyoming; Dr. J. Allen Hynek of the Center for UFO Studies in Evanston, Illinois; and Russell Targ and Hal Puthoff, at SRI International in Menlo Park, California.

Perhaps what Owens did to fake his supposed successes was to fabricate the various affidavits and testimonials that were then sent to the scientists. The truth is that this is, indeed, a possibility. I have not personally interviewed every alleged witness to Owens' demonstrations. Many of them are now deceased, in any case. However, I have interviewed many, and my research colleagues have interviewed many. *Never once* did an interviewee contradict Owens' account regarding any material facts. Some, of course, would refuse to confirm Owens' interpretation of these facts, such as James Harder who would not interpret a strange light in the sky as a UFO.

Many facts in the Owens' case still stand unchecked. I have used them for purposes of context, not for purposes of evidential proof. Other demonstrations are sufficiently documented to carry some evidential weight.

I have no reason whatsoever to think that Owens engaged in deception. That he had many psychological problems and character defects I would not dispute. He would, for example, try to take credit for a wide range of events that he did not specifically predict. I think that he deceived himself in this regard. But there is no inkling of evidence to support the conventional skeptical theory that Owens engaged in outright deception. In fact, I feel comfortable using the same phrase most often mouthed by skeptics that there is not one shred of evidence supporting *their* hypothesis that Owens, for all his many human faults and frailties, engaged in deception!

Another viable skeptical position is that I, myself, am the trickster. After all, I wrote this book with the idea of obtaining some financial gain. Miracle stories are often popular, and readers are especially vulnerable to authors who make up such tales. It is now well accepted in the academic community that the shamanistic tales written by Carlos Castaneda in his many popular books, such as *The Teachings of Don Juan: A Yaqui Way of Knowledge*, are fictionalized in important regards. This is especially disgraceful, as Castaneda received his doctoral degree in anthropology from UCLA for this same body of work. And, today, he has many followers who are completely unaware of the many errors and loopholes that scholars have found in his writing.

Similar charges have been leveled at other writers as well— George Adamski, author of *Inside the Spaceships*; Lynn Andrews, author of *Medicine Woman*; Courtney Brown, author of *Cosmic Voyage*; Dan Millman, author of *Way of the Peaceful Warrior*, who acknowledges that aspects of his book were fictionalized; David Morehouse, author of *Psychic Warrior*; Marlo Morgan, author of *Mutant Message Down Under*; and Phillip Corso, author of *The Day After Roswell*. In most of these cases, I do not know the specifics regarding the charges of fabrication. Still, rumors can serve to arouse a reader's level of distrust. If you cannot trust these popular authors, why should you trust me?

How am I to defend myself against such an accusation? Fortunately, I am not alone in dealing with this problem. The accusation of researcher fraud is one that has bedeviled parapsychologists for decades. It is, after all, the last refuge of a debunker, and unfortunately, there is just enough fraud among writers and researchers to justify the suspicions of many.

The best defense against accusations of research or literary fraud is to be able to produce multiple witnesses so that the testimony of an author need not be relied upon in and of itself. This is, indeed, the situation with regard to Owens' demonstrations. Although many leading observers of the Owens case have died (i.e., D. Scott Rogo, J. Allen Hynek, Max L. Fogel, and Otto Binder), not all of them are deceased. If I were actually fabricating the reports in this book, it would have to be with the collusion of other independent researchers and witnesses: Hal Puthoff, Russell Targ, Larry Maddry, Charles Jay, Wayne Grover, Leo Sprinkle, and many others. Furthermore, I have my original files on the Owens case intact—neatly organized, month-by-month, in two file drawers. These include the original letters from Owens and copies of hundreds of newspaper clippings, all dated and annotated. Also included are articles and notes on the case, written by many of those who have now passed on.

As time and resources permit, I will make this database available to concerned skeptics and interested researchers via the Internet (www.WilliamJames.com). Science is ill-equipped to explain the phenomena reported herein. Nevertheless, persevering investigation should be able to rule out fraud. I invite those who traditionally criticize and debunk to *first* take a good, hard look at the data.

" . . . Less Than One in a Billion"

None of the scientific disciplines that rely upon statistics, i.e., all the social and behavioral sciences, are able to eliminate the factor of chance coincidence as an explanation of the data. The laws of probability tell us that extremely improbable events do occur. On one occasion, for example, the roulette tables in Monte Carlo recorded forty-two black numbers in a row. Some events can be so rare that they occur only once in the entire history of the universe, assuming both a finite universe and a very specific description of events. Indeed, there is a sense in which every moment in our lives is such an event.

With regard to the demonstrations described in the previous chapters, it is extremely difficult to assess the probabilities in any precise way. My intuition is that the probability that chance alone accounted for the dozens of unique occurrences is less than one in a billion. Let us assume, for purposes of argument, that I am correct. So what? Even if the odds were less than one in a billion trillion, a skeptic is still perfectly entitled to maintain that chance alone is a more reasonable explanation than the alternatives. And, furthermore, we can count on skeptics to argue that, surely, the real probabilities, could they be known, would be closer to one chance in ten than one chance in a billion trillion.

The skeptical argument will be bolstered by the following factors. Virtually none of the Owens demonstrations occurred under scientific conditions—so, from a statistical sense, they carry no weight whatsoever. Furthermore, the account presented here has failed to provide a complete reporting of all of the many statements made by Owens. Perhaps there are tens of thousands of incorrect claims that have been hidden from the readers. If one had a complete picture, one might see that the unusual coincidences were just "lucky hits." Even in those instances that appear to be uncanny "hits," is it possible that the reports have been embellished or distorted?

I regard these as valid objections. From my perspective, the best test of the "chance" hypothesis would have been ongoing testing with Owens. The so-called paranormal, in my view, will only fully enter into the realm of science when we know how to use it reliably for some sort of practical application. It was my hope that research in this direction could have been initiated with Ted Owens during his lifetime. However, this proved not to be possible. The best alternative I can now imagine is to seek other individuals who may have similar talents. Short of that, the historical record itself is still available for scrutiny. I am in possession of what is probably the most complete database of statements made by Ted Owens during his lifetime. These documents can be made available for careful scholarly analysis. My personal assessment is that about a third to two-thirds of Owens' statements seem to have been more or less supported by the facts, depending upon how precisely one wishes to interpret these statements. This is a much higher "hit rate" than has generally been found for psychics who make popular predictions. But how can I quarrel with a skeptic who would prefer to interpret the historical record as nothing more than happenstance, anecdotes incapable of demonstrating or illustrating any scientific point whatsoever?

My next recourse would be to refer to the background database available for the phenomena associated with Ted Owens: psychokinesis, precognition, and UFO-related occurrences. Here, we are not limited merely to anecdotes. We can draw upon both highly organized and analyzed naturalistic observations of thousands of spontaneous cases going back to serious nineteenth-century studies of spiritualism, plus an additional database of hundreds of well-controlled parapsychological experiments starting with J. B. Rhine's research on controlling the fall of dice at Duke University in the 1940s. Excellent summaries of the research have been written by Gertrude Schmeidler and published in the *Advances in Parapsychology* anthologies, edited by Stanley Krippner. Given this context, the case of Ted Owens, while unusual, is not totally unbelievable. There are skeptics, of course, who regard the findings of parapsychology and ufology as so far-fetched and distasteful that they still refuse to accept the data. However, they are on weaker ground because this data was collected using the recognized methods of science.

"He Knows His Predictions Will Come True Because the SIs Make Them Come True"

One of the reasons that parapsychologists settled on the use of the term psi to refer to all ostensible psychic phenomena is that, from a philosophical perspective, it seemed impossible to distinguish between precognition and psychokinesis, as well as between telepathy and clairvoyance. In the case of Ted Owens, for example, how are we to tell whether he predicted various unusual events or, as he often claimed, whether he was instrumental in causing those events?

It was just this precognition versus psychokinesis issue that led to a major boost in Owens' career. One day in 1970, Owens walked to the mailbox outside of his Virginia home and found a letter from a writer named Otto Binder. The writer, corresponding from New York State, had heard about Owens and his abilities and was intrigued by what little he had read. He thought he might like to write a magazine article about Owens and wondered if the psychic would send him some material. This letter to Owens from an anonymous writer was the beginning of a four-year collaboration.

As Owens passed on to the writer hundreds of files, reports, and newspaper clippings, Binder realized that there was more than just a magazine story here. Having recently become interested in the UFO mystery, Binder began to understand that the Owens case might be one of the most important, though unrecognized, cases that could be used to prove the existence of alien intelligences in the universe. As he studied the case further, Binder also realized that the critical issue at stake was to determine whether or not Owens' powers were basically precognitive or psychokinetic in nature. If he could show that they were psychokinetic, Binder theorized, this would go far to prove Owens' claims that some alien intelligence was working through him.

Otto Binder was primarily a science writer who eventually wrote two books on UFOs. He was the author of many science pamphlets and worked for NASA as a technical writer for years. He was a professional at his job, no mere hack. He was an original thinker, and a hard-working investigator, but never pretended to be a scientist. Long before von Daniken started promoting the idea, Binder had already suggested that mankind was seeded on Earth by extraterrestrials. His book on this theme, *Flying Saucers are Watching Us*, was still being reprinted a decade after it was first released in 1967.

While Binder's theories and interpretations are questionable, there is little doubt that he honestly believed what he wrote and based his theories on cases and reports that he had studied seriously. His boldness in presenting unwelcome viewpoints and data made him the ideal person to study and promote the Owens' case. At the time of his death in 1974, he had written no less than four lengthy *Saga* magazine articles on Owens and had spent countless hours organizing and studying his friend's files.

When he died, one of his last requests was that all of this material be returned to the psychic. It was a disappointment for Owens that Binder was never able to begin a biography that would incorporate this material. Owens once mentioned that Binder was the only one capable of writing a book about him. As an added bit of irony, Binder and Owens, despite their four-year collaboration, never personally met.

Binder was more than just a writer since he was also a researcher and he realized the value of getting the Owens story out to the public. He knew the value of placing Owens' predictions in print before they came to pass. *Saga* was a *perfect* medium for him, and anyone interested in the Owens affair might begin by studying these articles that appeared in 1970 (August and September issues) and 1971 (March and April issues). Aside from merely recording Owens' achievements, Binder also tried to evaluate them. This ultimately led him to reject the precognition theory and adopt the view that somehow Owens could directly cause weather changes, UFO appearances, lightning attacks, and other assorted phenomena. Binder reached this conclusion only after a long and detailed evaluation of Owens on whom he reported in his first two *Saga* articles.

Binder's first article was an introduction to Owens and his claims. The crux of the piece was an interview with the space prophet interwoven with material drawn from Owens' book, *How to Contact Space People.* While focusing on Owens' ability to affect weather and "hex" football and basketball teams, Binder made the public aware of the many predictions Owens had made, based on information presumably relayed to him by the Space Intelligences. One of the most notable of these concerned a warning Owens sent to then President Richard Nixon. On July 30, 1969, Owens wrote to the president, saying: "The SIs told me that there is a plot already under way . . . has been completely planned . . . to kidnap you at your Key Biscayne residence. The 'bad guys' (Cubans) know how well protected you are . . . but they are going to strike at night, by water . . . "

Within a month, the *Miami Herald* ran the headline, "Spy Plot Shatters Prospects For Renewing US-Cuba Ties." The story, released on August 24, went on to explain that some of Castro's United Nations diplomats had been caught doubling as espionage agents and that their plan dealt with matters concerning presidential security. It also reported that the plan "was to study President Nixon's movements at his Key Biscayne home, using scuba divers as part of the surveillance team."

But even in his first article, Binder was more intrigued by Owens' apparent PK abilities than his precognitive ones, and publicly announced for the first time that Owens had interfered with the Apollo 12 space shot. This may have been the first time Owens consciously attempted to interfere with our space program, which had such an outstanding success in 1972. Binder reports that on the morning of November 14, 1969— just as Apollo 12 was in its final countdown at Cape Kennedy— Owens told no less than three residents of Virginia Beach, Virginia, that lightning would strike either the launching pad or the spacecraft itself.

"Seconds after the giant rocket roared into the overcast sky," writes Binder, "the control crew at Cape Kennedy was alarmed to see a sudden drop-off of telemetric data from the spacecraft. Through an alternate voice-circuit, astronaut Charles Conrad told how light had gone out within the spacecraft." Conrad could only report back to base that, "I don't know what happened," but added, "I'm not sure we didn't get hit by lightning."

It is tempting to think that the U.S. government would have wished to recruit Owens, given his apparent prodigious PK powers. Surely they were monitoring him, as he did everything in his power to get their attention, including issuing numerous threats. To me, it is evident that the government was no more capable of understanding, accepting, or working with psychokinesis than any other element of our society. Psychokinesis has been almost a taboo topic in science, education, and business. Even many parapsychologists are uncomfortable with the idea. In this context, it seems clear that no government official would dare risk his career on behalf of Ted Owens.

In this germinal report on Owens, Binder didn't attempt to analyze what process was behind Owens' talents and took his claims of possessing PK abilities at face value. He gave a similar treatment to the Owens matter in his second article, in which he again quoted material from *How to Contact Space People*. However, in this article he publicly stated that Owens had tried to warn Lyndon Johnson, then president, of a threat against his life.

Owens wrote to President Johnson on May 10, 1966, claiming that a man was planning to crash a plane loaded with explosives into either the White House or into Johnson's ranch in Texas. He also warned that the would-be assassin was either an ex-Army flier or serviceman. This prediction didn't come to pass until May 4, 1967—almost exactly one year later—when, as the *New York Times* reported, "A former Air Force pilot has been jailed pending sentence because of an alleged threat to plunge a plane into the White House."

This is an impressive case indeed, since there can be little doubt about the coincidences in Owens' warning. His letter contained three direct hits—including the information that (a) someone would attempt an air assault on Johnson; (b) that this crash would occur either at the White House or at Johnson's Texas ranch; and (c) the would-be assailant would be a serviceman. The only problem with the prediction was that its fulfillment did not come to pass until a year later. But it occurred almost on the very anniversary of Owens' announcement.

This time-lapse phenomenon impressed researcher D. Scott Rogo as one of the most convincing aspects of this unusual case. If Owens were lying about writing to Johnson, or if Binder had merely made the story up in order to highlight his article, either of them could have done a better job of it instead of marring a good story by adding a one-year time-delay factor. Yet—and surely neither Owens nor Binder realized it at the time—this odd one-year "delayed phenomenon response" is consistent with some fascinating data about precognitive experiences reported from Germany by Dr. Hans Bender.

Bender was the former head of the Institute for the Study of Borderline Areas of Psychology and Psychohygiene at the University of Freiburg and Germany's leading parapsychologist. For nearly nineteen years, Christine Mylius, a German actress and psychic, had been having precognitive dreams and had been filing them with Dr. Bender. From this large database, Bender was able to isolate several characteristics of Mylius' dreams. One of these features was her habit of precognizing an event that would eventually occur exactly one year later. These have been called "anniversary cases."

Although Owens' prediction was not realized in exactly one year's time, it was fulfilled close enough to the anniversary of the prediction to suggest that it and its denouement were possibly more than merely a coincidence.

Binder's article ended with a brief list of validated predictions Owens had made over the previous several years. These set the stage for Binder's third and most important piece on Owens, in which he directly attempted to resolve the precognition versus psychokinesis issue. This was a problem he had never clearly raised before, but that had obviously been in his mind for some time. Published in the March 1971 issue of *Saga* with the eye-catching title, "Ted Owens—Flying Saucer Missionary," Owens believed this article to be the authoritative statement on the nature of his abilities.

In his previous articles, Binder was primarily concerned with the accuracy of Owens' predictions and the authenticity of his claimed contacts with the Space Intelligences. But in this third article, he squarely confronted the parapsychological aspects of Owens' powers and devoted the crux of the discussion to Owens' alleged PK abilities. He was especially concerned with Owens' weather-control talents. On the basis of his success at psychic weather control, Binder wrote that Owens was "not really a prophet at all, looking blindly into the future. He knows his predictions will come true because the SIs make them come true. Ted is merely announcing them in advance."

Binder went on to point out that Owens' ability to foul up space launches (see chapter 10) suggested that a psychic could induce a direct long-distance PK effect. To reinforce this suggestion he cited two specific examples where such a mechanism seemed to have been efficacious:

> In November 1964, the Mariner 4 space probe was launched from Cape Kennedy to Mars. On December 13, Ted wrote NASA that he was putting a "PK Light" on Mariner to follow it all the way and affect its mission in adverse ways.
>
> Mariner reached Mars on July 14, 1965, and swung around the planet as programmed. But what was entirely unprogrammed was Mariner's reappearance on the planet's other side eight minutes late. NASA scientists were utterly bewildered and shocked.

After UFOs were reported over both the deep-space Goldstone tracking station in California and the Tidbinbilla facility at Canberra, Australia, all kinds of "conflicting signals" came from Mariner. It failed to shut off maneuvering systems, and it kept power circuits on that drained its batteries. In short, Mariner went "wild" and violated its built-in electronic control systems.

August 1965. Ted had put a PK hex on the Gemini 5 flight, calling for a power failure, and promptly on August 22, its fuel cells malfunctioned. NASA authorities debated whether to bring the manned ship down and abort the mission.

But the SIs communicated with Ted and said they would, on their own, return the power as a gesture of good will to the President of the United States. And the next day, full power magically returned to the Gemini craft, although the fuel cells were still faulty according to telemetric data. Ted calls this another "on the button" feat in partnership with the SIs.

The preceding words are taken directly from Binder's article. Since the files on the incidents are not in those to which I have access, I could not check Binder's accuracy. However, after checking Binder's articles, researcher D. Scott Rogo was able to find only two minor inaccuracies in Binder's treatment of the Owens material. So, Rogo was tempted to think that these writeups were probably correct.

After citing these two cases, Binder, through a long line of reasoning, began his argument that Owens' power was basically PK-mediated. If PK could control the roll of dice and other moving systems as J. B. Rhine postulated during his pioneering 1940s Duke University research, Binder thought that there was no reason to reject the possibility that it could affect weather or missile flights. He also pointed out that no one had ever discovered a fixed limit to how ostensible PK could function, or what potentials it could reach. After making these two points, Binder finally addressed himself directly to the precognition problem.

> Is Ted Owens unwittingly using pure precognition? That is, does he have the power (miraculous in itself) to peer into the future and see coming events that turn out true 85 percent of the time? The SIs and his contacts with them could then be mental "window dressing" out of his subconscious mind, as it somehow delves with uncanny accuracy into the future. This would mean too that his so-called powers are imaginary—that he does not control or make hurricanes and has never spoiled a space shot with a PK shot.

By way of an answer, Binder returned to the subject of J. B. Rhine's experiments at Duke, starting in 1930. When Rhine first became interested in precognition, he tested his subjects by having them guess the order of cards in a twenty-five-member deck, each card being imprinted with one of five different geometrical figures, before it was shuffled. The results of these tests were meager, but statistically significant. Binder, drawing upon these results, argued that they decidedly indicated that precognition is a weak ability and could not be used on a grand scale with any accuracy—the very kind of scale and accuracy needed to explain the Owens' effect.

Second, argued Binder, the SI-PK theory is a better explanatory model for Owens' feats since it explains the process behind his demonstrations. He supported this theory by outlining two principles: (a) that UFOs are seen all over the world, therefore (b) these craft exist and their occupants must be far more intelligent than we are, and are capable of endowing us with extraordinary abilities.

Binder ended his line of reasoning by pointing out that the existence of ESP, which had been aptly demonstrated in the laboratory, could therefore be a very likely method of communication between humans and the extraterrestrials. By applying this chain of logic to the Owens' case, Binder believed all of his friend's abilities could be explained within a simple framework. He wrote, "The pure precognition theory is barely possible, while the SI-contact explanation is more highly probable."

Although one can be sympathetic to Binder's arguments, researcher D. Scott Rogo found them unconvincing in the long run. Rogo wrote:

> In fact, his argumentation is often rather misguided. To begin with, he missed one very obvious point. If the success of Rhine's PK tests does not preclude the existence of more powerful PK forces controllable by man, then the results of his precognition experiments likewise do not preclude the possibility that we are capable of extraordinary feats of prevision. If seen in that light, Binder's whole theoretical edifice crumbles around him.
>
> Binder's point about the extraterrestrials is also dubious, since it is based on a non sequitur. It is indeed true that UFOs exist and are a real phenomenon somehow invading our skies. The evidence as to their existence is overwhelming. But it does not necessarily follow that they are being manned by beings from outer space.

Over the last three decades many ufologists—including J. Allen Hynek himself—have come to revise the extraterrestrial hypothesis. They have argued that such a theory cannot explain the number of UFO sightings reported each year from around the world, the behavior of UFO occupants, and so forth.

Hynek, taking his lead from the writings and research of other leading UFO experts, suggested that UFOs were somehow the result of a psychic or paraphysical process, perhaps similar to those that cause the production of materializations or apparitions. That they are somehow produced by our own minds or by our culture is a possibility many ufologists are now entertaining. They do not deny that these flying discs or cigars are physical objects, but they feel that they are based here on Earth and brought into being only temporarily by our own minds under conditions still to be determined.

Despite the fact that Binder's arguments were not too convincing, it may well be that he came to a correct conclusion but by the wrong line of reasoning. PK probably played some role in Owens' demonstrations, the extent of which has not been determined. But it is also obvious that precognition played just as great a role. One must always remember that precognition and psychokinesis are not discrete phenomena. During the process of precognition, the human mind is somehow interacting with physical reality and drawing information from it. During psychokinesis the mind is interacting with physical reality and manipulating it. They are two sides of the same coin; so, it doesn't seem unusual that a psychic gifted in one ability would also be gifted with the other. They are interchangeable abilities.

CHAPTER 8

SUPER FAN

PK might be used to determine the outcome of a game or even an entire season. And not only the athletes might contribute their psychic abilities to this endeavor but the coaches, too, could exercise PK. Spectators at games could use it. Even fans watching the game on their TVs at home could use PK.

Rhea White

In Front of the TV Set with a Bottle of Scotch

During his Cleveland and Chicago experiments, described in chapter 5, Owens apparently affected a system more complex than the weather, more sophisticated than a NASA missile, and more unpredictable than an erupting volcano. It appears that he was able to influence the workings of the human brain in order to make people behave in erratic and bizarre ways.

The odd, lunatic behavior of so many local residents during these demonstrations, such as people claiming to hear the voice of God or receiving messages from outer space, may have been mitigated by several factors. Living in the decadent and stagnant confines of this country's poverty-stricken inner cities can create pressing conditions that may cause people to act in socially unacceptable ways. So it is hard to tell if Owens really had anything to do with the activities reported from these two Midwestern cities. Despite such factors, there were more specific instances when it did seem that Ted Owens had made people behave just the way he wanted them to. This fact was no better illustrated than by his ability to influence sports events. Owens was an avid sports fan, and he had been trying to sway the outcomes of football and basketball games for several years.

Just how Owens manipulated a football game was fascinating, especially when he did it through TV. This procedure is simple. First he sat down in front of a wide-screen color TV, armed with a healthy stock of beer (Dutch imported, no less) and a bottle of Scotch. He leisurely sipped away during the course of the game and let his PK go into action. Owens claimed that he could do little to actually help a team. He could only hinder their opponents. From there, claimed the psychic, the team he was assisting must take advantage of the situations that arose.

"It is up to them," the psychic stated. "If they aren't going to take advantage of what I'm doing, I can't help them either."

During a football game, for instance, Owens felt that he could do little to affect runs or kicks, so he focused on passes. Each time the opposing quarterback was ready to pass, Owens would point his hand at the TV—almost as if giving the sign of the evil eye—and would concentrate on blurring the player's vision so that the pass would be incomplete. He also constantly focused his attention over the opposing team in order to imbue the playing field itself with his force. And if he got mad enough, he would start shouting, "Enemy! Enemy!" each time the cameramen came in for a close-up of an opposing team member. The demonstrations were nerve-wracking to watch, and Owens usually locked his family out of his study while he attempted to manipulate a game.

Owens' sports interest represented a quiet bit of irony in one respect. For years he had been trying to persuade scientists and parapsychologists to take his claims seriously, and had urged them to publish his predictions, demonstrations and successes. But he had generally failed in obtaining this type of public attention. Yet his ability to influence sports events, which was perhaps the most flippant way in which Owens used his psychic abilities, earned him headlines in sports columns across the country and in some of this nation's most prestigious papers.

Just as with his weather demonstrations, Owens' sports exhibitions covered a wide range of forms, guises, and effects. Sometimes he would attempt to influence the overall outcome of a specific game; at other times, he would try to control, for better or worse, a particular player. And if he got sufficiently riled, Owens was likely to hex a team for an entire season.

"PK Might Contribute to the Outcome of a Game or Even an Entire Season"

None of these claims should strike anyone as strange, since a sporting event—especially team competition—may serve as a perfect setting for ESP and PK manipulation. We know that an athletic competition is a random system of sorts. During a basketball or football match, for instance, people dart about every which way, balls are thrown with dizzying regularity, and the slightest error in judgment, movement, or skill can significantly alter the outcome of a play, game, or even an entire season. It is for this reason that a few parapsychologists have long wondered to what extent psychic factors might interact during athletic competitions. Could freak plays, miraculous outcomes, or bizarre maneuvers on the playing field have been mitigated by ESP or PK? Could psychic ability be the athlete's edge?

We needn't just speculate on these questions, since strong anecdotal evidence exists that suggests an inherent relationship between psychic phenomena and the state of mind the athlete enters during competition.

"Competitive sports demand a great deal of the participating athlete," wrote Rhea White in her classic book, *The Psychic Side of Sports*, co-authored with Michael Murphy. White is a sports fan as well as a highly regarded parapsychologist who has made a detailed study of the role psychic abilities play in sports.

"They must be strongly motivated," she goes on to say, "employ intense concentration, yet remain relaxed, visualize their targets, and drive themselves beyond the normal limitation of their muscles. It shouldn't seem strange, then, that some of these athletes, as they push themselves up to this extra mental and physical output, are using PK."

White went on to point out that an athlete gifted with psychic ability would have a considerable edge in such games as golf, football, or basketball. An athlete, like a laboratory PK subject, is constantly trying to will a certain outcome to take place, and there seems little reason that this type of willful volition couldn't become a real but unrecognized factor in sports. Baseballs that take odd turns in the air leading to base hits, players who always seem to be in the right place at the right time, inexplicable errors and fumbles—all these might be manifestations of psychic forces inadvertently unleashed by athletes in the heat of a game.

"Moreover," suggested White, "PK might be used to determine the outcome of a game or even an entire season. And not only the athletes might contribute their psychic abilities to this endeavor but the coaches, too, could exercise PK. Spectators at games could use it. Even fans watching the game on their TVs at home could use PK."

White isn't the only parapsychologist who takes the idea of "spectator PK" seriously. Our U.S. chess teams have never been comfortable about the fact that the former Soviets regularly employ psychics to "whammy" them during international competitions. This most pragmatic use of ESP and PK brings us back to the issue of Ted Owens' claims that he has been able to produce just this type of effect over the TV.

It is nonetheless interesting to note that, years ago, experimental parapsychologists discovered a curious effect that represents a laboratory analog to the spectator PK effect. This discovery was made back in the 1940s when a few of the original Duke University researchers began conducting "help/hinder" tests. These were relatively simple dice-throwing tests in which two subjects were used. Sometimes both subjects would try to influence a series of dice throws in the same direction, by trying to make one specific die face come up more often than chance could account for. These attempts would alternate with other trials in which one of the subjects would attempt to offset his partner's success by focusing his attention on a different target. The first help/hinder experiment was published by the Duke University Parapsychology Laboratory in 1947.

It was Betty Humphrey, a young research associate at the lab, who reported that extra-chance results had been obtained during the "help" condition, while only chance scoring had been achieved during the "hinder" condition. From these results one might suggest that a spectator at a PK experiment could significantly influence the outcome of that test.

The Humphrey experiment has only been replicated once, some twenty years later (1968) by two other parapsychologists working at the same Durham, North Carolina, lab (now off campus) where Humphrey had conducted her original work. Their experiment showed no consistent results, though. Nonetheless, the fact that help/hinder PK tests have been successful in the past suggests that Owens' claims about his ability to influence sporting events is not impossible.

Perhaps most psychokinesis by spectators goes unnoticed because the influences of many different people cancel each other out. A clear, coherent mind, full of both self-confidence and mental focus, is rare enough in our world. Psychokinetic talent, of the type apparently exhibited by individuals such as Uri Geller or Ted Owens, is also extremely rare and controversial. So, it should be no surprise that our understanding of PK is so meager.

"I Will Take the Eagles Apart with PK"

Sometimes Owens would focus his PK directly on a specific player in a more overt way than merely making him fumble a pass. One such incident occurred in 1968 as a result of the psychic's long-standing feud with the Philadelphia Eagles.

In 1965, Owens approached the Eagles' management with the offer that, for a fee, he would assure the team's victory that year and lead them to the Super Bowl. The management wouldn't even meet with the psychic to discuss the matter; so, in retaliation, Owens decided to hex the team for good. The hex was publicly announced when Philadelphia newspapers published a story about Owens versus the Eagles in October 1966. The papers flippantly quoted the story when it became obvious that the Eagles were putting on a poor showing that season. Joe McGinnis, a sportswriter in Philadelphia, met with Owens to discuss the situation and later assured his readers that Owens had indeed written the owner of the team that "since you will not take me seriously, and graciously meet with me to discuss the matter, from now on, in each Eagle game, I will use my PK system."

"I don't like using PK against the Eagles," Owens told the sportswriter. But he was finding the team's management hardheaded. "The only way I can make them believe in it," he added, "is to clobber them with it."

Owens explained to McGinnis how he enacted one of his PK curses. "When I use it against a football team like the Eagles," he explained, "it blankets the field and attaches itself to each man. Basically, what it does is magnify human error. Everything goes wrong for the team under the spell. The other team will get ten scoring opportunities for every one the team I'm working against gets. If they take advantage, even a little bit, well, they win the game."

The Eagles didn't have a cheery 1966 season, and in 1968 Owens went on the attack. Before the commencement of the 1968 season, the psychic, then still living in Philadelphia, wrote to several local sportswriters to say that he would "take the Eagles apart with PK" and that he would cause no less than twenty injuries to the team during the season. It looks as if he made good on his claim, too. The Eagles lost eleven straight games after Owens made his threat, and suffered thirty injuries by the end of the season. But what may have been the highlight of the team's bad luck came on September 29. This is the incident to which I alluded at the beginning of this section.

Stan Hochman, a sportswriter for the *Philadelphia Daily-News* and one of the writers Owens had first contacted, had begun to take the psychic seriously when he saw how badly the Eagles were doing that year. Hochman became so intrigued with Owens that he decided to take the psychic with him to a key game scheduled against the Dallas Cowboys on September 29.

"I figured I'd pin him down as to his claims of hexing the team," Hochman wrote in his September 30 column after the game had ended in a rousing defeat for the Eagles.

Hochman went on to report that, throughout the game, Owens attempted to beat down the Eagles, but wasn't getting much help from the Cowboys, who had begun the game by playing decidedly under par. The Eagles' star fullback, Tom Woodeshick, was having a field day at Dallas' expense and was taking advantage of his opponents' poor showing by gaining yardage on nearly every play.

"The SIs are going to have to get Woodeshick," Owens finally told Hochman who quoted the conversation word for word in his column the next day. He also said that he had heard Owens invoke the Space Intelligences by saying, "Get him out of the game. Bull's-eye on number 37. Shift your target to Woodeshick."

What happened next is a matter of public record. Several moments after Hochman overheard Owens invoking the Space Intelligences against Woodeshick, an altercation developed between the Cowboys and the Eagles over an interception. A pushing match between the two teams ensued. It didn't seem that the fight was too serious until Woodeshick, who was sitting on the bench at the time, suddenly jumped out onto the field like an enraged bull and tried to rip the headgear off a Dallas player. He was immediately ejected from the game and all within a few minutes of Owens' psychic invocation. Owens later told Hochman that the Space Intelligences had caused Woodeshick to behave wildly so that he would be tossed out of the game for the day. It was a more humane way of getting rid of him than through an injury, he implied.

The game ended as a disaster for the Eagles. Interceptions abounded, fumbles were the order of the day, and the Cowboys, despite their shaky start, ended up trouncing Philadelphia by 45 to 13 in a game more comical than inspirational.

"I Am Out to Get the Team"

The Eagles, however, were not the only team toward whom Owens felt a certain amount of animosity. In 1971, he decided to hex the Baltimore Colts for the same reason he had hexed the Eagles. Before the season began, Owens had written to Carroll Rosenbloom, who controlled the Colts, suggesting that, for $100,000, he would insure the team's success. Rosenbloom wasn't thrilled with the idea, but according to an April 27, 1971, *Virginian-Pilot* story, he offered Owens $25,000 for his services if the psychic would get permission from Pete Rozelle, the National Football League (NFL) commissioner. Negotiations broke down, as Rosenbloom no doubt expected they would, and Owens never got the money. He got even angrier when Rosenbloom wrote him a further letter explaining that, even if he were able to come up with some money, his fellow owners would never forgive him for taking Owens seriously.

Since Carroll Rosenbloom is now dead, we will never know whether he was serious about his offer or whether he was merely humoring the psychic. But the Colts had a miserable season that year, whatever the case. The Colts also sustained six major injuries within a short time span from the time Owens originally notified Rosenbloom that he would destroy the team by placing it on a list of five NFL teams he was going to help defeat. It is a matter of record that Rosenbloom did, in fact, write to Owens twice during the season specifically asking him to remove the Colts from his list of hexed teams.

However, on December 1, 1971, Owens attempted to influence the Baltimore Colts (world champions at the time) so that they would suffer setbacks and fail to reach the Super Bowl that year. He notified a friend in Florida that he would help the Miami Dolphins win game after game until they were strong enough to beat the Colts, but warned that he would desert the Dolphins after they beat the Colts in the playoffs so that they would lose at the Super Bowl.

During the next several weeks, Owens' influence seemed to have spurred the Dolphins, who suddenly found themselves on a winning streak. After trouncing Baltimore, they seemed headed for the Super Bowl. But their luck ran against them, just as Owens had predicted, and they lost to the Dallas Cowboys.

This case may not seem particularly impressive, but it must be remembered that Owens had to successfully predict or cause a number of individual outcomes in order to implement his long-range plan in bringing the Dolphins to the Super Bowl only to make them lose at the last minute. Luckily, we also have clear confirmation as to the specific nature of Owens' predictions because his friend in Florida wrote out a complete affidavit in February of 1972 about the psychic's forecasts.

Owens' animosity toward Rosenbloom did not end with the Colts affair but may have followed the owner to a new team when he bought the Los Angeles Rams. With Rosenbloom now in charge of Los Angeles' prize team, Owens decided to go after them during the 1972 pro football season. He added salt to the wound by advising Rosenbloom in advance that he was out to get the team. That he made good his threat is once again a matter of public record. The Rams had a disastrous season! The *Los Angeles Herald Examiner* went so far as to run a story on the Rams' bad-luck streak in December and labeled 1972 their "strangest season." The story especially noted the large number of heart-breaking losses the team had undergone because of freak accidents, goofed-up plays, and plain old incompetence.

Even the Rams' coach, Tommy Prothro, admitted to the *Examiner* that his team was playing as though accursed. "I can't ever recalling [sic] any team I've coached having more misfortune on the field than this one," the *Examiner* quoted the coach as saying after a disastrous game against the Cardinals that week. "We've had so many unfortunate things happen to us this season that maybe our luck will change this weekend."

"Put the Blame Where It Belongs . . . On Ted Owens"

Nor were Owens' feats being recognized only by newspaper sportswriters. *Sports* magazine was impressed enough with Owens' psychic record that they ran a story on him as part of their July 1971 issue in their "Sport Talk" column. That was the year Owens decided to go after the Baltimore Bullets basketball team when its management refused to act on Owens' offer to help them out. Owens' specific animosity against the Bullets is another case that cannot be understood unless viewed within a larger context.

Owens had not started the 1971 basketball season with any particular spite against the Bullets, even though they had rejected his "psychic protection" offer. But his attitude changed drastically during the April championship finals when the team was playing against the Milwaukee Bucks in Baltimore. Although the Bullets had rejected Owens' offer only five days before, the psychic had at first decided to take no action against them. But then an unfortunate remark by a Baltimore sports commentator changed the whole picture—and may have helped insure Baltimore's defeat in the playoffs. As *Sports* tells the story:

> To all Baltimore Bullets fans, a plea for justice: Don't blame the team's failure in the NBA championship series on Lew Alcindor or the Big O. Don't blame it on the Baltimore players, either. Put the blame where it belongs. Blame it on Ted Owens.
>
> How's that? Ted who? Just a moment, fans. Ted Owens happens to have super-human power. By simply concentrating, Ted Owens says, he can control events anywhere on Earth or in space—all without leaving his living room. And when the Bullets made Ted Owens mad, he used his power.
>
> It happened during the first quarter of the second playoff game. The Bullets were trailing the Bucks, but not by much, when telecaster Keith Jackson mentioned that "a man in Virginia has offered to cast the evil eye on Milwaukee to help Baltimore win." The man from Virginia (Norfolk) was 51-year-old Ted Owens and he had made that offer to Bullet coach Gene Shue, who politely declined it. "That was

bad enough," says Owens, "but when Keith Jackson made it public on TV, I immediately called the Baltimore Sun and told them: 'I'll wreck the Bullets in the second half. Watch it. I'll make them miss their baskets and I'll throw their timing completely haywire.'" The Bullets trailed by four at the half; they lost the game by 19. The rest of the series was a Milwaukee laugh-in.

The *Sports* story serves to augment an April 30 AP news release that documents the Bullets' terrible showing during their third play-off game. The story related that the Baltimore team, having played well enough to make it to the NBA championships, was missing their shots to a staggering degree, and had seven percent more misses than their year's average. The AP story described the team as "frustrated and humiliated" and caustically remarked that the team was bound to achieve the worst NBA championship showing since 1958-59, when the Minneapolis Lakers lost four straight to the Boston Celtics.

"They [the Bullets] have the right to refuse the PK man," was the only thing Owens would say when the *Baltimore Sun* interviewed him about the affair. "But not over television."

Competing with "The Great Kahuna"

On April 30, 1972, in a letter to John Kerr, vice-president of the Virginia Squires basketball team, Owens predicted that he was going to use his PK powers to cause Kerr's team to lose its American Basketball Association (ABA) playoff series against the New York Nets. At the time the letter was written, the Squires were ahead 3-2 in the seven game series. Owens stated in his letter that he was angered when he received a call from a representative of the team asking him to help out, but refusing to pay him a fee for his service. Furthermore, the Squires had hired a

"PK Master" called "The Great Kahuna" to help them win the series and to entertain the audience at halftime.

Newspaper clippings indicate that the Squires lost the next two games and thus the series. One article states that, in the final game, the Squires missed 57 of 91 shots and made the fewest number of points since moving to Virginia two years previously.

There are dozens of similar cases in the files in which Owens has apparently used his PK abilities to affect the outcome of basketball and football games with success. Sportswriters have generally received Owens' claims favorably and presented him as something of a hero opposing the big business management of the teams. His exploits have even received coverage in several national sports magazines.

"Owens, at Times, Deliberately Picked Underdogs"

Owens had for years asserted that he could manipulate not only particular games, but whole seasons, and he had been more than willing to back up his claims with demonstrations. This led him, in 1973, to contact Dr. Max Fogel of Mensa in hopes that the Baltimore psychiatrist would help evaluate one of his experiments.

Owens contacted Fogel about the experiment in September when he decided to design a foolproof test to prove his claim that he could influence sports events even at a long distance. Fogel consented to monitor the experiment, and the following protocol was agreed upon.

As the basis for the test, Owens would try to influence a lengthy series of pro football games. Only those games listed in *TV Guide* for telecast would be used as "target" games, and the experiment would run through the entire 1973 season. Owens proposed that he would stay at his Virginia home and watch two TV sets simultaneously, if necessary, so that he could influence two games at once. He also announced that he would not be adverse to influencing three games at any one time. In order to keep the experiment as controlled as possible, each week Owens agreed to send Fogel a list of the games he would attempt to influence and which teams he would try to help win. A success rate of 75 percent was his goal.

The experiment was conducted precisely as Owens and Fogel had agreed upon. Tabulating the results was an easy matter as well since Owens also agreed to send the Mensa scientist published notification of game scores along with tear sheets from *TV Guide* showing exactly which games should be incorporated into the final results.

The eventual outcome of the experiment was just a little short of Owens' goal. The psychic tried to influence a total of 62 games; he achieved 44 wins and 16 losses, and there were two ties. This tallied up to a success factor of between 71 and 73 percent, depending on whether the ties are considered as failures or are deleted from the sample.

This certainly is an impressive success rate, but it is difficult to translate these figures into probability statistics to determine if they are meaningful. The question we have to ask ourselves is rudimentary. Was Owens' success during this 1973 experiment more significant than what might have been expected by chance? This is an extremely difficult question to answer. The outcome of a football game does not rest on simple fifty-fifty odds since a sporting event can be "loaded" by several factors. This is why so many amateur athletic matches, such as bowling and golf, employ handicapping in order to even up the odds between the competitors. Although pro football teams do not use handicaps, any sports fan knows that one team will always have an edge over another based on such factors as its past performance, who is in the lineup, and so forth. This is why gambling on sports events has become a virtual science. All these factors must be taken into account before one can properly evaluate the Owens-Fogel experiment.

"It is difficult to know how to interpret these findings," wrote Dr. Fogel in an affidavit dated February 21, 1974, describing the experiment. "We cannot use typical parapsychological statistics since the predictions were not based upon chance observations. Rather, Owens did have information about the worth of each of his teams, information that undoubtedly influenced his predictions one way or another. However, it would not be valid to compare Owens' predictions with those of, say, sports page predictors since Owens, at times, deliberately picked underdogs in order to attempt to demonstrate his abilities. So his work and intentions should not be called either guesswork or straight predictions, but something in between."

Unfortunately, Fogel did not offer his readers any statistics showing how successful Owens was in specifically influencing underdogs. It would have been helpful to know this data to see how the psychic's success in these instances compared to his overall accuracy.

It is unfortunate, also, that this experiment was designed so loosely that it cannot help us to understand much about Owens' psychic abilities. It is impossible to judge from the results whether Owens was predicting the winners or using his psychic abilities to influence the outcomes. This experiment would have been much better controlled had Fogel randomly determined which team he wanted Owens to help psychically. Any significant outcome would probably then have been the result of a PK process. It might also have been wise had Fogel asked Owens to try to aid only the teams that were considered the underdogs. If he had then achieved a fifty percent success rate under such conditions, it would undoubtedly have been significant. Of course, no one can blame Fogel for the various difficulties one faces in making any meaningful sense out of the Owens experiment. Fogel was, after all, monitoring an experiment primarily designed by Owens himself. But the way things stand, we have no way of determining the extent to which PK played a role in Owens' 73-percent-win record, and to what degree unconscious precognition influenced him when he chose which teams he wanted to win.

Owens gave Fogel another demonstration of his spectator PK effect in 1973, one that was above and beyond his long-range attempts to influence the NFL season that year. On November 4, he notified Fogel that he was going to try to exert a significant influence over an upcoming Washington Redskins versus Pittsburgh Steelers game slated for November 5. The Steelers were considered the underdogs, and professional odds-makers were wagering on a clear-cut victory for Washington. Besides the fact that the Washington team had played a better season, one of the Steelers' key players was out of the lineup due to an injury. Despite all this, the Steelers pulled the match out of the fire during the last few minutes of the game—and all because of a freak play. The Redskins had control of the ball just as time was running out. During what could have been the final and winning play of the game, the Redskins fumbled, and the ball landed in the hands of a Pittsburgh safety. Then he fumbled it, too, but another Steeler gained possession of the ball and was able to run out the clock, in order to maintain the victory.

The play was so weird that even the Steelers didn't know what to make of it. "We've got someone up there taking care of us," was the only thing Joe Greene, a tackle for the team could say after the game.

"The Cowboys Are About to Be Destroyed"

During Owens' 1974 Texas demonstration, which is more completely detailed in chapter 5, in addition to fouling up the Texas weather, he wrote to Ed Busch promising to hex the Cowboys forever. While it is debatable just how efficacious Owens had been in permanently destroying the team, 1974 was an awfully bad year for the Cowboys. Although one of the NFL's most colorful teams, their performance began to ebb as soon as Owens focused his negative intentions on them. A story published in the November 20 issue of the *Virginian-Pilot*, a little over two weeks after *Owens'* announced his curse, summed it up best. It read, in part:

> Dallas Cowboy Coach Tom Landry said he can't pinpoint the decline of his perennial NFL powerhouse but admitted "some strange things are going to have to happen" for his team to make the playoffs a record eighth consecutive year.
>
> "Our chances are slim and obviously, because of the tie breakers, Washington will have to lose three out of its last four games, and we've got to win all four to get the wild card," Landry said.
>
> Dallas is 5-5 in the National Conference East Division—two games behind Washington and three behind pace-setting St. Louis.
>
> Landry said No. 1 quarterback Roger Staubach, who was hospitalized with an infection of his throwing arm, was to be released from the hospital Tuesday night and will play Sunday against Houston.
>
> "We've been giving Roger some antibiotics, and his elbow is progressing well," Landry said.
>
> Asked what was wrong with his club, Landry said, "Your guess is as good as mine. We've lost a lot of close games. It's been an unusual year. You don't see many teams playing good football—maybe Oakland and now Miami—that's about it."

It is also significant that Owens specifically predicted the injury to Roger Staubach. On November 3, he sent a telegram to Frank Vehorn in which he stated that Staubach "will be injured" and that the Cowboys were about to be destroyed. Staubach had to be hospitalized two weeks later when his elbow became inflamed due to an injury to it a week prior.

"The Football Games . . . Should Be Wild, Freakish, and Quite Funny"

Ted Owens' 1975 "Chicago Demonstration" has already been discussed in chapter 5, in which some details were provided regarding his hexing of the Chicago Bears football team. Specifically, Owens, in a letter to WCFL radio announcer Doug Dahlgren, predicted that he would cause:

> . . . Poltergeist phenomena . . . I will send hundreds of poltergeist entities into the area . . . to cause all sorts of mischievous, prankish, freak happenings. This will cover, of course, . . . the stadium in which the Chicago Bears play football. I will especially request that the poltergeists not harm anyone. . . . But the football games of the Bears in that stadium, in the months ahead . . . should be wild, freakish, and quite funny.

In the *Chicago Tribune* of October 29, 1975, columnist Jack Mabley remarked on Owens' demonstration as follows:

> The Bears Are Bugged: I've come across an interesting theory about what's happening to the Chicago Bears. Poltergeists. From flying saucers. When a team loses a close game because on one play they had only 91 per cent of their team on the field, you've got to look for more sophisticated reasons than bad coaching or missed signals.
>
> The poltergeist theory is contained in an "I told you so" letter from one Ted Owens, of Cape Charles, Virginia, who calls himself "The UFO Prophet," to one Doug Dahlgren of WCFL.
>
> Apparently Dahlgren challenged Owens to produce a UFO phenomena in Chicago. On October 8 Owens

announced he would "send hundreds of poltergeist entities into the area . . . to cause all sorts of mischievous, prankish, freak happenings."

He says he has connections with the occupants of the flying objects, and set this up with instructions that nobody was to get hurt.

. . . Of the caliber of the Bears' play I'd say the poltergeists had some of their greatest moments Monday night when the Bears had only 10 men on the field as Tarkenton tossed the winning touchdown. I could almost see the little men sitting in their saucer over Soldier Field with the lights out, hugging their sides in mirth. What's cooking for the next game, fellows?

On November 3, the sports headlines were: "Have Mercy . . . Don't Laugh At Bear Comedy." And on November 17, "Bears Can't Win For Fear Of Losing."

Did He Do It by Telepathy or PK?

Cases such as the above could be cited ad infinitum. There would be little point in doing so, though. The examples I have cited give substance to Owens' claim that he could affect the outcome of sporting events and the behavior of particular athletes. This finding, in itself, should be no new revelation to parapsychologists since, as pointed out earlier, they have long suspected that psi might be a hitherto unrecognized factor in sports performance. Even some of this country's leading parapsychologists have thought about trying to experimentally demonstrate this possibility. We have often heard this idea bandied about in conversations with both American and European researchers.

The most important aspect of Owens' sports demonstrations is that they help us to understand a little about the nature of the psychic's abilities. So let's turn to this fascinating issue.

There are two ways in which an athlete's performance might be influenced by a psychic. (1) He could affect the player himself so that he loses coordination or makes serious errors in his decision making processes, or (2) the psychic might be able to psychokinetically affect such items as moving balls, pucks, and so forth. If PK can deflect a rolling die, it certainly should be able to influence a rolling golf ball. Now there is some evidence that Owens has been able to employ both of these psychic processes during his sports exhibitions. It also seems clear that he has the ability to directly influence the minds of the players he is trying to manipulate.

The Tom Woodeshick incident will seem a good case in point. Owens may have somehow influenced the fullback's brain, thereby causing him to act wildly and violently in a situation in which such behavior was totally out of keeping. He may well have exerted a similar affect over those Cleveland and Chicago residents who began acting bizarrely as a possible result of his demonstrations in those cities. As pointed out earlier, Owens has long maintained that some of his predictions come about when individuals—even people unknown to him—carry out inexplicable compulsive acts that fulfill the requisites of his forecasts.

This idea is not simply a matter of wild speculation, either, since there is copious evidence on file that suggests that a psychic can directly affect the mind of a person unknown to him. In order to demonstrate the point, we need only to examine one such incident from parapsychology's rich lore.

Pascal Forthuny was one of France's greatest psychics. Born in 1872, he was extensively tested by European parapsychologists during the 1920s. Although educated as a man of letters, he discovered his psychic gifts accidentally in 1919 when he suddenly began receiving automatically written scripts from his dead son. He soon decided to devote most of his time to giving public demonstrations of psychometry and of his other psychic talents. Unlike many psychics, though, Forthuny was intellectually fascinated by his own abilities and often offered his services to scientists wishing to study them. Some of the most notable experiments were conducted by the Institut Metapsychique International in Paris, and most of them were designed by Dr. Eugene Osty, the director of the Institut and one of France's most original researchers. One type of experiment designed specifically for Forthuny was called the "chair test." The psychic would be asked to describe the individual who would eventually be seated in a specially designated chair chosen by the experimenters several hours before one of Forthuny's public demonstrations.

A remarkable test of this kind was conducted by Osty on April 21, 1926. The lecture hall seated 400 people, but Osty and his colleagues asked Forthuny to make a series of predictions about the person who would sit in one specific chair of his or her own choosing. After contemplating the target chair, Forthuny made a long list of highly specific statements about the target person. He told the investigators that the subject would be a woman, that her summer vacation plans had twice been canceled, that she was concerned over a grave, and that she had liver problems. A young woman did, in fact, occupy the chair that day, and all of Forthuny's predictions about her were on target.

Osty, however, was not content merely with proving that Forthuny possessed psychic abilities, but was just as interested in determining what mechanics lay behind the psychic's predictive powers. So, after the talk was over, he asked the young lady to explain just how she had found her way to the lecture. She explained that she had only heard about it during lunch that same day, and had suddenly felt compelled to attend despite the fact that she had been feeling ill. She even admitted that her illness mysteriously vanished as she approached the hall, and described how she had become inexplicably "obsessed" with the idea of attending the lecture after she had heard about it.

These facts tend to indicate that the lady in question had not attended the talk by chance, but had been compelled to go there specifically to fulfill Forthuny's prediction—as though the psychic were somehow directing her to his talk.

Owens may have possessed the same ability as Forthuny to influence the minds of people he had never met to do his psychic bidding. If he *could* influence people in this way, our next question becomes obvious. Did he do it by telepathy or PK? This is an issue every bit as thorny as the precognition versus psychokinesis paradox that we dealt with earlier. The issue might also be moot. It could be that two different kinds of telepathy exist, one of which is PK action. The first type of telepathy parapsychologists have isolated in their laboratories might be labeled "mind reading," during which the "receiver" in an ESP test delves into the mind of the "sender" to extract information from it. Several parapsychologists, however, have theorized that another type of telepathy exists during which the sender somehow directly impresses his thoughts onto the mind or brain of the receiver. This type of ESP has been called "agent-active telepathy."

Such a process would be indistinguishable from PK, and several parapsychologists have argued that agent-active telepathy might occur when the sender is able to psychokinetically cause alterations in the brain of his receiver, causing him to behave or to perceive whatever the sender wants him to. This type of telepathy may be a clue to Owens spectator PK abilities. We are not talking about mind-to-mind communication when we posit the existence of this form of telepathy. We are talking about a psychokinetic action directly onto the tissues of the brain. This theory has more recently been dubbed the MOBIA model, a term that stands for "mental or behavioral influence of an agent" upon the receiver.

Parapsychologists in the former Soviet Union had long been interested in this form of ESP-PK action and in the past had actively tried to experimentally demonstrate its existence. Their research into the nature of agent-active telepathy followed a diversity of lines. Some of their most famous research included attempts to hypnotize experimental subjects telepathically. Many of these original experiments were designed by the late Dr. L. L. Vasiliev, a Soviet physiologist who was, for many years before his death in 1966, affiliated with the Institute for Brain Research in Leningrad. This work is chronicled in his book, *Experiments in Distant Influence*, in which a chapter is devoted to the issue of agent-active telepathy. As Vasiliev reports, sometimes he and a colleague would clear out a ward room at the institute and hypnotize a volunteer subject. Then they would stand behind the subject and silently command him or her to carry out simple motor acts. Vasiliev noted that, by silently commanding them to do so, their subjects would exhibit certain facial expressions, raise specific limbs, or open and shut their eyes.

In light of this research, it seems plausible that Ted Owens could have exerted a similar influence on sporting events through telepathy. In fact, it seems plausible that many of us may be vulnerable to the mental intentions of other people broadcast telepathically. What is the antidote? How can we protect ourselves from such potential negative influences?

My years of experience in considering such matters suggests that the answer lies in the ageless wisdom of the perennial philosophy. As Socrates stated so soundly that his words have reverberated for 2,500 years, "Know thyself." We must be aware of our own thoughts. We must cultivate, as a regular habit of mental hygiene, the practice of noticing any negative thoughts that may chance to pass through our minds—so that we can replace them with positive affirmations. Many seminars and self-help materials are available to train these skills. For over 100 years, they have been the basis of the American New Thought movement. These very techniques are the ones that Owens eventually taught me and are presented in chapter 11.

CHAPTER 9

CONTACTING THE SPACE INTELLIGENCES

In my own experience, and in that of other UFO investigators, the Ted Owens case is not an isolated one. It is only the most extraordinary modern case out of many others. This suggests that the total picture does indeed deserve serious attention, and that this most salient case should provide more insights than those derived from cases with lesser strangeness.

James Harder,
former research director,
Aerial Phenomena Research Organization

There is a story connected to the Owens case that may be the most incredible of all. This is Owens' claim that one can learn to contact the Space Intelligences, that he has developed a training procedure to help one achieve this ability, and that he has, in fact, trained several students who have succeeded in making this contact.

"Powers from . . . Another World Are Flowing in to You"

Even as far back as 1969, Owens was claiming that anyone could form a link with the Space Intelligences, and he wrote notes on this subject in his book, *How to Contact Space People.* While Owens revised and broadened his techniques since that time, his book originally outlined the germinal steps one could take to make other-worldly contacts possible.

The basic procedure is simple, and Owens described it briefly. One need only visualize the "chamber" he uses to make contact with Twitter and Tweeter, the SIs, as described in chapter 4, and, if the conditions are right and the subject has properly prepared his mind, contact with the Space Intelligences will result. The key to making contact is visualization exercises, especially as developed through auto-hypnosis.

Owens' first professional career was as a hypnotist and, to the end of his life, he practiced the art and was willing to use it in order to train students to develop their minds so that they could make personal contact with the Space Intelligences. Owens therefore developed a two-day training program in mind dynamics.

Owens first developed his training program after his 1965 Texas UFO encounter. He wrote the following in an unpublished description of his methods:

> Shortly thereafter, ideas began to flow into my mind. These were ideas on how to use hypnosis and auto-hypnosis to teach other people. So many ideas came into my mind that I began to put a book together. And the intelligence kept coming, in steady flow and continuity.

For the first stage of the program, Owens instructed the student in the art of auto-hypnosis so that he could learn to enter into a deep state of relaxation. The auto-hypnosis was taught after the student had been allowed to explore the hypnotic state as induced by Owens himself. After the student had mastered this technique, he was instructed in such mind dynamics as memory improvement, pain control, and other mind control abilities. Suggestions were also given for the development of ESP abilities. The goal of these instructions was for pupils to learn to teach themselves to control their sleep patterns, increase their physical strength, and raise their IQ as well as improve the keenness of their mental capabilities. In short, the first part of the training program was designed so that, through the students' own powers of mind, they would be able to take control of their mind and body.

The second, and critical, part of the training came next. Through hypnosis and by aiding the students with their auto-hypnosis, Owens built "triggers" into the self-programming the student was trying to implement. In other words, Owens instilled in the student's mind certain suggestions that were coded, via trigger words or phrases, that the pupil could use at any time to instantly enter back into a state of auto-hypnosis and control any desired aspect of behavior.

This may sound insidious, but it isn't. In essence, Owens trained his students so that, by relying on self-suggestion, they could instantly relax, reduce tension, recall forgotten memories, and enhance their lives. In this regard, the goals of Owens' training program were not essentially any different from many self-hypnosis courses or mind dynamics training programs. His specific techniques, though, were uniquely his own.

It was also Owens' belief that, since these techniques were imparted to him via the Space Intelligences, anyone undergoing them would automatically become linked to the UFO intelligences. Owens wrote:

> One very interesting aspect of this special training is that I am able to utilize other dimensional powers from my UFOs in the training with you. That is, not only are amazing "mechanics" set up in your mind to help you in your life in many ways, but during this training itself, powers from another dimension, another world, are flowing into you, to help you.

The entire training, as mentioned earlier, took two days to complete. If any difficulties arose, the training was extended to a third day. The sessions constituted six hours of work, with breaks every hour or so, depending on the endurance and stamina of the student. Owens asked potential students to check into a hotel near his home, where the sessions were carried out. The psychic allowed his students to bring along an observer or onlooker, and the price for the program was one thousand dollars.

These techniques may sound simple, almost too simple, but several of Owens' students have testified to their efficacy.

"We Called These Fast-Darting Craft 'Zippers'"

Janice Leslie took Owens' training course in 1978. To date, Leslie has developed the ability to make UFOs materialize and to psychically intuit when and where they will appear. She has given several demonstrations of her ability, and a book could be written about her experiences. Leslie's adventures began shortly after the death of her husband in 1978. A month later, she was taking a vacation, to get away from her home and children, and was staying at a hotel in Portland. One day at breakfast, she saw an ad Ted had placed in a local newspaper advertising his psychic readings, development courses, and other services.

Although Leslie had never visited a psychic before, she decided to call upon Owens. She met him shortly afterwards and decided to take his SI training program.

Her serious study began on August 27. She was accompanied on the visit by her sister-in-law, Jade Swan, since Leslie was afraid of hypnosis, which is an integral part of the training. Both women took the course, and after they completed the training, Owens predicted that the Space Intelligences would appear for them as a result of their newly acquired mind dynamics. Leslie wrote an unpublished report on her experience:

> We left Ted's about 11:00 P.M. to return to Vancouver. We were driving slowly down a dark curvy road, in an isolated area, between Silverton and Woodburn. As we approached a curve in the road I looked out the window and saw several beautiful beams of light coming from the heavens down to the earth above a maize field. The sky in this area was a beautiful pale blue, the light beams bright, but soothing, while the rest of the sky around was very dark in comparison. Jade pulled over and we jumped out of the car, excitedly watching in awe. We had no idea what we were watching. To the right of the beams was a beautiful, large, supernaturally bright object (a "low-hanging" star?). The object moved slowly, then stopped, then moved again. The movement was *no optical illusion!*

Leslie was overcome by the numinous beauty of the scene, but her reverie was interrupted by the untimely arrival of a policeman who stopped to see if the women needed help. He, too, saw the beams of light and was at a loss to explain them, but suggested that they might be reflections caused by nearby city lights. The two women decided to explore this possibility by driving along the road to a point where they could have a clear view of the horizon. This, they felt, would give them a better position from which to view the lights of surrounding towns. They returned to the curve in the road where they had originally stopped. Leslie wrote:

> We returned to the spot in the curve of the road, got out, raised our hands and the beams brightened enormously. My sister-in-law turned her head to comment on how dark the sky was behind us (towards Silver Creek Falls) when a low-flying light came moving slowly, silently from that direction. As the ball of light came over us we heard no noise but watched with mouths open as the craft gave off a beautiful yellow aura. The object disappeared as quietly and quickly as it had come.

The night's adventures still weren't over. As the women entered Portland en route to Vancouver, they sighted a red light maneuvering in the sky over a downtown building. As they watched, the ball seemed to grow larger and then darted quickly along a horizontal path across the sky and grew even larger. Then it burst in the air in a brilliant flash of light.

By the time the witnesses returned home, the beams of light could still be seen in the sky. Now, though, they seemed to draw together to form an arc. A cloud-like form detached itself from the arc, according to Leslie's report, and approached in the direction of the witnesses' house before suddenly vanishing.

Leslie had her next odd encounter two days later on August 29. Ever since the first incident, Leslie had become aware of an odd "low-hanging star" in the sky that she had come to believe was a UFO. That night, she took her two children outside and showed them the star and tried to make telepathic contact with it. "Within fifteen minutes," reported the witness, "several darting lights began shooting around the star. My daughter was convinced that I possessed some sort of power. About ten minutes later, we spotted a red ball of light falling straight down."

The next day, Leslie was able to give a demonstration for her father-in-law. It was an extraordinary night:

> I invited my father-in-law, a skeptic of almost anything supernatural, to ride in the country with us. We stopped, I telepathed [i.e., attempted to send a mental signal to the UFO entities], nothing happened. My daughter insisted that we'd chosen the wrong road and should return to the area in which we'd called the night before. She was correct. Within five minutes after I telepathed (with the help of my daughter), a bright, white, darting object shot from the lower southern horizon across the sky to the northern horizon, forming a perfect arc. This was not a shooting star, but much larger. The speed at which this craft traveled was incredible!
>
> When we arrived home and got out of the car, my daughter commented on the cloud formation above the house. The sky around us was perfectly clear, yet just above us was, in her words, "a hand" of red clouds. I thought little about it, actually, but glanced up and saw two white lights (tiny, for they were at a very high altitude) shoot enormously fast through the clouds. We call these fast-darting craft "zippers." They definitely are not shooting stars. A few of these had appeared at Silver Creek Falls.

These UFO visitations lasted throughout the first week of September, during which time the entire Leslie family continually saw UFOs darting about the skies near their home. Some would look like bright stars that mysteriously dimmed when a plane approached too near them, while others would glow in the sky and then recede into the distance until they couldn't be differentiated from other stars. Like so many close-encounter witnesses, the Leslies found their domestic life disturbed during this time by poltergeist antics in their home. These incidents lasted until September 10 when a climax seemed to be approaching.

That night, Leslie decided to take a friend named Irene out into the country and show her a UFO. She didn't expect what was about to happen. The women had driven to a deserted river outside Portland, Oregon. It was a glorious, clear night, and the UFOs weren't about to be shy.

> We first saw "zippers," then across the horizon, between two hills, moved a beautiful white beam of light. It moved slowly, steadily, too close to the earth to be made by a jet, and too silent. The trail of light remained for about fifteen minutes, never losing its perfect linear form. Then, the top of one of the hills lit up in white. I thought a craft had landed. Suddenly we heard a definite rustle in the trees, not like the rustle of an animal but more like a wind-force moving only in one area and moving towards us. A clanking noise accompanied the rustle. The car's antenna began to vibrate. I was a little frightened, as was Irene, but sat quietly, willing to "make contact" if the unknown force chose to appear. Suddenly we couldn't hold our heads up. We were almost knocked out—or maybe we were totally. Neither of us had been sleepy before. I think we were hypnotized, perhaps our minds were being "trained" as future receiving stations. Who knows? Time passed quickly. As we left, an enormous full orange moon rose slowly from behind the hill.

Encounters of this type lasted through September and finally came to a head on September 30. Leslie had been at a birthday party that night when, at 2:00 A.M., she received a telepathic message to the effect that she should drive out into the countryside alone. In response to the message she obediently drove to her usual UFO viewing spot outside Vancouver. There she waited, and a silent, blinking red light passed over her car as a faint arc of light formed in the sky. Once again she felt that she was receiving a psychic message. This one instructed her to go to an even more isolated area up the river in the mountains. According to Leslie:

> Being alone, I was frightened. Finally, my daring was not enough to keep me there, so I turned on the ignition to leave for home.
>
> I was startled and surprised to see two friends of mine, Terry and Bill, walking up the road. Terry said he saw the large ball of light accompanying my car.
>
> I felt that maybe the SIs had arranged for Terry and Bill to be there with me. Terry told me later that he'd "felt a compulsion" to go out to this spot less than an hour before I arrived.
>
> Because the road along the river is sometimes steep and curvy, I asked Terry to drive for me. The starlike UFO led the way.
>
> Forty-five minutes later, we'd accidentally passed the spot from which I usually telepath (now I wonder if perhaps this was intended to be) and had ended up at a place called Dugan's Falls, an area of trees and a waterfall. Not too far away, down the river, was a camp of some sort, but at this hour of the morning there was no noise and no chance of interruption by passersby.
>
> The wind was strong. Terry and I got out, leading the way, and Bill quietly followed. I telepathed, waited. Nothing. We looked around for our leading star. It was gone. Suddenly the blue became dark, filled with mist.

Because we're at a fairly high elevation, this seemed normal.

We waited a while and began to think we'd see nothing. After all, there were no stars visible in the sky. Then I spotted a beam of pure white light rise over the hill just to our left. I was getting excited when Bill said, "It's probably just a truck." But where it came from we couldn't figure out.

However, as the object moved further over the hill, at least four white beams shot out. We had no flashlight so couldn't decipher the shape, but from the position of the beams, I would say it was round or close to it. It made no noise.

Terry and I walked towards the hill. The craft began to move, as though on wheels of some sort, down the hill through the trees, moving to our right so that it was directly in front of us. A couple of faint beams seemed to shoot up into the air. Then it turned off all its lights. Total silence.

We were frightened. I grabbed Terry's arm and asked, "Are you going if they ask?" We both agreed to cooperate.

We waited a few minutes, then Terry and I walked closer.

We couldn't see well, and Terry said that, without a flashlight, we'd never make it across the rocky terrain through the trees. "Well," I said jokingly, "here we are. Come on out."

Suddenly, we heard a clinking noise, like a chain rattling. Something indescribable brushed against me. Terry, having felt the same thing, said, "Did you do that?" "No," I said, "I thought you did it." We all agreed that something or someone else was with us. Bill went running to the car. He wanted no part of this.

We waited about thirty minutes and decided to drive around the mountain to see if the ship would follow. Half an hour later, we spotted two large, brilliant globes of light on a hillside. Terry remembered that he had binoculars in the car. We all got out and took turns looking. The globes were yellowish-orange and sparkled like crystal in sunlight. At times, they didn't appear as globes, but seemed concave. Then again they may have been V-shaped. Because of the sparkling effect, it was impossible to tell exactly what the shape was, and we couldn't tell what they were attached to. The object looked something like a concave saucer with two sparkling headlights. But we couldn't be sure because we had no flashlight.

We watched a while, then drove around and headed home. We returned to the spot where I had met Terry and Bill, and as I talked with Bill, Terry began to yell, "Look, look!" I turned too late. Terry said a glowing orange object shaped like a pole with an arrowhead came closely towards him and suddenly darted backwards and disappeared.

It had been an exciting evening. Terry and I talked about going out again. Perhaps had we not been frightened, the SIs would have made an appearance—if they can be seen.

I arrived home between 5 and 6 A.M. My daughter and her friend both awakened and insisted that something—or someone—had been in the house while I was gone.

Denise and Linda explained that they heard and felt something "move like wind" through the window in her bathroom, enter the bedroom, and progress down the hall. The baby's bed rattled, and the side kept falling down so that Denise had to periodically get up and reset the catch to secure it. Both girls insisted that there were sounds like footsteps in the kitchen on the spots where the floor squeaks.

Leslie's UFO encounters, which seem to be related to her initial contact with Owens, have been a continuing saga. Whether or not her experiences led up to an actual UFO close encounter or abduction is not known. Over the intervening years, I have lost track of her. So I can offer no conclusion to Leslie's bizarre story.

Luckily, Leslie—like Owens himself—appreciated the value of corroborative evidence. She supplied D. Scott Rogo and myself, since we began taking an interest in this affair in conjunction with the Owens case, with signed statements from several people who have shared in her adventures. For instance, the following report is from a friend of Leslie's who witnessed one of her demonstrations.

The witness, whom we'll call Betty, witnessed one of Leslie's demonstrations on September 15, 1979, after she had been invited to go UFO hunting. Betty accompanied her friend willingly, although she stated in her report on the incident that "I didn't really know what to look for at the time," and that "I was not really sure of what I thought Janice [Leslie] might be seeing." Accompanying her on the trip was her thirteen-year-old daughter with a school friend, as well as Leslie's two children.

While out in the country, the group saw several odd stars that would blink when they were waved at. "I didn't talk hardly at all," writes Betty, "mostly because I just wanted to see more. All of a sudden the animals, dogs and horses, all became agitated, and the horses across the road were running around in a type of frenzy. We all looked around, and to the east behind us, a bright beam of light shot up like an aeroplane [sic], but there was no noise. Then it went up . . . I could see it was shaped round and had what appeared to be porthole windows." The object shot across the road and then flew up into the sky where it took on the appearance of a star.

On the way home after their adventure, they stopped by a mist-filled field. Betty watched Leslie go out into the field and hold her hands in the air towards the sky. The mist rose and then shaped itself into an arc. This eerie episode so frightened the children that Leslie aborted her demonstration, and the group decided to drive home.

One could go on citing the testimony that Leslie has collected from her friends and fellow UFO hunters. But for the present, the affirmation quoted above will substantiate the fact that Leslie seemed to be having genuine UFO contacts and experiences. In a sense, this makes the Leslie case a vicarious corroboration of Ted Owens' own claims and contacts. Although Leslie reported that she had seen UFOs on occasion as a child, it was her contact with Owens that initiated her recent adventures. What the precise connection between Leslie and Ted Owens was remains a mystery.

The case of Janice Leslie suggests that Owens was not only psychic, but that the Space Intelligences were at least somewhat independent of Owens' mind. But just what was the nature of this intelligence?

The Strange Case of Andy Eastman: "I Knew Ted Owens . . . and Became an SI Contact"

In July 1998, as I was in the process of preparing this manuscript, I received a most unusual e-mail from one of Ted Owens' early contacts, a man living in the Australian outback and calling himself Andy Eastman. He suggests that there still exists a network of individuals who have been trained by Ted Owens to contact the SIs, which he refers to as "Space Intelligence Masters" or SIMs. He also refers to an unusual document that can be found on the Internet that provides detailed information about one individual's experience of the SIs. Excerpts of his message to me are quoted here:

> I knew Ted Owens from 1970 to 1977 and became an SI contact. Ted sold me a few of his little red plastic PK disks over the years and I still retain one on my person. Our acquaintance soured after Space People were disemboweling too many cattle in my home state of Colorado and nearby states (and countries like Mexico and Canada) in the mid-1970s. I basically wrote the message "Nuts to You" to SIs in a letter and never heard from Ted again. Even to this day I do not like animals being mistreated by space entities.
>
> Ted used to eat cigars and chew on one inch thick steaks. Me, I'm a vegetarian, like Gandhi. Anyway, this is only a preliminary message to you to let you know that some others of us are still out here and know quite a bit. I have a technical paper outline at www.sumeria.net/cosmo/simi.html that details my own contacts and thoughts about Space Intelligence Masters (or SIMs, a highly elevated type of SI) and their hierarchies. This was written when I worked at the University of Adelaide in their Computer Science Department in the late 1980s. Now I live in the bush in a shack without electricity, gas, plumbing, etc.
>
> Sometimes I search the Web for "Ted Owens and UFO" and come up with a few hits. Needless to say, your posting sent me through the ceiling.
>
> About myself, I started having increased SIM contact in the early 1970s and became an SI operative. I went on a mission for SIMs into the U.S. military in 1973 and sparked a U.S. military red alert from within a nuclear weapons storage depot in October 1974 that occurred about the same time as an airliner carrying

some top military officials and a team of FBI agents crashed into Mount Weather (a secret U.S. government enclave). To this day I regret this happened as it caused the deaths and great pain to some innocent people. The purpose of an ultimatum I issued from within the red alert umbrella I created was that the U.S. government should finally disengage itself from the senseless Big Money war in Southeast Asia.

The red alert I helped spark resulted in a cylindrical UFO appearing at the periphery of the nuclear weapons depot, and I spotted plenty [of] "Lucy in the Sky with Diamonds" UFO stars going overhead at the time.

The red alert purportedly cost the U.S. government about $25 million. I was never put in jail or disciplined over it though, as I had done nothing wrong except send an ultimatum to the U.S. Senate. And the U.S. military KNEW that it was probably best to pull out of Southeast Asia. (Especially while their spy satellite network was always going down in the wake of interference by SIMs and Space People.)

Thinking back about Ted and SIs, I remember much. One time, I had SIMs or SIM helpers inside my skull, too, doing their little operations while trying to establish my worth in contactability. This did not last long since they probably found out that I suffer from far too much nicotine, alcohol, and other drug abuse that could have prevented my brain from functioning the way they wanted it to. At the time of the red alert and sighting of the UFO cylinder and UFO stars, I had a vision of Tweeter and Twitter as they made interface with my brain consciousness, and to this day I'll remember the numbing and crumbling effect it had on my awareness: I always felt very heavy at the time, with long periods of sleep, as if a very heavy weight had rested itself on my brain. I developed a stutter to my speech and partial retardation. These eventually lessened over the years, and now I have become one of the "smart" nitwits who knows a little more than the other nitwits in life.

More about Ted: his real name at the time was given with the initials H. T. O., that I'll guess were Harry Theodore Owens. Ted always seemed a little paranoid himself, warning others not to let other people know about their contacts with him and/or SIs. In time I heard from others that there was a large incidence of deaths among people who had known Ted. Ted would encourage people to beware of the "Devil" or "Satan" in some of his more evangelistic messages.

Amazing thing is, there are Australians (Aborigines) here in Oz that can do similar things, even on their own. It is embedded in their folklore that their women had powers to influence the weather, and they knew about "Yowies," their equivalent of the Hairies [I assume this refers to Yeti or Bigfoot types of entities]. To the Australians, UFO and un-human advanced beings were more of the "norm," and white people who were amazed at these were considered "unusual." I think this is because most white people are still evolving their logic to be able to deal with nonphysical brain consciousness activities that earlier types of mankind had easy ability to deal with and wield.

To summarize: I've been a contactee with beings who are to humankind what people are to simple, single-celled bacteria. These are detailed in the Web link previously mentioned. Also I knew Ted Owens and for the most part he seemed like a really good guy, who like many other psychics, including myself, seem to have an aversion to criticism from others, even other psychics. I guess Ted became sickened from receiving too much criticism though, as would anyone. Humanity has a deep unconscious aversion to dealing with anything or anyone who is of a nonhuman origin.

I responded to Eastman's e-mail, requesting his permission to use excerpts of his message and his Website in this book. He responded positively, so below are excerpts of his essay "Space Intelligence Master Interface":

Guidelines.
The best tool for interface with SIMs, SIM helpers, and other Nature entities, was and is love. Love is a great asset to create soul channels that carry thoughts. Love also maintains healthy attitudes and intentions in life.

SIM Time Windows.
SIMs view time differently than people do. What people experience in great detail over years may be seen, before mental eyes of SIMs, to be just a matter of minutes or seconds. SIM attentions are not weighted-down [sic] with precise physical awareness, and worldly concerns, as experienced and enjoyed by most humans.

Healthy Tolerances.
Exposures to SIMs and life-forms SIMs associate with are most comfortably taken with patience and tolerance, since reactions to the unusual may be present. SIM contacts can be stressful. Amnesia and loss of brain logic, are sometimes induced by emotional distress, in addition to powerful SIM telepathic energies. Emotional impairments can be prevented, curtailed, or reduced through self-suggestion, meditation, hypnosis, and other forms of inner emotional management.

Pictures in the Sky.
SIMs of the outer space variety are usually present around a planet. To contact these SIMs by visual images: 1) go outside on

a clear night, 2) point a hand up at the sky, and 3) paint on the sky, with the mind's eye, a picture of desired items or events.

SIMs make and change weather and other nature phenomena. Use of the technique to paint a picture of a thunderstorm, that bristles with lightning and deluges a landscape with torrents of rain, on the night sky, can draw SIM attention to the request for rain. SIMs and SIM helpers will consider bringing the desired weather, to nearby areas, within a few hours or days. Experiments with these techniques can have high direct correlation between visual requests, and SIM-induced weather and other miracle activities.

SIM Activities Internal to the Skull.

Creatures in other dimensions can seem to be the size of small insects compared to people. Yet because they live as extremely advanced intelligent beings, their proficiencies in memory-related skills, to change the brain for instance, can be evident and effective. People seen this way might appear to be like dinosaurs.

After a series of contacts, SIMs may interface some of their helpers with brain consciousness. A person subjected to this is probably already well-acquainted with SIM and SIM-helper abilities to enter the skull and modify brain areas. Voices and visions in the skull, caused by other creatures, can be real. A SIM helper, interfaced with the brain, can resemble a bee, hornet, or other markedly intelligent life-form. They can alter the brain or interpret telepathic languages for SIMs. Exposures to these hornet or bee-type creatures often retard the brain: powerful telepathic radiations from them can cause the brain's functional structures to collapse in over-stressed "muscle failure," and some amnesia follows.

Sources of Advanced Guardianship.

People domesticate animals for the benefits of having companionship, clothes, protection, transportation, food, and additional help with plants and other animals. Mankind can give other creatures protection, guidance, increased fertility and liveliness, medical aid, and other basic assets for increasingly healthy and happy lives. In [the] same ways do SIMs relate to the people-variety of creatures: if mankind-type creatures come to know and pleasantly associate with SIMs, so also can their lives improve, and provide sustenance and extensions for SIMs. Definite protection from danger, and other even greater benefits, are acquired by people who become SIM friends and servants of SIM projects.

SIM Reflective Shields.

SIMs can be emotionally and mentally sensitive. A definite danger to those who annoy SIMs is SIM use of mental reflective shields: unhealthy actions directed at SIMs can be reflected back at offenders.

Conclusion.

Any interface between the minds and mindful activities of SIMs and humans requires adaptations in the human mind. SIMs have an awareness advanced far beyond human levels. SIM gifts, like miracle talents or exciting electric PK energies, can be more valuable than large sums of money. Attainment of any interface with SIMs should add great rewards to a person's life!

Intelligent information and techniques, such as these, can be used to contact Space Intelligence Masters, perhaps the most highly evolved creatures to ever visit Earth.

I suppose that, if I had not had so much personal experience with Ted Owens and his lengthy files, I would be predisposed to dismiss Andy Eastman's essay as the ramblings of a schizophrenic. However, based upon my own experiences and studies, I am inclined to think that—on the contrary—Eastman is potentially referring to an extraordinary, and little understood, aspect of human consciousness. I suspect that no understanding of psychokinesis, shamanism, or UFO phenomena will be complete without an appreciation for what Owens and Eastman refer to as Space Intelligences or Space Intelligence Masters.

Is it possible that we are living in the vicinity of other-dimensional, conscious life-forms who are invisible to our normal senses? Of course, all ancient cultures held such beliefs regarding a virtual zoo of spiritlike creatures. Today, we pride ourselves on a modern outlook that is free from such superstitions. People such as Ted Owens, Janice Leslie, or Andy Eastman, who make such claims, are often viewed as cranks or kooks, beneath any serious consideration.

But what if the most advanced theories of science pointed to the existence of additional, hidden dimensions of space beyond the three we experience with our normal senses? This is, in fact, the case—as witnessed by the growing significance of super-string theory in physics today. We, as a civilization, have hardly begun to look at the implications of this work. But, clearly, it calls for us to re-evaluate our old prejudices against shamanistic thinking. An overview of scientific progress in exploring hyper-space is presented in chapter 12.

CHAPTER 10

THE DARK SIDE
OF THE FORCE

*Owens became a kind of an outcast who embodied
the American archetype of the villain-hero
renegade memorialized in countless movies. He
was Jesse James, Clyde Barrow, and Dillinger
using weather disturbances instead of guns.*

James P. Driscoll

*I believe that Ted Owens suffered needlessly because
he invested so much time and energy into trying to
convince his peers that his abilities were real.
Skeptics either dismiss this altogether or become
extremely hostile. Hostility is rooted in fear and
overcoming fear is the function of initiation. Every
ritual initiation has a segment that challenges the
courage of the initiate. Understanding the life of
Ted Owens could be just such a challenge.*

Awo Fa'lokun Fatunmbi

*The Ted Owens story then becomes the very arche-
type of exploring both the positive and negative
aspects of our destiny. It will hopefully become a
wake-up call towards a new morality that could
ensure a sustainable future for all of us traveling
on spaceship Earth on the threshold of relating
with our greater purpose.*

Brian O'Leary

To say that Ted Owens' demonstrations often had a negative
or dark side to them would be an understatement. As early as July
21, 1965, Owens again wrote to his CIA contact, George Clark,
a wild letter in which he stated that the Space Intelligences "will
begin an attack campaign in the U.S. with lightning . . . lightning bolts striking everywhere and everything." The reason for
this destructive display, according to Owens, was "to further
prove that PK Man [Owens] is their representative, and that they
can communicate with PK Man."

The circumstances of Owens' warning apparently came to
pass. By the end of August, there were no less than ten recorded
deaths due to lightning accidents in the United States, while a
Polish airliner was struck by lightning on August 10 over
Belgium. Since lightning only rarely strikes people, this series of
accidents was unusual. Owens had also warned that UFOs
would be seen over "one of our major cities," and UFOs were
seen over Washington, DC, before the end of the month.

"Owens Told Me That . . . Planes Might Crash . . . "

In June 1972, Owens claimed that he received a message from
the SIs telling him to set up a demonstration involving PK influence on a radar installation. Owens had little experience with
radar, so he called a friend of his, Bill Richards, a radar expert in
Cape Charles, Virginia, who had access to a radar dome and

screen. Owens did not mention in his letter how Richards had this access or where the screen was located. This information was kept confidential, as Richards, apparently, had no authorization to conduct the test. In an apparently sworn affidavit (no notary seal), Bill Richards stated that Owens' description of a radar experiment was accurate in every way. Owens explained what had happened in a letter to acclaimed UFO researcher J. Allen Hynek dated June 27, 1972:

> Yesterday afternoon [June 26, 1972], the UFOs communicated with me and told me to get to a radar screen and try to demonstrate phenomena on a radar screen. . . . So I phoned a man I know who by chance is a radar expert. . . . The upshot of it was last night I wound up in a huge radar setup, sitting before a radar screen with my friend sitting beside me. This was not done through official government channels. . . .
>
> First my friend patiently explained what was what. Then mentally I called the SIs to appear on the radar screen. Then a strange ring of objects appeared on the screen in a concentric circle. My friend, who is a top expert, would not identify these objects. He could readily point out ships, airplanes, etc. After a bit, the ring of strange objects faded out and vanished. Then after a bit, they reappeared again. Before my session was over another ring of strange objects appeared inside the first ring.
>
> The big result was this: I'd been concentrating for about an hour on the screen when suddenly what my friend called "spokes" or "strobes" began to appear. These were heavy, straight lines of light revealed when the sweeping arm went over them. My friend explained that sometimes these spokes could be seen at sunup or sunset, but never at 10 to 11 P.M. at night

(when we were working on this demonstration). My friend got very excited at these spokes which began to appear at different points of the circle. After checking he stated that these spokes were caused by something very powerful RIGHT OVER THE RADAR DOME WHERE WE WERE OPERATING!

. . . I used my regular excitatory technique, same as I use on TV screens to control pro football games, exuding PK power from my brain, backed by verbal exclamations. AS SOON AS I DID THIS, CLUSTERS OF SPOKES APPEARED CLEAR AROUND THE CIRCLE, IN EVERY DIRECTION! Up until I used this PK "attack" technique, there had only been a spoke here, a spoke there. But immediately when I began to exude PK force, psi force, the spokes appeared in multiples, everywhere. This lasted for a brief time, then the spokes vanished entirely. The radar expert told me that he had *never* seen this phenomenon in all his years of radar work.

The above quotation is taken from a copy of a letter by Owens to J. Allen Hynek, which Richards, in his affidavit, states is accurate. Richards' affidavit added further details regarding the experiment:

Furthermore, Owens told me personally the night that he did his radar screen experiment that the technique which he was using on the screen could probably result in immediate rainstorms, because he was using on the radar screen lightning coming from his fingers which was the same technique that he used to make storms at other times. (And the weather was clear.)

Last night, following the experiment, there was a huge rainstorm here in Cape Charles, Virginia, then again today, two days later, there was yet another rainstorm; rather two, one in the afternoon and another tonight.

Furthermore, on Monday night Owens told me that as a result of his use of psi force over the radar screen ships might sink and planes might crash in the Chesapeake Bay area (which the radar screen denoted). Tonight a Navy Phantom jet airplane crashed in the Chesapeake Bay area (this is Wednesday night, two days later after Owens' prediction). And furthermore, Owens told me on Monday night to watch the television and newspapers for just such a happening! This news of the plane crashing appeared on local television tonight! (June 28, 1972)

I swear that all of these statements are true and accurate to the best of my knowledge.

Subsequent to Richards' affidavit, the files indicate a number of other crashes and accidents in the Chesapeake Bay area. Up to three inches of rain was reported in some Tidewater locations on June 28, and there were also many power outages throughout the area. On June 29, a newspaper clipping reports a variety of unusual "gremlin" type phenomena interfering with a Navy change-of-command ceremony for the vice admiral of the Atlantic fleet in Norfolk. Also, a Navy jet was almost lost near Chesapeake Bay when a wheel dropped off while the jet was flying. Only tremendous flying skill got the plane down without crashing.

On July 10, 1972, a fire aboard the U.S. aircraft carrier *Forrestal* caused $12 million in damages. A sailor who was caught setting one small fire was charged with arson, and newsclips mentioned a possible death penalty. On August 6, Owens wrote a lengthy letter to the attorney defending the sailor suggesting that he, Owens, was responsible for the fire as a by-product of his radar demonstration. The attorney's reply indicated that, while he was very interested in Owens' argument, he didn't know if it would hold any weight in a court of law.

On July 28, a small twister hospitalized two people and damaged several motels and automobiles in Virginia Beach. On July 29, 1972, lightning struck and killed two people in Norfolk, Virginia. On August 1, a civilian pilot was killed in a crash near Zuni, Virginia.

An accident occurred with a Navy Blue Angels Phantom jet on August 3, 1972, in Kingston, North Carolina, which was within the 150 to 200 mile range of the radar demonstration. On August 10, another Navy jet crashed at the Ocean Naval Air Station in Virginia Beach after returning from field-carrier landing practice at Fentress Air Station in Chesapeake. The pilot was killed. Another Navy jet crashed off the Virginia coast on September 14, 1972. Eventually, after fourteen such mishaps, the Navy grounded all 139 of its multimillion-dollar F-14 fighter planes because of suspected engine problems.

On September 21, 1972, an empty barge, drifting in high winds and heavy seas, slammed into the Chesapeake Bay Bridge tunnel, heavily damaging the structure and forcing it to close for about three weeks. A survey showed no fewer than thirty impact points. Owens claimed that this bridge was the main focus of his PK radar demonstration. The storm, which occurred at the time of the accident, was the worst in that area in over ten years.

This rash of incidents can be more readily explained as a product of PK than as the fulfillment of a non-causal prediction. The fact that Owens could willfully produce odd and unprecedented effects on the radar screen and that these readings were not apparently picking up any physical objects flying or cruising in the area, indicates that he was either (a) somehow PKing the radar unit itself or (b) was causing physical alterations in the target area (Chesapeake Bay) the radar was monitoring. Either way, PK seems to have been the cause of the phenomena. But which of these possibilities is the correct one?

The answer to this puzzle may well lie in the airplane crashes that occurred within just a few days of the experiment, just as Owens predicted. Could he have actually caused a physical change in the Chesapeake Bay area during the course of his experiment that made it dangerous for air travel? This is a distinct possibility, and there is even some experimental evidence that could be cited to support this suggestion.

Parapsychologists have sometimes described a curious phenomenon called a "linger" or "lag" effect. This effect was first discovered by some of the Duke University workers during their initial attempt at training subjects for PK ability back in the 1930s and 1940s. These tests were dice-rolling tasks, in which the subjects tried to make the dice land on certain faces more often than chance could account for, to make doubles show up at a rate beyond chance expectation, to land on certain desig-nated areas of a platform and so on.

However, a few of the Duke workers ran into a complication during these tests, which resulted in the discovery of the linger effect. They learned that, if a subject was attempting to make one specific die face show up repeatedly, and then shifted away through the experiment to a new target face, the original target would sometimes still show up to an extra-chance degree. The Duke researchers were puzzled by this effect and originally thought that the lag effect was a psychological phenomenon, i.e., that the subject, being unable to reorient to a new target, became unconsciously fixated on producing the one he had been originally asked to make.

Subsequent research on the linger effect, however, indicated that this curious phenomenon might be the result of a physical process and thus have nothing to do with psychological factors. These findings have been made primarily through the labors of parapsychologists working at the Foundation for Research on the Nature of Man in the early 1970s. This is the name the Duke Parapsychology Laboratory adopted when it was reorganized off-campus in 1967.

Graham and Anita Watkins, a husband-and-wife research team, rediscovered the linger effect during a series of experiments they were conducting on psychic healing. The design of their experiment employed animal targets. Two mice from the same strain, after being anaesthetized with chloroform, were placed next to each other on either side of a platform. The subject was asked to make one of the mice recover consciousness before the other. Several trials, using different pairs of mice were conducted one after the other during each experimental session. The Watkins procured good results with their experiment, but only if certain conditions were met. Their main finding was that, in order for the test to succeed, they could not ask the subjects to alternately arouse the left-hand or right-hand mouse by focusing back and forth between the corresponding sides of the platform. It would only work if the subject focused only on one side of the platform consistently throughout the session.

This finding indicated to them that their subjects were not merely arousing the target mice but were setting up some sort of PK field, which was affecting the specific side of the platform they were using for the trials. The experimenters later found that if they placed a pair of mice on the platform area after the subject had left the room, the mouse placed on the side that had been used as the target would still arouse quicker than the control animal. This linger effect usually lasted for about twenty minutes.

The Watkinses were able to reconfirm their findings during subsequent experiments, when Felicia Parise, a psychic from New York, took part in some experiments at the Foundation. For one test, Graham Watkins asked her to use PK to make a compass arm deflect. She was successful, but in a curious way. After the test was over, Watkins discovered that the compass would deflect every time it was placed in that part of the lab room where the test had originally been conducted. The effect lasted for about 20 minutes, even when Parise was out of the room.

Somehow, the psychic had momentarily set up a psychic field in the area where she had worked, one which only gradually dissipated.

In light of these findings, there is no reason to reject the possibility that Owens, when producing a PK effect, could have temporarily produced a long-lasting alteration in that area of space upon which he had been focusing. He might simply have produced a linger effect, but an effect of a much greater magnitude than has so far been isolated in the laboratory. If this theory is correct, then Owens did not merely predict the air crashes around Chesapeake Bay. They may have been the inadvertent result of his experiment.

And it certainly could not have been the first time Owens has produced such a bizarre result. The following report from my files on Ted Owens is a second strong case of presumed PK:

On September 13, 1972, Larry Banko, a feature writer for the *Norfolk Star-Ledger*, interviewed Owens as part of a news story he was doing on the psychic. Owens told the writer that he was currently aiming his PK at NATO exercises then being conducted in the Atlantic and would attempt to make two ships collide. The very next day, the newspaper ran a story reporting that two ships had collided off the coast of South America. Of course, while the event Owens predicted came to pass, the psychic was way off in his calculation about where it would occur. So, this incident could be dismissed as a lucky coincidence. But this accident occurred under strange circumstances: it was broad daylight, the sea was calm, and neither captain could explain how the accident had happened. This is just the sort of remark that individuals unknowingly involved in Owens' demonstrations so often make. So this might be classified as a prediction, or demonstration, and is impressive because of the bizarre conditions that accompanied its fulfillment.

It should also be kept in mind that psychics are sometimes poor at guiding their PK abilities. In the former Soviet Union, for example, several Russian scientists were engaged in studying the psychokinetic abilities of Nina Kulagina, a housewife who could apparently make small objects move across tabletops and counters just by concentrating on them. She would usually sit at a table, upon which several small household items had been placed, and she would pass her hands above them in a rotating and angular movement until they started to move in little jerks. The objects would usually follow either a straight or curved path. Many films of Kulagina's PK demonstrations, conducted under controlled conditions, have been shown in the West. However, both Soviet and Western researchers who had worked with her noted that sometimes, while she was concentrating on a specific test object, such as a pen or matchbox, another object on the table would suddenly begin to move instead. This is known as a "displacement" effect.

It is therefore feasible that Owens sometimes produced this effect on a much grander scale. The collision off South America could have been one such instance.

In evaluating Owens' moral culpability for the aforementioned accidents, a few things may be said in his favor. It does not appear that he was acting out of any particular malicious intent. I don't think that he really understood the potential harmful consequences of his Chesapeake Bay radar demonstration. This, it seems, only dawned on him, or was communicated to him by the SIs, after the area had already been the target of Owens' PK concentration. It seems as if Owens simply behaved like a child might, testing his own limitations. And who else could provide any guidance or oversight in a society that studiously avoided serious inquiry into such matters?

But this excuse does not apply to the Atlantic ship collision. Even if the actual collision were a mere coincidence, Owens is not off the hook. He did, after all, express his intention to create such an event. His excuse was that such an extreme was needed in order to awaken the U.S. government to the potentials of psychokinesis. However, the whole project was poorly conceived. The U.S. government, as best I can tell, always kept Owens at a distance. His flamboyant negative demonstrations, I believe, served more to reinforce his own ego than to do good in the world. As such, they tend to reinforce the esoteric teachings of many cultures that the display of psychic powers is a detriment to the path of spiritual enlightenment.

"The Worst Single-Plane Disaster in the History of U.S. Aviation"

A few years after the Chesapeake Bay crashes, Owens found himself in an airplane. Ironically, he was carrying a copy of an article in *Saga* by Otto Binder. It included a drawing of a Phantom jet and a reference to the earlier plane crashes. Perhaps, this drawing ended up functioning as the equivalent of one of Owens' PK maps, because, as he was landing at Kennedy Airport in New York, the airplane directly in front of his mysteriously crashed. Owens described the incident in his own words, in a letter sent to his correspondents on July 23, 1975:

SCIENTISTS . . . .
In this file you will find some strange documentation re the Kennedy airplane crash. I was returning from Egypt, from Cairo via Rome . . . and showing my *Saga* magazine writeups to the stewardesses and others . . . particularly the page where the artist has my face looking up into the sky . . . where an airplane is being struck by lightning . . . and on the page are the words "Tornado Winds Rip Area." Then my plane began its approach to Kennedy Airport and the pilot told

everyone to buckle seatbelts for landing. But the plane, going down, veered off . . . circled over the ocean . . . went to another airport for a while . . . then returned to Kennedy and landed. When I went through customs, the customs officer looked at my flight ticket . . . said, "You are lucky to be here. You know that, don't you?" I asked what he means . . . and he told me that the plane ahead of ours had been struck by lightning; had crashed.

In the file with this letter is a newspaper clipping about the airplane crash at Kennedy Airport, dated June 25, 1975. The article states, "More than 100 people were killed in the crash, the worst single-plane disaster in the history of U.S. aviation." It also says, "At least two witnesses said they saw lightning strike the aircraft just before it tore through three landing-approach light stanchions and plowed into an area of parkland north of the airport." Owens includes a xerox of his flight ticket for TWA flight 491 into JFK Airport on June 24 from Cairo. A copy of the *Saga* article and illustration is shown, as Owens described it in his letter. In a news clipping of June 26, 1975, winds are now cited as the cause of the airplane crash. Only one other time in U.S. aviation history has there been a case where lightning had been cited as the cause of a crash. And never had lightning destroyed the airframe or damaged it to the extent that the plane couldn't fly, according to a spokesman from the National Transportation Safety Board.

What are we to make of this? Was it just a coincidence? Perhaps. Yet, I see it as a prime example of how Owens' need for recognition and attention warped his own good judgment. He did not seek to harm another airplane. But he allowed his own personal needs to cloud his thinking with regard to the harm he could inadvertently cause. Yet it is hard to judge him harshly for this since no one else has ever thought through the ethical implications of psychokinesis. And we have seen many other technologies introduced without concern for their harmful side effects. Would that Owens' wisdom had been as evolved as his psychokinetic power.

"I Promise I Will Never Do That to You Again"

From the very beginning, the PK Man story has contained many shadowy shades. Playing with forces of nature, such as lightning and hurricanes, necessitates the inevitability of human casualties—and not all of these were accidental. I had my first experience of Ted Owens' dark side on December 31, 1976, during the period covered by our San Francisco experiment. At the time, in spite of the excellent UFO sighting a few weeks earlier, all of the conditions specified by Owens for the demonstration had not been met. I reminded him of this during a telephone conversation and, perhaps to tone down his own arrogance over what had been accomplished, I added the statement, "You're not 100 percent accurate, you know!" Immediately after that remark, Owens slammed the phone down, hanging up the connection. Within about forty-five minutes, I began to feel ill. A sore throat developed of such severity that I assumed I might be fighting a cold for the next ten days or so.

Then, about two hours later, I received another telephone call. "Jeffrey, I apologize," said Owens. "I promise I will never do that to you again," he said without specifying just what it was he had done. And, just as suddenly as it had begun, my sore throat began to recover. It was then that I developed the principle, for myself, that Ted Owens was something of a psychic mirror. If I treated him with respect and courtesy, I felt confident that I could expect the same in return. And, in retrospect, that principle served me well in the years I worked with Owens. However, the files are full of examples of individuals who treated Owens with hostility, sarcasm, and contempt. Apparently, the energy that they directed toward the PK Man was returned to them, amplified by Owens' own psychokinesis.

Of course, the anthropological literature of shamanism and sorcery is resplendent with similar examples.

"Now California Will Become a Hell on Earth"

During the summer of 1977, I received an unplanned Northern California visit from Owens. This time he was not in a magnanimous mood. Owens had traveled to San Francisco that summer to take credit for ending the drought. His first plan on arrival was to make contact with several newspapers in the Bay Area and urge them to publicize his mission and to publish messages imparted to him by the Space Intelligences. Unfortunately, the San Francisco media wasn't taken with the space prophet. Two newspaper offices had him unceremoniously ejected by the police.

When Owens left California, he was steaming. One of the first expressions of his anger was to write letters to me, Sprinkle, Targ, Puthoff, and others, warning them that he was about to punish California. This time, he threatened to level "fire PK" at the state. "Now California will become a hell on Earth," he declared in his letter. Drought conditions, electromagnetic interference, and poltergeist infestations were predicted.

Owens was again going out on a limb by threatening California with fire danger. The summer of 1977 had been blessed with minimal fire damage. In fact, an article in the *San Francisco Chronicle* on July 21 noted that the U.S. Forest Service was considering the summer as California's mildest fire season in fourteen years. While the average number of fires for the season up until mid-July was usually about 1,400, causing the destruction of 30,000 to 40,000 acres of forest land, only 474 fires had occurred during the 1977 season, consuming only 3,967 acres. But this luck didn't hold out for long.

Two weeks after Owens' angry outcry, California was struck with a number of lightning storms and freak accidents that resulted in hundreds of forest fires. A UPI story, issued on

August 8, reported that California was plagued by its worst outbreak of forest fires in fifty years. Despite the U.S. Forest Service's earlier optimistic announcement, it ended up the worst—not the best—fire season since 1970. Over 300,000 acres of forest were destroyed between July 25 and August 10; over 1,000 forest fires struck in August alone.

If not merely a coincidence, Owens certainly had his revenge— to his everlasting discredit. I regard this incident as a prime example of Owens at his most distasteful. At the time, however, he was almost broke and virtually homeless. He and his family were traveling with all of their possessions in a rented U-Haul truck, for which he lacked the money to pay. His failure to attract the acclaim he felt he deserved led him to become increasingly frustrated, vindictive, and difficult to communicate with. The social alienation forced upon him by the constant rejection of his claim to possess psychokinesis that could be used for the benefit of humanity contributed to the dark turns his life was to take, exacerbating the many flaws already existing in his own character.

"The SIs Say Time *Is Short*"

On February 1, 1980, Owens sent Rogo and me a personal letter stating:

> A book . . . maybe, perhaps, if, etc., could be published about my work . . . a year from now. A long year. But the SIs and I haven't a year to delay . . . to lag. (While I struggle along, broke, just barely making it day to day, week to week . . . while basketball and football stars make hundreds of thousands.)
>
> Therefore, I am entering into a new high level of activity. A new plateau. And for once, my SIs, the UFOs, will not help me. I am calling in my alternate (but in no way inferior) power . . . Pyrcre, the Egyptian power, with

which I am linked, like a brother. [Pyrcre was Owens' abbreviation for Pyramid Creature.] Together, we will strike out *at all power sources ALL OVER THE WORLD. Electric . . . you name it . . .* we will work to neutralize it. To hell with a time limit . . . I am not working with scientists, so what do I care about a time limit.

All over the world . . . power out . . . all kinds of power . . . starting with electricity. That is what we will be working on.

Then on February 16, Owens dashed off a handwritten letter to Rogo, me, and his other scientific observers proclaiming:

Today my UFOs communicated. They stated: either I get the Hearst Castle in California for five years, as our base, plus $100,000 per year for expenses . . . or they, the SIs (UFOs) will *destroy California. . . .* This has a 90-day time limit [to March 16]. The SIs say *time is short.* It *has* to be this way, let the chips fall where they may.

A month later, on March 16, Owens issued another proclamation:

My UFOs today communicated.

Because time is so short (before a nuclear shootout, which will involve the whole world directly and indirectly) . . . they are raising "the ante" now in order to try and get the base they want so desperately (five million).

They are going to attack the higher-ups in the U.S. government. I do not know what they have in mind, but it should be quite bad.

Owens' PK Attack against the world's power supply was, in his view, producing results. In April 1980, he sent me a package of newspaper clippings that included the following items, among many others:

March 8, 1980. *Miami Herald.* ATHENS, Ala. A reactor at the nation's largest nuclear plant was mysteriously shut down three times in less than a week. . . . The first shutdown occurred Feb. 10 . . . The reactor turned itself off again on Feb. 12 and 15.

March 11, 1980. *Miami Herald.* The Nuclear Regulatory Commission has ordered inspections of 11 nuclear power units nationwide, including the Turkey Point unit south of Miami, to detect possible cracks in the Westinghouse turbines in use at the plants . . . one Westinghouse turbine failed last month at the Yankee Rowe nuclear plant in Massachusetts.

March 12, 1980. *Miami Herald.* The Crystal River nuclear plant, shut down by an electronic failure two weeks ago, will stay down for two or three months for repairs and refueling, a Florida Power Corp. spokesman says.

March 15, 1980. TOKYO. (AP) A nuclear power plant in the Mihama district of western Japan shut down automatically Sunday when the water level in a vapor-generator rose abnormally, a plant official said . . . . The 826,000-kilowatt power plant is Japan's second largest generator of electricity.

March 24, 1980. (AP) Equipment problems prompted the shutdown Sunday of reactors at two nuclear power plants, including one in Connecticut that went out of service for the fifth time in five weeks.

April 1, 1980. (AP) A single picket shut down Portland General Electric Company's coal-fired plant in Eastern Oregon [on] Monday.

April 12, 1980. *Portland Oregonian.* Portland

General Electric Co. shut down the Trojan Nuclear Plant at 5:22 P.M. Friday for refueling and extensive maintenance.

April 13, 1980. San Juan, Puerto Rico (AP) Power was restored and life returned to normal across this island of three million people Saturday after a blackout that lasted through the night.

I Confront Ted Owens: " . . . You Seem Evil and Dangerous"

In his letter, Owens seemed to be particularly gloating about his "power knockout" across the island of Puerto Rico. This, he warned, was just the beginning. "Bigger and more dramatic happenings will occur." For my part, I was less than infatuated. I found the evidence itself meager in relationship to Owens' grandiose claims. For all I knew, these power problems were nothing more than chance occurrences. But, more than that, I did not approve of Owens' plan to intimidate the world into supporting him. In the first place, it was an unrealistic assessment of his own powers. In the second place, it would have been unethical even if it had been realistic. So, I wrote him a confrontational letter in the naive hope that I could persuade him to become the sort of civilized psychic about whom a credible case could be built for a positively oriented research and application effort. In part, my letter read:

> As you know, I've been receiving your information about shutdowns at nuclear power plants lately, and I think that this is very interesting. Of course, I have no background statistical database regarding these events, and as I've told you many times, this is necessary to make any logical evaluation of your demonstrations. However, as I recall, you originally stated that this one was not for the scientists.

Back in 1976, when we first met and I started following your career, it was my intention then to help you establish some credibility for your work in the eyes of the larger public. My attempt was in terms of well-written, logical letters, and the scientific report on you. The impact of this has been largely minimal. I think there are two reasons for this that I shall list as follows:

Probably most important, what you have done is mind-boggling. Many people are simply not willing to accept that weather control or prediction is even possible. In fact, they are not even willing to seriously examine data, such as the report that suggests such a possibility. It is too much of a challenge to people's belief systems.

There are a number of people, however, who accept the reality of psi. They don't exactly disbelieve your powers; rather they dislike your flamboyant style. It will be to your advantage if you can understand their point of view with sympathy, even if they cannot understand or sympathize with your position. To many of these people you seem evil and dangerous (injuries, plane crashes, forest fires, droughts, accidents, storms, deaths, etc.). To some people, you seem crazy, with your insistence on exorbitant, or at least unrealistically negotiated, fees for your services. To some, you seem paranoid in your belief that government agents are out to destroy your career, with apparently little thought as to how you, yourself, interfere with your own best interests. To others, you seem, at times, like a braggart and egotist—even if your abilities are real. From my point of view, frankly, you are all of these things and also none of them. I think you understand me.

Now that I have finally received my doctoral degree, I am in a position where what I have to say is given greater legitimization and credibility. I have the ear of the newspapers, wire services, the business world, and the academic world—at least to a larger extent than before. So, to a degree, the first objection that I mentioned above is being overcome. This leaves the second one for us to deal with, if we wish to achieve mutual goals.

"Look into My Eyes and You Will Have Wisdom, Knowledge, and Understanding"

Clearly, I did not appreciate how enchanted Owens' life had become after so many years of psychic work. I had known of his capacity for mental agility and brilliance; after all, he was a member of Mensa, and I was hoping to engage him at the rational level. But Owens was operating on too many other dimensions for that. Indeed, he responded to me, but in his own way. A few weeks later, I received a nine-page letter from him detailing his adventures in the jungles of the Yucatan, where he had gone to commune with "the ancient Mayan entity left by my UFOs ages ago to guard the Mayan mental treasures." Even though he was broke, he had managed to generate sufficient funds from his small coterie of faithful followers. The highlight of the trip was the following epiphany:

> I found an old tunnel beneath the pyramid of Uxmal, and telepathed to Control and Pyrcre and asked their assistance in making friends with the Mayan power that exists in Yucatan in the same way that Pyrcre, the Egyptian power, exists in Egypt. I told them that I came as a friend, not to rob the pyramids or try to seek treasure . . . and that I respectfully request permission from the Mayan power to

approach it, telepathically. Then Pyrcre and Control of the UFOs made a cross (or "X") of light over my location . . . each one made a beam of what seemed like light so that they intersected over my location . . . at Uxmal . . . they showed it to me in my mind . . . and evidently this is the only way that I could approach the Mayan power that exists . . . so I wait now to see what happens.

I have just met with the Mayan power [i.e., Xtolac]. It wasn't what I thought it would be at all. It was a huge face, like that of Pyrcre, but completely different. This was the face of a wrinkled old man, but it had great beauty in it. Peacefulness. It had a headdress on top, with all colors of the rainbow . . . like feathers . . . I told this old man I was seeking wisdom, knowledge, and understanding . . . I was a friend request[ing] permission to approach him. He said then, "Look into my eyes and you will have wisdom, knowledge, and understanding" . . . and I looked into his eyes and there were no eyeballs at all, like human eyes would have . . . but there was the sky and nature and azure . . . blue sky, blue water . . . all of Nature and Nature's secrets were in his eyes. His eyes weren't like your or my eyes . . . they were like windows that you could look through . . . there was beauty that words could not express. After a short while he said, "It is enough for now." And the face faded, and I had knowledge that, while I had been looking into his eyes, I had been receiving encapsulated knowledge that would unfold as time went by and as my mind would be able to absorb it.

So there is no doubt now . . . I have linked up with the Mayan power. It's a great relief . . . because I don't know what to expect . . . whether it would be like a jaguar, a snake, or whatever. But instead, a leathery old, crinkled, reddish-colored face . . . humanoid. I didn't notice a nose or mouth or ears much . . . just the face and eyes and headdress . . . but great beauty and peacefulness emanated from the Mayan power. Tranquility, if you will.

I just thanked Control of my UFOs and Pyrcre, the Egyptian power, telepathically, for making it possible for me to approach the Mayan power. Without the cross of light that they laid down over this location, I'm sure that I could not have approached the Mayan power. It is sort of like a secret door . . . or a time window . . . that they opened for me . . . and only they could have provided it. Amazing.

Wednesday night . . . I am explaining the Mayan power to Teddy [Owens' young son]; that it covers the ancient key Mayan pyramids and temples like an invisible blanket . . . or an x-ray effect, guarding them—but that its "personality" or characteristics are totally different than its brother Egyptian power, Pyrcre, in that it is not destructive. Pyrcre, the Egyptian power, can be infinitely destructive, to a degree beyond human comprehension. And the SIs (my UFOs) can be very rough when they want to be, too, with their powers. But the Mayan power deals with beauty, tranquility, creativity, wisdom, knowledge, understanding . . . its makeup is entirely different from Pyrcre or the SIs, and to get what it is . . . the essence of it . . . down onto paper in English is well nigh impossible. I have seen it and experienced it, but can hardly describe it to others of the human race. Just to look through the eyes of Xtolac . . . is an experience of indescribable beauty and perhaps I should say "goodness."

And, it appeared that something good did, indeed, come out of this trip.

"It Was an Accident"

In May 1980, Mount Saint Helens exploded with sufficient violence to flatten twelve miles of Washington forest. Owens, as it so happened, was living nearby in the town of Vancouver, Washington. Was this yet another synchronicity? The day after the eruption, he telephoned me apologetically to explain that it was an accident. He had not meant to activate the volcano. He did tell me that he was working with one of his PK Maps at the time of the eruption. He was out picnicking with his family and was holding up the PK Map and focusing his energies in the direction of the volcano. He promised me that in the future he would be more careful. In later communications, he referred to the eruption as a warning from his Space Intelligences. He even suggested that the proof of this is that, in spite of the enormous explosion, no lives were lost (There were fifty-seven lives lost in the eruption). Owens even sent me a copy of the PK Map he was working with at that time.

"The War Will End When the Book Is Published"

By August 1980, Owens was furious at the delays that had developed in finding a new publisher for the manuscript that D. Scott Rogo and I had written about him, *Earth's Ambassador*, and he issued a proclamation saying that his Space Intelligence allies had decided to take matters into their own hands:

> Today the SIs (my UFOs) communicated to me the following intelligence: "When the book you have written about me and my work appears in bookstores across the land, as it is written . . . then they will

withdraw their war against the U.S. government. . . ." This is their word on it. "So the sooner your book is published and in bookstores, the sooner the U.S. government will begin to 'get the breaks.'"

At this point, I was confronted with a man who could apparently end droughts "on behalf of suffering humanity" as he was then doing in Australia (see chapter 5), accidentally set off volcanos through the inadvertent use of his psychokinesis and launch "poltergeist attacks" against the U.S. government. Owens had demonstrated his unusual talents in dozens of different ways, and I had been documenting them for years. Few scientists had ever had the vision or tenacity to pursue a case in which a great breakthrough in human potential was being exhibited by a man with criminal propensities.

On top of these difficulties, my disenchantment with Owens was further accentuated after I received an urgent phone call from Owens, followed by a handwritten letter, postmarked August 4, 1980. He warned that his Space Intelligences were readying an 8.0 earthquake for California, one that would shake the length of the state within a matter of hours, days, or weeks. Of course, the earthquake did not manifest. This event was probably the single most dramatic *disconfirmation* of Owens' reputed talents. I think that even he, an incorrigible egomaniac, was flabbergasted. Owens phoned me on October 6, telling me that he was calling off all of his negative demonstrations.

"Because the U.S. Will Not Protect or Help Me, Their Only Human 'Ambassador'"

By November 1980, Owens had developed a new rationale. He sent me a letter on November 16 stating that his Space Intelligences were no longer allowing him to write or draw PK Maps. Therefore, he could no longer perform any demonstrations at all. Nevertheless, the Space Intelligences on their own planned to continue a wide range of attacks against the United States with dire results: pilots of planes will become confused and lost, everything will go wrong for the U.S. government that possibly can, and all forms of power will be knocked out. Owens explained it this way:

> The reason for all of this negative, aggressive behavior on the part of the UFOs is because my "host country" the U.S. will not protect or help me, their only human "ambassador" [to use the Mishlove/Rogo term, which is accurate]. And the U.S. will not furnish the base which is an absolute necessity if the SIs are going to be able to step in and save the United States (and probably the rest of the world) from extinction.

Once again the news clippings began pouring in: power blackouts; major American and world leaders becoming hospitalized. In February 1981, Owens sent me a letter specifically threatening to destroy the space shuttle about to be launched for the first time. The following month a shuttle accident killed one worker and injured five others. Many other bizarre communications followed. In one letter, Owens described how he witnessed food items jumping off the shelves at a local grocery store. In another letter, he claimed that he and his son Beau were abducted by aliens. This letter was accompanied by newspaper clippings of UFO sightings in the Columbia River area of Oregon and Washington where Owens was then living.

"Have You Been Willing to Learn and Grow Spiritually?"

Then I received a package of files from Owens describing his famous 1960s knife-throwing act, billed as the world's "most dangerous and exciting." Primarily, however, the files sent in by

Owens contained disaster after disaster with Owens claiming, on behalf of the Space Intelligences, *post hoc* credit for everything. In January 1982, I finally sent Owens the following letter, which read in part:

> I would like to leave you with a thought I have been wanting to tell you in many ways for a long time. Under the best of circumstances, it would be quite difficult—but not totally impossible—for you to achieve more recognition for your talents. Perhaps the Space Intelligences have been using you as a barometer of what society is ready for. However, I think that your own behavior has done much to make your circumstances far less than optimal. Perhaps, with extraordinary effort, you could correct this situation. Your "attacks on higher-ups" and "warfare against the U.S.A." is absolutely futile. It is like the proverbial gnat in the ear of an elephant. (The gnat makes his home in the elephant's ear for many years. But when he bids the elephant goodbye, the elephant doesn't even realize he has been there.)
>
> Your potential powers are so frightening that they activate an equally powerful human defense mechanism in people to deny that they exist. I think this is why I have had absolutely *no* response to the report I wrote on you, or to the book Rogo and I prepared.
>
> There may be several viable ways to counter this defense mechanism: (a) consistent demonstrations of positive uses; (b) a more saintly appearance on your part; (c) formation of a more socially effective support network; (d) a more artistic approach; (e) a more coherent, logical approach.
>
> In many ways, I think you have acted with great integrity. You have always consistently been yourself.

But have you been willing to learn and grow spiritually? One pattern I observe in the data is continued behavior on your part of a type that simply aggravates this defense mechanism that causes people to want to deny your reality. You wish to be a diplomat, but you haven't honored the power within you by learning diplomacy. You are an extraordinarily bright man, but have you used your intelligence for self-scrutiny, to see what changes in your behavior might make your work more effective?

Do you really think, for example, that you can simply sit there and take credit for every quirk and bizarre pattern that shows up in the newspapers? Surely you can step outside of yourself and see how this claim must appear, even to sympathetic observers.

I'm sorry this letter is all I have to offer you. I hope that it will help you to better honor the force within you.

A week later, I received Ted's response:

It would be so much more fun for me to answer your letter if you were not my friend. Ever since my younger years . . . when I fought in the ring so much . . . I always said to myself, "Aw darn" . . . when a friend would step into the ring to spar with me and I knew I'd have to pull my punches.

Now perhaps I can "do you a favor" too. Let me show you the current accuracy of your thinking processes. You submit a "flea and an elephant" illustration. You completely overlook the fact that the flea can, albeit obliquely through allied powers, control the weather over cities and entire countries and control the happenings over thousands of selectively chosen people. And that's just for starters. I do not believe your elephant would survive that flea, once the elephant became the enemy of the flea; i.e., if the flea could bring three-quarters of the United States into utter chaos through weather control, then that flea would have small difficulty in taking on one single pachyderm.

Now, Jeffrey, you advise me to change my "image" with a more "saintly" appearance on my part. It appears to me that you are greatly concerned with my image . . . with what others think. Rhine didn't try to change his image and he didn't really give a damn what his peers thought . . . and for twenty years he took a beating from them . . . until he proved what he was doing and became world-famous. And that is my message to you: if you ever want to amount to anything at all in the field (and of course you do) you will have to change your own approach to the entire thing and become more of a fighter and scrapper, doing what you perceive to be right and true at all times . . . and the devil take the hindmost. Jeffrey, the United States is crawling with thousands of doctors of science clutching their diplomas in their hands . . . all neatly dressed, all conforming, all peering around timidly at their peers lest they do something to make their peers angry at them. And they will all fade away, in time, into the vacuum of mediocre nothingness. I learned long ago something you have never learned . . . and I learned it fighting in the ring, fighting on the judo mat, fighting in the streets, if you will . . . a special "way of mind." You know that you are going to get hurt fighting this tough opponent, but then . . . that's to be expected. You know you may get knocked down, so you have to be prepared to get up and resume fighting when that happens. But above all . . . you know you have to win the fight. Well, you can't win them all . . . I lost a few, just a few, in my time . . . but after I'd gone past that stage of my life, I knew one thing for damn sure . . . that I was tough, that I was a fighter . . . not only in the ring or in judo or on the street . . . but in every phase of my life.

And it is this very element . . . that is missing in you and that you need in the worst way, before the Establishment turns you into just another jelly-spined, anaemic scientist bowing to all his peers who are bowing to their peers and so on, sickening on. The truth of it is simply that you are sitting on the very greatest parapsychological find in history . . . but you are afraid to do anything about it. You made a beginning, after realizing the material was valid . . . but you dropped it when confronted by peers tougher than you are.

You state: "Your 'attacks on higher-ups' and 'warfare against the U.S.A.' is futile." Now, there is some scientific statement. In the first place, it is *not my* attacks on higher-ups. I am not doing it. It is the UFO, Mayan, and Egyptian powers that are currently engaged in these activities. And . . . *futile?* As compared to what? When my UFOs tell me that they are going to escalate their attacks against the U.S. 100 times and then bury three-quarters of the United States in snow, ice, rain, mud, flood, hurricane winds, and so forth . . . frankly, Jeffrey, I'd like to know your definition of "futile."

In closing . . . I must assume that your *very same letter* must have been sent to Moses while he was attacking the Pharaoh and the Egyptians. Moses' people didn't like his attitude or behavior either. And may I ask . . . how "futile" was that little flea, Moses?

Of course, now, with the perspective of time, I can see that Owens and I were both right. His efforts were indeed archetypally futile. He lived in poverty throughout most of his career as a psychic, and he died in poverty. Whatever powers he did have were vastly insufficient to force the United States government to give him any serious consideration whatsoever. But, Owens was right about one thing: I have never been much of a fighter or a scrapper in my life, up until the present time.

In fact, the publication of this book has been delayed by me for over two decades—until it seemed to me that public attitudes had evolved sufficiently so that Owens' story might receive a fair and understanding reception.

Owens' cause is clearly a double-edged sword. For not only would I have been fighting in behalf of "the very greatest parapsychological find in history," I would also have had the burden of defending the actions of a man who had penchants both for greatly overstating his own significance in the scheme of things and for using what talents he did possess in a careless or negative fashion. That is the superficial reason why this manuscript has sat in storage for nearly twenty years, waiting to be rewritten and released. Other deeper reasons for the delay, I believe, are related to the larger question of the timing of the unfoldment of psi consciousness within humanity.

Communications from Owens became more infrequent. In October 1982, Owens sent me a copy of a medical report showing a CAT scan of his brain. The final result showed "no abnormalities." I interpreted this as a lack of evidence that extraterrestrial entities had operated on Owens' brain, making him "half alien." From his point of view, it was simply a confirmation of how very clever and subtle they were, to operate and leave no traces.

On April 5, 1983, Owens sent me a letter claiming that he expected a major earthquake on the West Coast soon, "nothing less than 7.0 on the Richter and perhaps an 8.0. Destruction will be devastating." On May 3, the newspapers did report an earth-quake of 6.5 in the San Juaquin Valley community of Coalinga. Owens claimed this as a hit. I did not think so, and began to pay very little attention to Owens' communications.

"I Had Been Ignoring Owens for Too Long"

Then, on July 22, 1985, Owens sent me a letter threatening the NASA space program once again—specifically the space shuttles. He wrote:

> There are four space shuttles at NASA . . . *Challenger, Atlantis, Discovery* and *Columbia.* As of July 22, my UFOs were directing destructive powers at these shuttles and the NASA program. Heretofore my UFOs have tried to be compassionate . . . simply destroying major experiments aboard spacecraft. But now time is short . . . they need their UFO base in order to hold back war on Earth . . . help the human race . . . and help the face of the Earth itself. So, in order to try to pierce the armor of the bureaucracy blocking the UFO base they intend to attack one or more of the above-mentioned shuttles. They warn that any astronauts going up in these shuttles do so at their own peril, having been fairly warned in advance.

I remember vividly the evening in late December 1985 when Owens phoned at about 8:00 P.M., telling me in an angry tone of voice that I must warn the U.S. government to cancel the next space shuttle flight. "This is one of the most important phone calls you will ever receive," he said. "The SIs really mean business. They will destroy the shuttle. It's up to you to prevent it." Of course, I felt completely helpless. I had no influence, whatsoever, with the U.S. government. Nor did I have any great confidence in the precision of Owens' forecast. Most of the time, his threats were only partially fulfilled. However, a month later, on January 28, 1986, I was shaken to my bones when the Challenger disaster occurred. The space shuttle exploded, killing all seven crew members, including thirty-seven-year-old teacher Christa McAuliffe. Later I learned that journalist Wayne Grover had received a similar warning from Owens.

I realized that I had been ignoring Owens for too long. In spite of the seeming criminality of Owens' or the Space Intelligences' behavior, assuming it could be taken at face value, a point about which I was—and am—still uncertain, I was motivated by an intuition that there was still a core of goodness to this phenomenon. I had always treated Owens with respect and, for the most part, he had reciprocated. I deeply suspected that the unpleasant side of this phenomena was largely a reflection of the dark human emotions that other people projected on to Owens. I wanted to learn more, and I intuited that the next step for me would be to take Owens' training course. This will be described in the following chapter.

CHAPTER 11

THE FINAL GIFT
OF THE UFO PROPHET

*As a culture, we are faced with the most awesome
technologies for destruction that humanity has
ever known; torn by religious and political differ-
ences; searching for a deeper synthesis of knowledge
than that attained by earlier generations. As a
culture, we are looking for a balance, a unity and
harmony of spiritual and material values. I feel . . .
that we are very close to a higher equilibrium and
that, perhaps, we stand at the brink of a new era.
It is within this context that I wish to place psi
research and the questions surrounding the
training of psi abilities.*

Jeffrey Mishlove,
Psi Development Systems, 1980

"I Give My Soul, Mind, and Body to Nature and God"

In February 1986, I arranged to take Ted Owens' training course. We met together in a San Francisco hotel room near Fisherman's Wharf. The program ran for two days. During most of that time, I was lying on the king-size bed in a hypnotic trance. The training was audiotaped, and I still have the complete set of cassettes.

I was no novice when it came to hypnosis. I have used hypnosis and self-hypnosis since a cousin, who was an amateur magician, taught me at the age of sixteen. The hypnotic suggestions I received from Owens, as imaginative as they are, were not at all outside the range of what one might experience in a variety of hypnotic programs. The fundamental message was one of positive thinking, and it is fair to say that the positive thinking, or New Thought, movement has been associated with hypnosis and suggestion for well over a century. Owens, however, insisted that his training was not merely hypnosis but that it involved a PK effect as well as the influence of the Space Intelligences who were always working through him.

He began the session by asking me what I wished to accomplish at that point. My answer was clear. I had little desire to influence weather patterns or call down UFOs. I stated succinctly, "I want to be very effective in communicating parapsychological information to the public." At that point, my life was at something of a low ebb. I had been fighting a libel suit for five years. During that time, I had minimal income. I had been depressed and mortified by a *Psychology Today* article about me that claimed I did not deserve, and possibly did not even receive, my doctoral degree in parapsychology. Even though I knew it was full of untruths, I was reluctant to show my face at gatherings of my parapsychological colleagues. Instead, I received training as a psychotherapist. I learned computer and business skills. I felt that I no longer had the credibility to be an effective spokesperson for parapsychology. So, my focus for this training session was heartfelt. Although I never lost belief in myself and in my life's mission, I seriously doubted that I would ever achieve the ambitions that I once had held.

Much of Ted Owens' career might be characterized by the term "dysdaimonic," i.e., a dysfunctional use of the powerful psychic energies with which he was in contact. Rather than developing a career as a master of these energies, Owens often seemed to be a slave to the anger and resentment that had built up within him over the years. However, throughout my training session, his behavior could much more appropriately be characterized as "eudaimonic," an expression of the positive side of his powers.

The hypnosis sessions typically lasted for about half an hour. We took fifteen-minute breaks between sessions and then continued. This lasted for two days, with short breaks for lunch. What follows now, are the actual hypnotic suggestions that Owens used. He informed me that almost all of these specific techniques had been given to him by the Space Intelligences, along with hundreds of others that he reserved for his own use. Some of these are named below. I recommend that, for you to gain the most insight into this process, read each statement slowly and repeat it to yourself three times before moving on to the next one. These statements are all in the first person, as they represent the hypnotic suggestions I was to repeat to myself while in a trance.

The Power of Nature is Working within Me. I have complete faith and confidence that universal consciousness, God and Nature can give me whatever I want and need to build a good life, a better life, a happy, healthy, useful, and successful life ahead of me in time. I know that if Nature can make the flowers bloom and be beautiful, Nature can also make my own life bloom and be beautiful. I know that if Nature can repair a cut on my arm, Nature can also repair any damage to my mind, body, and soul that has happened or will happen.

The Power of Auto-hypnosis is Working for Me. Deep down, I will be at peace and will be friends with myself from now on. My subconscious mind will absorb the suggestions that I can use the most. The secret to tremendous power for myself is to use auto-hypnosis all throughout my life. All the words and techniques that I am taught here in this training will fix themselves in my mind, will be deeply engraved in my mind, will always remain fixed and deeply engraved—permanently impressed—so that I can use the words and techniques as tools to shape my life ahead of me as I wish without having to use willpower. There will be deep, inner peacefulness more and more in my life. It will be like a rock and a foundation for me.

Strengthening the Power of Suggestion Within. The suggestions will keep on working until the benefits are obtained in time ahead. My nervous system is relaxed, like a relaxed, open hand. I will be able to smile and shrug off upsets and tension. This will continue for two years. Then I will be able to accommodate just enough tension for a happy, healthy, alert balance.

These suggestions are more powerful than the negative conditions that have influenced my life in the past.

There will be improvements in every part of my life. These improvements will grow within me just as if I were a young child. There will be a thousand and one joys and accomplishments ahead. My will to live becomes stronger with each heartbeat. My ESP abilities and psychic abilities will grow and become more powerful for me. The frequency of my life field will be raised to a much higher level. I am able to adapt and get along with anyone.

Day by day, I will be calm and confident. I will have a solid, inner balance. I will be happier and more powerful. My confidence will become rock solid, deep inside. My mind will be clear. My sleep will be good and restful. My concentration will be powerful.

The Wonderful Circle. Whenever I want to see something very clearly, I will create a "wonderful circle" in front of me. As if I were looking through a telescope, everything will be in clear, sharp focus. Like a camera, I will see clearly. My troubles are dissolving. I will know myself completely. I will be in control of my own life, like the captain of a ship on a clear day. I will no more be in a fog. From now on, I will experience a new day and a new life.

My mind is in perfect balance and timing with my body. All the little clocks in my body are being put now in perfect order and synchronization.

Contacting Subconscious Control. I will now see in my mind's eye a person sitting at a control panel. I now give that person a name. This name will never change for me. I will consider that person my subconscious.

I will create a circle with my thumb and finger. Whenever I wish to contact this person, I will use my auto-hypnosis mechanism. Then I will create a circle with my thumb and finger.

I will see this person. I will address this person by the name I have chosen. With the control panel, this person has the ability to create events and situations for me that will manifest in my life in time ahead.

The Life Principle within Me. Long ago, the life principle came to Earth. Nothing could defeat it. It struggled on, upward and upward. Dangers and hardships were a new incentive. It is inexhaustible. It developed new features to meet each new challenge: shell, sting, poison, coloration, gills, fur, feathers, webbed feet. It is set to survive, to resist.

This principle lies within me—as a human creature, working within, but only to a slight degree. More often than not, it has been asleep. But now it will become fully awake.

Using my auto-hypnosis mechanism, I can create a special telephone with a direct line to the life-principle. I am calling it now.

It will become awake with all of its infinite powers from all ages, making life healthy, happy, and useful—above all to Nature.

For my life does not belong to me alone, but to Nature, that will improve me and improve my life. That way, I will improve and help others and the human race. From now on, the life principle will be dynamically awake within me.

The Secret Place. From now on, I will also have an alternative method for talking to my subconscious mind. This is called my secret place. I see a large, glass ball floating in a blue sky, among beautiful pink and white drifting clouds. Then I seem to melt and pass inside the glass ball. Inside, I can look around. There are two soft, comfortable chairs facing each other. There is absolute peace and quiet. This is my secret place. Here I can have clear, undisturbed contact with the forces of God and Nature.

I see myself sitting down in one of the two soft chairs. It will become my own. I lose connection with my body. Mind alone is all that is. Look ahead at the other chair. A man is taking form there. He does not ever make a sound or use his voice at all. His face is strong and kind, with gentle, soft eyes. He is dressed in a white robe and sandals. He has a beard. Rays of white light coming from his hands are soaking into me.

Whenever I wish, I can come to this secret place and share with this friend. He will hear me and help me. He controls all the power of Nature. He controls our world. He will never speak out loud. But, as he looks into my eyes from his chair, his great infinite wisdom will pass into me.

When I leave my secret place, my questions and my wishes will all be answered in time ahead on a deep level of which I will not even be aware. Later on, they will be made known to me, at the proper time. I will be helped. I know this: my friend and I in the glass ball can absolutely bring about any good thing that I wish or strive for in this world.

The secret place is as far inside my mind as the stars and sky are outside. Whenever I am in the glass ball, a lustrous, pure white light will be present. It will intensify and increase the frequency of my vital force or bio-field—while I am exposed to it.

I Give My Soul, Mind, and Body to Nature and God. I am experiencing more relaxation and concentration this time than I have previously. I hereby give my soul, and mind and body to Nature and to God completely, without reservation. In exchange for this, I am to receive from Nature and from God love, wisdom, understanding, happiness, and peace of mind. I am making this arrangement with Nature and with God because I wish to live a good and happy life, a moral, ethical, and spiritual life. I understand that I am not guaranteed material comfort or wealth at all times. But I am guaranteed the things mentioned before. Although my words and mind are now being guided by a friend, I sincerely believe that Nature and God brought this about and made it possible for me to make my human choice at this time and in this way.

I have connected myself through this system with all the powerful powers of Nature that can heal a cut on my arm. All of the doctors in the world cannot do that. Only Nature can do that. Nature that makes babies, provides for birth, holds the planets in their place. I no longer belong to myself now because I have given myself to Nature and to God. For the rest of my life, this mysterious and wonderful power of Nature, that I have drawn to myself, will fill my mind and body, and make me happier and healthier than I have ever been. From now on, my life will flourish more and more, like the green fields growing in the springtime, like a flower unfolding. From now on, I will have a new and better life of happiness, hope, and good health. I will see. It will be so. And nothing can stop it.

Positive Memories Always Available to Me. From now on, if at any time I begin to feel negative, downhearted, or depressed or lack confidence in myself, if I feel out of step with the world, or if I feel everything is going against me, this is what will happen. My subconscious mind will automatically bring forth memories of good, happy, positive things that have happened to my life in the past. These good, happy, pleasant, positive memories will push out and replace any feelings of blues or depression or lack of confidence with stronger feelings of cheerfulness, hope, optimism, and confidence in myself, automatically.

Resynchronizing My Vibrations. I am returning in my mind to the moment of my birth, on a deep level of which I will not consciously be aware. Here, I adjust the timing of my heartbeat and brainwaves to synchronize with each other and with Nature. This will bring me into perfect timing, perfect balance and perfect focus—physically, spiritually and psychologically. I will remain that way, coming back to the present, and I will stay that way for the rest of my life in perfect balance, perfect focus, perfect timing.

Now, as I count from ten to one, my mind will play itself backwards, just like a tape, to my moment of birth on a deep level. And I will be just born in the mind. Ten, nine, eight, seven, six, five, four, three, two, one. Now my heartbeat and brainwaves will be instantly adjusted into perfect balance—physically, spiritually, and psychologically.

When I count now from one to ten, my mind will come forward in time back to the present, keeping this perfect balance and perfect focus, for the rest of my life.

Auto-direction. Attention: subconscious mind. In the time ahead, I will be in the right place at the right time with the right abilities. I will be in the best geographic location for me to do the most good. I will arrive there when my own skills and abilities are needed at that certain place. You, subconscious mind, will help me "find myself" and make the most out of the rest of my life, bringing out the best in me for the service of humanity and self. Turn your infinite power to the satisfactory fulfillment of this assignment.

Bank Eight. From now on, I will have superhuman control to set moods. Whenever I say one word out loud eight times, the vibration of the word will expand and fill my entire being, with happiness, peace, courage, patience, confidence. Whenever I say it out loud eight times, this will happen.

IQ, What to Do? I will always have the ability to remember my past experiences so as to put them to good use. To trigger this, I will repeat the phrase, "IQ, what to do?" I'll just say this, and the appropriate answer will come from my subconscious mind.

Power Control Fifty. I can increase my mental power fifty times. I just link my little fingers together and say, "Power control fifty."

Pain Control Fifty. I can withstand fifty times more pain, whenever I need to do so. I just link my little fingers together and say, "Pain control fifty."

ESP Control Fifty. I can increase my psychic abilities fifty times. I just link my little fingers together and say, "ESP control fifty."

Auto-binoc Fifty. I can remember anything from the past. I just link my little fingers together and say, "Auto-binoc fifty." My subconscious mind will go into action, with binocular-like power, to scan my memory banks and locate and deliver memory material fifty times faster and more accurately than could be done normally.

Hypnosphere. I will become a powerful human magnet, drawing great knowledge, wisdom, and understanding from the invisible reservoir of universal knowledge, both now and for the rest of my life, to use as I wish—great knowledge, wisdom, and understanding that I would never had have under ordinary conditions.

Whenever I wish, I will be able to send my mind back to the great minds of the Incas, the Aztecs, the Mayans, and the Egyptians. Before I fall asleep each night, I can use these suggestions to learn from these great minds while I am sleeping, if I wish. My mind will return automatically to the present moment when I awake. In this way, I can be trained by the best minds of these ancient civilizations, if I wish.

The Kink Eraser. I now regress back to my childhood. Then I will use the power of childhood learning and time acceleration as a healing process. I now go back to the day I was born to straighten out the kinks in my subconscious mind.

Auto-weekly. For the next ten weeks, once a week, all the techniques I am learning now will repeat through my mind on a subconscious level. This will reinforce these techniques.

Mind Wall. There will be an impenetrable wall around my nervous system to protect me. It will be in effect for one year.

Picture Frame. I now see an empty frame. I see my own shadow. Then I see it saturated with pearly white foam. This will unleash Nature's healing power within my subconscious mind.

Dream Projection. I now picture a problem or situation that I wish to solve. I ask for dreams that will answer my needs and provide a solution.

Magnifying Glass Distance Technique. If I have a problem or situation, I can move my mind to exactly the right distance to understand this problem or situation clearly. I will position my mind at the best distance for clear focus, neither too close to the situation nor too far away from it. My focus will be clear.

Nature's Bank of Happiness. Anytime I wish, I can borrow from this infinite resource. The happiness I receive, however, must be repaid with interest. To do this, once a month, I must make a stranger happy. The loan will be repaid even faster for the kindness that I bestow upon my enemies.

Today and Every Day. I will be in a Bright New World. I will be in harmony with the principle of Right Action. I will be surrounded by well-wishers all around. I engage in no activity that is destructive or harmful. I am developing a third consciousness, an auto-hypnosis consciousness. It is closer to my subconscious mind than my ordinary consciousness.

With this exercise, the training session ended.

Reflecting on My Transformation

It is interesting for me now to reflect back and look at the life-changes I experienced after taking this training program, especially in light of my avowed goal of becoming a more effective communicator about parapsychology. Within a few months, I managed to launch a television interview series, in partnership with Arthur Bloch, one of America's most popular humorists and author of the *Murphy's Law* series of books. At first, the program was carried only on the public access channel of Marin County, California, in which I live. But then things began to happen almost like magic.

My partner and I arranged to bring one of our tapes to the program director of one of the local junior-college PBS stations, KCSM-TV, in the San Francisco Bay Area. It was an interview with Keith Harary, co-author with Russell Targ of *The Mind Race*, on the practical applications of ESP. He liked the interview, and arranged to give our program a prime-time slot once a week. The viewer response was very positive, and after a year, KCSM-TV offered to sponsor our series, now called *Thinking Allowed*, for satellite uplink to public television stations throughout North America. That was in 1987, and the program has now been out on the satellite every week for more than thirteen years. It is actually one of the longer-running programs on national television.

Of course, I cannot say that the Owens training was the sole cause of this success. There are too many other antecedents, such as my prior experience in radio, and even other synchronicities that I have not mentioned in this book. All I can say, definitely, is that the television series was initiated within weeks of my completing the training. It has been a vital, transformative part of my life ever since, enabling me to engage in intimate, in-depth conversations with the world's leading creative thinkers in philosophy, psychology, health, science, and spirituality. It has served as a vehicle for me to communicate parapsychological perspectives within this larger context to many millions of English-speaking people. Hundreds of colleges and universities now carry these videotapes in their libraries. Today, over 170 transcripts from the television series are publicly available on the Website of the Intuition Network (www.intuition.org). I can clearly say that my ambition of being able to communicate parapsychological information to the public at large has been significantly fulfilled. This book, I expect, will bring things to another level, since the information I have revealed here has been largely hidden from the public. With the hindsight of fourteen years, I owe a debt of gratitude to Ted Owens for this training.

Was Ted Owens, himself, a complete expression of the lofty, self-mastery principles embodied in his own training program? Clearly not. In many regards, his life was a failure. He was a man of many moods and habits. His efforts to communicate to the world at large were almost completely unsuccessful. His level of self-awareness was constrained by the myths he had created about himself. Even his ability to simply provide for his family was at an absolute minimum, by American middle-class standards.

However, in Owens' defense, it must be said that the principles that he taught me were themselves almost impeccable. In this sense, he resembled many great teachers—from Moses to the present era—whose lives failed to fully embody the teachings that issued forth from them.

"They Had Certain Time Windows Here That Meshed with Me"

In late 1986, Ted Owens and his family moved to Fort Ann, New York, a rural, upstate area where moose occasionally roamed Main Street. Owens wrote to one of his supporters, George Delavan:

> I spread out a map of the U.S. and asked my UFOs where they wanted me. They telepathed upper New York state. I told my son, Beau, that we would seek out a place in the country, isolated, because my UFOs want to rendezvous with the boys and myself . . . not

one at a time, but steadily. (My boys call these meetings with UFOs "haunts" . . . and we have had them on many occasions.)

Within a few months, it seemed as if strange lights and strange sights had become commonplace in the vicinity of the farm that Owens had rented. The local newspaper wrote an article about the unusual beams of light. Owens' next-door neighbor wrote a testimonial letter regarding his own unusual sightings. Owens explained the situation in a letter to me:

> [M]y UFOs *brought* me and my family here to Fort Ann and, through tremendous synchronicity, stopped us here. They told me that they had certain time windows here that meshed with me. They told me that their sole reason for bringing me and mine here was to make powerful contacts and communication.

These UFO sightings apparently continued from about July 1987 through November 1987, when I received my final communication from Owens. It was a lengthy letter full of drawings of a large, rectangular UFO that had hovered for some time directly over his farm house, and had begun changing shape. A few weeks after that, I received the news from D. Scott Rogo that Owens had died of sclerosis of the liver on December 28, 1987.

Wayne Grover is the *National Enquirer* journalist who had worked with Owens and is a military historian and author of four nonfiction books for children. He maintained an ongoing communication with Ted Owens and described his experience of the PK Man's last days:

> Suddenly, Owens went silent for months. Then in 1987, he called me from upstate New York and said he had moved his family there to be picked up by the

UFOs. He sent me several drawings his son Beau had made of vertically long, non-saucerlike UFOs that were hovering over his rural home—as well as newspaper clippings reporting local UFO sightings and an affidavit to the same effect from a neighbor. There was a flurry of calls and then one last one whose contents were very strange and [which] I choose to keep private.

Suffice it to say, the predictions of that last conversation changed my life and caused me to wonder where science leaves off and the unknown begins. My wife was witness to the events that followed and shares with me the wonderment of it.

I never heard from Ted Owens again after that last call.

In 1998, when Andy Eastman (see chapter 9) first learned of Owens' death, he responded with the following thought:

I'm sorry to hear of Ted's death and can understand why the SIs were doing materializations near his house. He was a great man! The work Ted did to turn this crazed society away from some of its ways was outstanding. He had more courage and fortitude than anyone I can remember. Rest in peace, Ted Owens. You did more than your fair share and we all "OWE" you a lot!

CHAPTER 12

IMPLICATIONS, APPLICATIONS, AND RAMIFICATIONS

Truth is a shining goddess, always veiled, always distant, never wholly approachable, but worthy of all the devotion of which the human spirit is capable.
Bertrand Russell

There are those who would deny the existence of the phenomena studied by parapsychologists and ufologists. Rationalists propose that the universe is governed by orderly mechanisms, well-understood for centuries by scientists. This is a comforting world view. But this chapter will present the academic context within which the Owens case does make sense. Arguments will be presented from the perspective of sociology, physics, ufology, and anthropology.

The hero of all rationalists, Sir Isaac Newton, well understood the problems with this perspective. Newton was greatly troubled by gravity. How could Earth, for example, hold the moon in an orbit? We take this fact of nature for granted. But Newton could not. He realized that this meant action at a distance, yet the classical principles of mechanics that he formulated could not account for that. It took almost 200 years before the paradox of gravity's existence was resolved by Albert Einstein as curvature in space itself. Newton also realized, of course, that his classical mechanics could not account for creation. In fact, he was a deep student of the Bible, realizing that his own theory implied the existence of a higher power.

In the twentieth century, Einstein's theory of general relativity introduced several more paradoxes. Gravity is adequately explained only by adding the peculiar assumption that space itself is curved. Furthermore, according to Einstein, time stops completely at the speed of light! This means that, if I have a twin who travels in a space ship at the speed of light, she may visit the end of the universe and return to Earth billions of years from now. You and I, of course, will be long dead, but my twin could still be a young woman!

Other scientific mysteries are equally profound. How is it that you and I are conscious, that we have subjective awareness? We are made of up physical particles, held together by physical forces. There is nothing we know of in physics itself—time, space, mass, or energy—that could logically engender subjective awareness. No matter how complex our brains may be, there is nothing in the electrical patterns of neuronal firing or the chemical patterns of synaptic discharge that suggests consciousness. The problem is so immense that, for most of the twentieth century, scientists and philosophers chose to ignore it altogether. Consciousness, they claimed, was not a problem for philosophy, but a categorical error: we only think that consciousness exists because we mistakenly speak of it as a noun, as if it were a thing unto itself. Today, in the twenty-first century, things have changed. Scientists and philosophers are at least in agreement that there is a problem, but an agreed-upon solution to the problem is not yet in sight.

From my perspective, it will not be possible to address the question of consciousness until we adequately understand the nature and power of subjective awareness. This necessitates that we come to terms with the claims of the paranormal. This necessitates that we seriously commit, as a society, to explore parapsychology and ufology. However, our ability to objectively do so has been, for the last century or more, hampered by social dynamics that further obscure the already elusive facts in question.

A revolution in science began in the early twentieth century with the shift from the orderly regime of classical, Newtonian physics to the breathtaking paradoxes of quantum mechanics and general relativity. A parallel revolution in modern art began with the nineteenth century shift from representational to impressionist art, followed by the twentieth century explosion of expressionism, cubism, futurism, and surrealism. Thomas Kuhn, author of the classic text of the paradigm shift, *The Structure of Scientific Revolutions*, suggested that those who espouse new paradigms almost never succeed in changing the minds of those whose careers are based on defending the status quo. The revolutionary shift only is complete when the older generation is replaced by groups who became familiar with the new approach during their formative years. And, some shifts are so enormous in their import that the transition takes more than just one or two or three generations. This is the case in the field of psychology, in which a comparable revolutionary leap into the depths of the human psyche was initiated 120 years ago by founders of psychical research, including America's greatest psychologist, William James.

William James was in good company. His colleagues included the brightest European and American minds. However, in the end, their revolution was aborted—or, perhaps, just prolonged. By 1920, psychology had taken a distinct turn away from the study of the far reaches of the human psyche. Although Sigmund Freud and his brilliant disciple, Carl Jung, achieved penetrating theoretical insights, even they were treated with disrespect by the academics. The effort to apply scientific methods to the exploration of psychic energy was ultimately relegated to a marginal position in society. For most of the twentieth century, consciousness itself has been a scientific anathema as the field of psychology was dominated by the behaviorist approach.

The Theory of Cognitive Dissonance: *When Prophecy Fails*

Sociologists already understand that the facts, taken by themselves, are often insufficient when it comes to changing the opinion of somebody who is staunchly committed to their preexisting viewpoint. It is interesting that the classic test case of this "theory of cognitive dissonance" involved a UFO cult. Leon Festinger and his colleagues published an influential book in 1956 called *When Prophecy Fails*. The authors conducted a participant-observer study of a group surrounding a Midwestern medium, referred to as Mrs. Keech, who believed she was receiving messages from alien intelligences about the end of the world. When the predicted cataclysm did not occur, Festinger observed that many cult members developed even stronger adherence to the group, and increased their proselytizing activities. Festinger took this as a confirmation of this theory—and it has subsequently become standard sociological doctrine. Festinger observed (in the sexist language common to his generation):

> A man with a conviction is a hard man to change. Tell him you disagree and he turns away. Show him facts or figures and he questions your sources. Appeal to logic and he fails to see your point. We have all

experienced the futility of trying to change a strong conviction, especially if the convinced person has some investment in his belief. We are familiar with the variety of ingenious defenses with which people protect their convictions, managing to keep them unscathed through the most devastating attacks. But man's resourcefulness goes beyond simply protecting a belief. Suppose an individual believes something with his whole heart; suppose further that he has a commitment to this belief, that he has taken irrevocable actions because of it; finally, suppose that he is presented with evidence, unequivocal and undeniable evidence, that his belief is wrong: what will happen? The individual will frequently emerge, not only unshaken, but even more convinced of the truth of his beliefs than ever before. Indeed, he may even show a new fervor about convincing and converting other people to his view.

The irony is that Festinger's theory itself was largely disconfirmed in the classic study that he believed exemplified its confirmation. Most of the cult members abandoned Mrs. Keech. But, in spite of these contradicting facts, Festinger successfully proselytized his theory of cognitive dissonance throughout the Western academic world. In fact, the cult members were possibly more willing to abandon their belief system in the face of contradictory facts than were the sociologists. This should not be surprising, for sociologists and other scholars purporting to be rational and objective are all themselves actors on the social stage—and just as susceptible to social forces as other people.

I make this point because this book is largely about bizarre facts that have been a source of cognitive dissonance, certainly for myself but even more so for a wide variety of conventional thinkers, scientists, debunkers, and skeptics. In spite of the fact that Festinger's well-known theory was only partially confirmed in the classic UFO-prophecy case study, it remains a useful guide for thinking about human patterns of irrationality.

Using the theory of cognitive dissonance as a guideline, it is likely that those who will denounce this book most strongly, assuming that it receives any significant public attention at all, will be those who have made irrevocable social commitments to worldviews that are inconsistent with the data herein presented. For example, I would expect the most hostility to come from those who are card-carrying skeptics, or, to put it more humorously, "Archie Debunkers," i.e., fellows and members of the Committee for the Scientific Investigation of Claims of the Paranormal (CSICOP). Festinger's theory, I think, would allow us to predict that, should this book, or other books like it, become extremely popular, it would be an occasion for CSICOP to expand its own proselytization and propaganda against the "rising tide of irrationality and occultism."

Similarly, one would expect that CSICOP fellows and members, among whom are many distinguished scientists, would be the least likely to be willing to engage in serious, quiet investigation of the actual facts and discussion of the theoretical issues. I think Festinger's theory argues that, because these socially committed debunkers consider themselves to behave according to rational principles, they are likely therefore to at least put on a display of fair-minded examination. This is necessary in order for them to reduce their own cognitive dissonance for, in spite of their almost irrevocable social commitment to secular humanism and rational materialism, they do not think of themselves as people who would unfairly suppress legitimate data that contradicts their world view. Therefore, it is necessary that, in the end, they develop some ingenious strategy for delegitimizing the data itself.

On the other hand, students of sociology might observe here that proponents of the paranormal also take steps to criticize the strategies of the skeptics. How, therefore, is one to make sense of this social discourse? The answer, dear reader, is to follow the details. If a heated debate should result, many people will not have the time or energy to follow point by point and make an informed judgment about the intellectual integrity of the various positions. The theory of cognitive dissonance suggests that most bystanders to the debate will take sides according to their pre-existing disposition. Ultimately, however, scientific disputes are settled by the facts themselves. Yet, with regard to parapsychology and ufology, the dispute is so deep and the facts are so elusive that it is reasonable to expect the controversy to continue for many decades, if not centuries, into the future.

In the meanwhile, real psychic practitioners will have discovered for themselves ways to work within the social chaos. Good humor and a sense of proportion will enable many to avoid the painful forms of social confrontation that are an almost daily reality for the pioneers of parapsychology. There are many other creative possibilities.

We must not forget that there are more than merely two sides to any potential debate that will emerge from this book, or books like it. Of course, there is the predictable battle between parapsychology and its critics. But there may also be an outcry of hostility from those who accept the factual nature of the account I shall present, but who fear that such exploration is little more than flirting with the powers of evil. Festinger's theory of cognitive dissonance, I believe, would predict that, if this book or books like it become popular, they will encourage a new round of proselytization among religious groups that view the growing reports of UFO contact as a sign of diabolical activity.

And I think, if I focus my sociological binoculars carefully, I can discern a third debate emerging. There will be those researchers in parapsychology and ufology who may criticize this book or books like it because they lack the support of hard-core, experimental science. To these critics, it does not matter how plausible this book or books like it may seem. The important questions of mind and universe, they will argue, should only be decided by the leanest and meanest of scientific evidence. Anecdotal accounts, clinical studies, case histories, and historical data, as interesting as they may be, have no important role to play in serious scientific discourse.

At first, such an argument seems to be honest, scientific conservatism. How can there be anything wrong with that? And, superficially, there is not. But, from the perspective of Festinger's theory of cognitive dissonance, a seemingly reasonable ideology could be yet another strategy for reducing the discomfort caused by highly bizarre, complicated, and ambiguous facts. The risk is we may be, thereby, filtering out the very data that most requires our rapt attention. And, let us not forget, the methods of naturalistic observation have served science very well.

Sorokin's Social and Cultural Dynamics: The Crisis of Our Age

Now, we will step back from the relatively minor theory of cognitive dissonance and examine the macro-sociological picture. According to sociologist Pitirim A. Sorokin, the major dynamic in Western culture during the past 2,500 years has been a shift between a metaphysical understanding of reality grounded in mind or spirit, and one grounded in physical, material reality as experienced through the senses. Sorokin's ideas are controversial, but he deserves to be taken seriously. After all, every year, the American Sociological Association presents the Pitirim A. Sorokin Award for the outstanding contribution to the field of sociology.

Sorokin founded the Department of Social Relations at Harvard University, and he used the resources of that venerable institution to develop his grand meta-theories. In his popular book, *The Crisis of Our Age*, published in 1938, Sorokin predicted the coming second World War. However, he argued forcefully that the issues of the day—communism, fascism, nationalism, internationalism, etc.—represented no more than a side show on the stage of cultural development. Sorokin saw that the materialist paradigm that had dominated Western culture since the Renaissance was undergoing a transition. For him, this was the underlying reason why the twentieth century was to become the most violent in all of human history.

Sorokin postulated that metaphysical ideas actually serve as the glue that holds cultures together. For example, he argued that during the medieval period, European culture was focused on a spiritual reality, the "kingdom of heaven," as the ultimate source of and reason for human existence. In support of his contention, Sorokin pointed out that the major economic activity of that period was the construction of the great cathedrals with their spires pointing toward the heavens. Virtually all medieval art depicted biblical scenes, glorifying the reality of Christ in Heaven, and depicting physical reality as a "vale of tears" through which we pass on our way to eternity. Medieval law was the law of the church. Medieval music was the music of liturgy. To the extent that medieval science existed, it was couched in theological terms. The realm of the spirit was the metaphysical idea that served to organize all of medieval culture.

The Renaissance, itself, was a period in which the ideals of materialism and spirit were held in balance. A great flowering of human creativity occurred during this period. But the balance proved to be unstable, and following the Renaissance, Western culture entered into the materialist phase that has been dominant since that time. Consider the parallels. Since the Renaissance, our major economic activity has shifted away from the building of cathedrals. Church spires are no longer the tallest monuments that ennoble the human spirit. These days they are dwarfed by the towers of commerce in every major metropolitan area. Prior to the twentieth century, all artwork glorified the life of the senses. The legal system changed its emphasis to focus on property rights. Philosophy developed dominant new schools of thought including utilitarianism and pragmatism. Science and industry flourished. The reality of the senses was king. Sorokin labeled this cultural paradigm "sensate."

The irony is that, according to sensate sociology, metaphysical ideas cannot possibly serve as the glue that holds cultures together. From the sensate perspective, ideas are shaped by cultural institutions, not the reverse. This viewpoint, championed extensively by Karl Marx and his followers, is still dominant in sociology today. Thus, while Sorokin is honored as the founding father of American sociology, his core idea about the primacy of metaphysical thought in holding cultural forms together is treated, in the halls of academia, as a quaint and archaic notion—as almost medieval.

In 1938, Sorokin already knew that the sensate paradigm was dying. The human spirit itself had been too large to be contained by the medieval paradigm, but it was also too large for the modern. Something else was needed. After all, in spite of all its triumphs, modern society has brought us to the brink of disaster—either ecological or military or both. Sorokin knew that the transition between such large social paradigms always spelled trouble. For example, the period between the sensate Roman era and the medieval period was known as the Dark Ages. So, although his theories and his vision enabled him to forecast World War II, Sorokin disagreed that it would be the "war to end all wars," as some were then arguing. He wrote that violence and social disruption and alienation would continue until the establishment of a new cultural paradigm—one, he hoped, that would recognize the realities of both matter and spirit.

Paul Ray's Trans-modern, Cultural Creatives

Another way to view the contemporary collision of paradigms has been articulated by demographer Paul Ray, who is my neighbor in San Rafael, California. Ray, whose company, American Lives, tracks social trends, believes that the American public can be thought of as consisting of three basic groups. There are the traditionalists. They cling to the values of past generations, particularly religious fundamentalism. For them, the world can be seen as a struggle between the spiritual forces of good and evil. For the most part, they would describe the sorts of phenomena reported in this book as the work of the devil. Then there are the modernists. They reject religious dogmatism and superstition. They espouse humanistic ethics and values. For them, the world is governed by natural laws and operates on rational principles. For the most part, they are equally certain that the phenomena reported in this book are not at all real, but are rather entirely explainable in terms of sloppy thinking, delusion and probably fraud.

Paul Ray describes the third, and fastest growing, segment of the American population as the "trans-modern, cultural creatives." I personally identify with this group. They are interested in spirituality but not dogmatic religion. They are committed to their own personal growth. They are very interested in environmental and social issues. For cultural creatives, the powers of the unconscious mind are not "demonic" in the Christian sense, but rather "daimonic" as the term daemon was originally developed by the ancient Greeks—encompassing both the positive (eudaimonic) and negative (dysdaimonic) faces of the psyche.

Of course, the situation is far more complex than these three simple groupings. There are many subgroups within each of the large categories. I believe that the situation is further compounded by the collision of worldviews, or paradigms, that takes place daily within each of us. The situation is further confused because, while the modernists and traditionalists have well-articulated positions, the trans-modern cultural creatives are still striving to develop a synthesis. Paul Ray discovered, to his astonishment, that the 40 million Americans who constitute this group do not even think of themselves as part of a population segment at all. They consider themselves as loners, as seekers, as thinkers striving to find a new balance, as outsiders (to use the phrase popularized by Colin Wilson).

Pitirim Sorokin himself suggested that the twentieth century was characterized by "chaotic congeries," or disconnected collections of ideologies. The New Age is not yet born. The integration of scientific and spiritual achievements will require the sustained support of large segments within the human community. We have not yet achieved a new, cultural synthesis capable of containing the awesome magnitude of the human spirit itself. Sorokin, I am sure, would label efforts to proclaim a new paradigm as premature syncretisms, i.e., attempts at synthesis. Paradigms are not consciously invented. They evolve as society itself evolves.

"I Do Not Believe in ESP—
Because I Do Not Want Anybody to Read My Mind"

Through my eyes, both the modernists and the traditionalists respond in a similar way when they encounter reports suggesting the paranormal at work. The modernists decry a rising tide of superstition. The traditionalists decry the work of the devil. But, both groups seem to be expressing an aversion to exploring the depths within the human psyche itself

This situation was clearly exemplified on the day in 1973 that the noted writer Arthur C. Clarke spoke on the University of California, Berkeley, campus. At the end of his talk, I raised my hand and asked him if he, who had written so eloquently in *Childhood's End* about psychic functioning, believed in ESP. *Time* magazine's science editor, Leon Jaroff, had just quoted him as pooh-poohing the recently publicized claims about the famous Israeli energy practitioner, Uri Geller. His response to me was emblematic of the core problem. "No," he said, "I do not believe in ESP—because I do not want anybody to read my mind."

Of course, Freud, in *Civilization and its Discontents*, among other books, had already shown that we do not even want to know what is in our own mind! That civilized aversion is the origin of the Freudian unconscious—widely understood by practicing psychiatrists but ridiculed in academic psychology programs. How could we then allow others to see in us that which we are hiding from ourselves? But the ultimate project of the trans-modern cultural creatives is different. We are engaged in facing ourselves, in making the unconscious conscious.

From a social dynamics perspective, one must appreciate that what appears to cultural creatives to be a movement toward enlightenment may seem like madness to a modernist, or like diabolical evil to a traditionalist. As a graduate student at UC-Berkeley, for example, I found a pamphlet in the physics library written by a physicist, Robert Birge, for whom one of the physics buildings had been named. In it, he reported on his investigations of parapsychology. He drew negative conclusions about this field of endeavor, but what intrigued me the most was his warning to other physicists: he claimed that they would risk their own mental health if they began looking too deeply into this subject.

Birge's warning, coming from within the modernist camp, is not alone. Traditional Jews, for example, have a proscription against the teaching of Cabala to anyone under the age of forty and anyone unmarried. Again, the tradition is that only the most stable humans can engage in mystical explorations without harming the soul, or—from the religious perspective—becoming possessed. I have also heard it said amongst yogis that one of the greatest risks of advanced practice is losing one's sanity. And, indeed, the standard psychiatric diagnostic manuals clearly interpret belief systems and attitudes that are positive with regard to bizarre paranormal occurrences as a sign of psychosis.

The situation is further complicated by the fact that many paranoid and psychotic individuals do, indeed, have fantasies that are strikingly similar to the factual accounts that are presented in this book. This twilight zone between mental illness and authentic exploration into the cutting edge of reality has, of course, been a theme that has been explored in many science fiction and fantasy films. In real life, the social stigma associated with madness is present in the background and serves to impede rapid progress in fields such as parapsychology and ufology. Only those who are sufficiently secure in their own self-knowledge and self-esteem, or otherwise sufficiently naive or foolhardy, or perhaps sufficiently mad, are likely to engage in the sorts of professional risks required for serious investigation of parapsychology and ufology.

In my own case, I think I was propelled into this exploration by a strong sense of mental stability, considerable idealistic naiveté, healthy curiosity, and an openness to consider my own inner life as a laboratory. I was also schooled, as an undergraduate psychology major at the University of Wisconsin, in the writings of such great visionary psychologists as William James (author of *Varieties of Religious Experience*), Abraham Maslow (*Toward a Psychology of Being*), Jean Houston and Robert Masters (*Varieties of Psychedelic Experience, Mind Games,* and other classics), Carl Jung (*Memories, Dreams and Reflections*) and R. D. Laing (*The Politics of Experience*). From these perspectives, the unconscious was not a murky quagmire to be feared and avoided, but a sacred cave to be explored.

"It Would Be a Mistake to Think Owens Himself Was Able to Produce the Events He Takes Credit For"

One of the most open-minded scholars acquainted with the Owens material has been James Harder, now emeritus professor of hydraulic engineering at the University of California at Berkeley, who served as a member of my doctoral dissertation committee in the 1970s while I was researching the Owens case. He also served as director of research for the Aerial Phenomena

Research Organization (APRO), then one of the foremost organizations investigating cases of ostensible alien contact. His conclusions about Owens are as follows:

> The extraordinary powers or abilities of Ted Owens—abilities to influence material phenomena such as willing the location and timing of lightning strikes, the ability to influence weather, and the ability to influence the outcome of athletic competitions, is far beyond the lesser powers attributed to other individuals. I am sure that particular instances of Owens' demonstrations can be successfully challenged by skeptics, but also believe that the entire story would survive such a challenge. In other words, the work in its entirety constitutes a credible set of extraordinary facts that echo a lesser set that we can find in other humans, but which have seldom made their way into public discourse.
>
> I am very aware of the methods used by the media, and the average person as well, in evaluating such controversial matters. This conventional method uses examples to prove a point. Lost in their understanding is the logical truth that no number of examples can prove a negative, although one example can sometimes prove a positive. When described in this stark way, it should be obvious to any observer. Nevertheless, the method of using a large number of examples that throw doubts on a phenomenon is routinely used by debunkers to discredit a phenomenon. The prevalence of this method of arguing is so pervasive that we hardly notice its fallacy.
>
> So evidence of a failed attempt to produce a seemingly impossible event (and I have been one of the witnesses to one such Owens attempt [described

in chapter 6]) does not invalidate a mass of other data. In my own experience I have observed less spectacular parallels to Ted Owens' unusual powers, and I have friends who have both observed and carefully recorded other such unusual cases. Only the sheer magnitude of Ted Owens' abilities separates him from other individuals in other cases.

I think it would be a mistake to think that Owens himself was able to produce the events he takes credit for. To fully understand his case one must go further into other cases where humans have displayed extraordinary powers. In those cases open to careful examination, it has been my conclusion that most turn out to be powers exerted by extraterrestrial groups or individual extraterrestrial beings. This is the most likely alternative to the claim that ALL the events reported in the Ted Owens case are fraudulent (and I mean *every* one). Lacking fraud, any other alternative explanation would still have to involve the collaboration of some other godlike power or undefined spiritual entity. Good evidence for such interventions is found in history, notably in the history contained in the Christian Bible, although it is usually assumed by modern critics that these are the result of fantasy or error.

Thus I heartily defend Dr. Mishlove in his giving serious attention to this most remarkable case and hope that serious investigators *will* follow his example in looking further into such remarkable phenomena. By taking note of this case, we open up investigations that may lead in directions that are so bizarre that many investigators *will* be turned off. But recall that many of the major advances in our scientific understanding have been due to a dogged pursuit in unpopular directions. Where we find the maximum strangeness we also may find the maximum chance of finding new truths.

Ted Owens always referred to the SIs as coming from a higher dimensional realm and not from some distant planet. Whether Ted knew it or not, all during his lifetime (1920-1987), the world of physics underwent radical changes in its view of reality, which I will review here. These changes lend support to Owens' claims and his vision.

A Brief History of Hyperspace
(written by physicist Saul-Paul Sirag)

Albert Einstein in 1915 introduced the idea that gravity is to be explained as the warping of four-dimensional (4-d) spacetime. Whatever doubts physicists had—and there were many—about the reality of the four-dimensionality of spacetime as a unified geometrical whole that could be warped were erased by the dramatic verification of Einstein's gravity theory, called the General Theory of Relativity, in 1919, when a group of British astronomers led by Arthur Eddington measured the bending of starlight grazing the sun during a solar eclipse. That same year, Theodore Kaluza, a Polish physicist, came up with the idea that not only the Einstein gravity theory but also electromagnetism, including James Clerk Maxwell's (1831-1979) electromagnetic theory of light, could be derived from the assumption that spacetime is actually a warped five-dimensional geometric structure. With Einstein's help, Kaluza's 5-d theory was published in 1921.

The decade of the 1920s was the most revolutionary decade in physics and astronomy. I will mention only the highlights. In quantum physics: deBroglie's wave-particle duality; Heisenberg's matrix mechanics and the uncertainty principle; Bohr's complementarity principle; Pauli's exclusion principle; Schrödinger's wave function equation; and Dirac's antimatter equation, which unified quantum theory and Einstein's special relativity. In astronomy: Eddington's theory of the internal constitution of stars, including the sun; the discovery of galaxies beyond the Milky Way galaxy; Friedmann and Lemaitre's theory of the expansion of the universe; and Hubble's observations verifying the expansion of the universe.

In the midst of this revolution, Einstein contributed seminal papers on the statistics of quantum theory and the stimulated emission of photons from atoms. These papers led to many later developments including the laser. But Einstein was primarily interested in what he called "unified field theory," which meant the unification of gravity with electromagnetism. Kaluza's five-dimensional version of such a unified theory was an amazing achievement, but it had the major flaw that it could not explain why we don't see the fifth dimension, which is supposed to be spatial. Another flaw was that it said nothing about the new quantum mechanics that was exploding throughout the 1920s.

The Swedish physicist Oscar Klein in 1926 spoke to both these questions by publishing his version of the 5-d theory, in which the fifth dimension is not visible to us because it is an extremely small compact dimension; in other words, each point of 4-d spacetime is replaced by a tiny circle whose radius is around 10^{-33} cm. This is the Planck length, which is named for Max Planck who defined this size as the basic unit of size in the quantum world. The Planck length is twenty orders of magnitude smaller than a proton (10^{-13} cm): so if the fifth dimension is a Planck length circle, it is no wonder we can't walk around in it; not even a proton could do that!

Klein's Planck-length circle, as a candidate for the fifth dimension, entailed both Einstein's general relativity, applied to 5-d spacetime, and quantum theory to provide the smallness of the extra dimension. As a bonus, the theory provides a geometric explanation for the quantization of electric charge; that is why every electron carries the same charge.

This 5-d theory, called the Kaluza-Klein theory, was forgotten in the world of physics for several decades during which the frontier of physics became the exploration of the nucleus of the atom, where two new forces were discovered: the strong and weak nuclear forces. The strong force holds the nucleus together against the electrical repulsion of the constituent protons, all carrying an identical positive charge (remember: like charges repel). The weak force causes the most common type of nuclear decay—changing one type of atom into another in a kind of twentieth-century alchemy. These forces were exciting things to explore, and it was obvious that any proposed "unified field theory" would be incomplete without taking them into account. In his last two decades, Einstein (1879-1955) was a revered grandfather figure, who was widely believed to be out of touch with the frontiers of physics—persisting in his doubts about the fundamental nature of quantum mechanics, and his fervent pursuit of the holy grail of physics, the unified field theory.

It was quite a surprise to physics that by the one hundredth anniversary celebrations of Einstein's birth, a unified theory had arisen: superstring theory. Discovered in 1971 by Raymond, Neveu, and Schwarz, *it required* ten dimensions of spacetime! Physicists suddenly began to read the old 5-d Kaluza-Klein theory papers, and translated them into English. In 1975, Sherk and Schwarz showed that superstring theory unifies both Einstein's theory of gravity and quantum mechanics and also provides for the unification of all the forces: gravity, electromagnetism, and the strong and weak nuclear forces. During the Einstein celebration year of 1979, John Schwarz teamed up with Michael Green and together, over several years, they proved that superstring theory is a self-consistent theory of quantum gravity that includes general relativity and quantum mechanics as subtheories. This was published in 1984 and created a sensation in the world of physics. Many, especially younger, physicists immediately jumped on this bandwagon, so that today the unified field theory—the gleam in

Einstein's eye—is a vast industry in physics. This is why physicists take the notion of hyperspace (ten dimensions of spacetime) seriously.

Of course, the idea of hyperspace goes back to Plato (427-347 B.C.) who suggested in his cave allegory that we are like prisoners of the 3-d world, identifying ourselves with our 3-d shadows, rather than the hyperdimensional creatures we really are. Plato never used the word hyperdimensional, but the idea is clearly in his story of the projection of the prisoner's shadows (a 2-d projection) on the cave wall. The prisoners, so securely chained, come to identify themselves with their shadows cast by a fire behind them; and they believe they, as shadows, are interacting with the shadows cast by people walking behind them.

One of the prisoners breaks free of his chains and escapes to the world outside the cave, where he sees the full 3-d world. He can now really interact with the other 3-d people and objects. However, he goes back to try to rescue his former fellow prisoners. They mock him and challenge him to tell them what he thinks he sees in their shadow world. Because he has been in the bright sunlight outside the cave, his eyes are not as keenly adjusted to the dark shadow-world in which his fellow prisoners live. They can make out the details of the shadows better than he can. This proves to them that he is merely mad.

It is worth considering that the bizarreness of the Ted Owens story is a modern-day version of Plato's cave allegory.

Even though Plato had said of his academy, "Let no one enter here without geometry," it took many centuries for geometry to extend to the fourth dimension. It was the fourth dimension as a doorway to the spiritual realm that inspired this geometric foray. The philosopher who attempted to geometrize the Platonic realm was Henry More (1614-1687), an influential colleague of Isaac Newton at Cambridge University. He taught that the spiritual realm extended into a fourth dimension, which he called "spissitude." But this sort of thinking caught on only when mathematicians began exploring the geometry of higher dimensional spaces.

August Moebius (1790-1868) is most famous for his discovery of the Moebius strip, a surface that has only one side. But in 1827, he described how a 3-d object, such as a right-handed glove, could be turned into its mirror image, a left-handed glove, by rotating it through four-dimensional space. Such a rotation could also be used to tie or untie a knot, whose ends are connected as in the mathematical definition of a knot, and to link or unlink a chain.

Johann Carl Friedrich Zoellner (1834-1882), an astronomer at the University of Leipzig, where Moebius taught, tried to prove that the spiritual realm was four-dimensional by having mediums such as Henry Slade link two wooden rings, one of oak and one of alder. Zoellner hypothesized that only by passing through a fourth dimension of space would this be possible. Slade never did this but succeeded in convincing Zoellner that he could move things through the fourth dimension by, among other things, tying four trefoil knots in a loop of string whose ends were sealed together. Zoellner wrote about these ideas in *Transcendental Physics*, a book that made the notion of the fourth dimension abhorrent among scientists.

Mathematicians, largely unconcerned with the application of their discoveries, continued to explore geometries beyond the fourth dimension. They were interested in the most general case—any number of dimensions.

Hyperspace—a word meaning space of more than three dimensions—was coined in the 1890s by mathematicians who were exploring the geometries defined by Bernhard Riemann (1826-1866) that were not only non-Euclidean (with any degree of warping—called "curvature"), but also were spaces of any number of dimensions. Riemann himself even proposed that non-Euclidean 3-d space might account for gravity. He was almost right. Einstein in 1915 showed that gravity could be accounted for by a curved 4-d spacetime.

Now physics is in the embarrassing situation of having ten-dimensional spacetime forced on it, at least in theory, if we wish to unify general relativity with quantum theory. The major experimental test of this theory is the search for supersymmetry partners for all of the ordinary fundamental particles. Ironically, this seems to be a replay of Dirac's 1929 unification of quantum theory and special relativity, which required the introduction of antiparticle partners for all the ordinary particles. The anti-electron (the positron) was quickly discovered in 1932; but the next antiparticle, the antiproton, was not discovered until 1955. Only then did physicists agree that the antimatter idea must be true for all particles.

Since general relativity and quantum theory are gigantic worlds unto themselves, and hardly on speaking terms with each other, it is not surprising that, in order to unify these two theories as subtheories of a larger theory physicists have envisaged many new consequences, chief among them being the hyperdimensional 10-d spacetime.

Some physicists argue that the extra dimensions used in superstring theory and other versions of unified field theory are mere mathematical tricks with no necessary implications for our philosophical understanding of the world. They may be correct. But often mathematical discoveries and the physical theories that are developed from them precede new breakthroughs, both in technology and in our picture of reality. It is certain that people at the end of the twenty-first century will have a picture of the universe rather different from today's mainstream view. It may well be that, by then, the implications of the Ted Owens case, and other similar ones, will be understood in terms of hyperdimensional physics. Higher dimensions of space could account for many psychic effects, as well as for the existence of other-dimensional aspects of consciousness, and entities such as the Space Intelligences.

"I Have Seen Shamans Invoke Rain and Have Watched the Rain Manifest"

Perhaps the debate as to whether Owens' manifestations were produced as the result of psychokinesis or as the result of SI intervention misses the point that, for millennia, shamans of many different cultures were said to produce similar phenomena. Shamanism, while still poorly understood, may be thought to combine psychokinetic talent with an ability to interact with hyperspace realms. I have had occasion to discuss these matters with David Wilson, also known as Awo Fa'lokun Fatunmbi, a Western-trained scholar and author who is also an initiate into the Yoruba Ifa tradition of Nigeria. He summarizes his view of the PK Man as follows:

> Dr. Mishlove makes reference to numerous examples where it appears that Ted Owens affected the weather and appears to have caused lightning to manifest. In *Ifa*, the invocation of lightning is used as an instrument of warfare. There are very specific and detailed rituals that are designed to produce and direct this natural phenomena. I have personally witnessed enough examples of *Ifa* initiates invoking changes in the weather that it now seems normal rather than abnormal.
>
> I have seen shamans invoke rain and have watched the rain manifest. I have seen shamans invoke the spirit of lightning while their invocations were punctuated by bolts of lightning hurling across the sky. I have seen shamans command the wind to blow and demand that it stop. On one occasion a wind storm disrupted a ceremony that I was participating in, and the *Ifa* initiate who was leading the ceremony poked his head out of the door of the room that we were in and yelled

at the wind to stop blowing. The wind stopped until after we had finished. When I asked how he did that, he answered, "You have to believe that you can." This answer is not flip. Believing that you can means that you have worked through doubt, fear, hesitation and confusion. These are all emotions that would restrict access to *ase* or inhibit the manifestation of kundalini (as *ase* is known in the yogic traditions).

In my own study of *Ifa*, I have identified at least forty different categories of interdimensional beings, and each category has a number of subcategories. The shamanism of West Africa and South Africa makes clear reference to alien life forms who visit the Earth from different dimensions of reality and some who claim to be from specific places in the visible universe. Similar material appears in the shamanistic traditions of Native Americans, most notably the Hopi who dance in honor of their alien visitors. The Hopi are extremely reluctant to speak about their relationship with alien visitors, not out of fear of being called "crazy"; their reluctance is based on a concern for the safety of the aliens themselves. Elders among the Zulu teach a form of sign language used to communicate with visitors from other planets. Efforts have been made by the Zulu elders to publish this material for the benefit of everyone. Some of the material has reached the printed page; most of it has been rejected by publishers as noncredible. It seems to me that the issue of credibility should be left to the reader and that any effort to edit ideas that are uncomfortable to the Western reader takes the entire concept of colonialism to a new level of insidious sophistication.

Honoring the Potential "PK Person" in Each Human Being

To me, the dramatic weight of the evidence is that an intelligent energy worked with Ted Owens throughout his unusual career as a demonstrator of paranormal phenomena. As a scientist, I realize that there is an alternative hypothesis. Perhaps all that has transpired can be explained as "odd matches" occurring in a random and meaningless universe, or, perhaps, a rational universe. The skeptics may just be correct about this, but I reckon that the probability of this is extremely low—less than one in a million, i.e., the probability of lightning striking the bridge to Camden in Philadelphia after Owens pointed his finger in that direction in response to the request of attorney Sidney Margulies.

The social dynamics that I have presented suggest that science itself has been handicapped in its pursuit of knowledge about the paranormal because we, as a society, are in a phase of conflict, controversy, and polarization regarding important questions concerning fundamental metaphysical issues. A new cultural paradigm is in the process of formation. However, progress in understanding and working with psychic energy will be limited, for humanity as a whole. We must evolve beyond denial. We must move beyond premature syncretism. We must move toward honest, authentic integration of the depths within us and the facts before us.

As for Ted Owens, it might be said that he has made a contribution worthy of being named after him. So, I propose that the term "Owens Effect" be used to refer to ostensible psychokinetic manipulation of large-scale, volatile systems such as hurricanes, tornados, earthquakes, volcanos, lightning, power blackouts, weather patterns, etc. Throughout his life, Owens tried—both valiantly and foolishly—to awaken public awareness regarding this potential.

At the same time, it is easy to criticize Ted Owens as his own worst enemy. He had numerous bad habits and even criminal propensities. To put it simply, the history of his demonstrations embodies many warnings about the potential harm that may be associated with the reckless cultivation of talents such as psychokinesis. Perhaps this is why the notion of witchcraft still raises shivers of fear in the general population.

But it is too late to revert back to medieval notions, and it is too late to point a moralistic finger at Ted Owens for the damage that followed in his wake. Our judgments about Ted Owens will neither change the past nor protect us against such abuses in the future. My own view is that Ted Owens and his powers, however they are to be explained, generally served as a mirror reflecting and amplifying the attitudes that were directed at him by those he encountered. Although Owens often acted recklessly and constantly used poor judgment, his malice was almost always reserved for those who treated him with contempt and disrespect. If humanity, as a whole, is to fully awaken to its own psychic potential—and harness it for good—we must all grow in wisdom. Specifically, this means we must learn to practice mental hygiene with regard to our own stream of consciousness—cultivating positive thoughts and attitudes while eschewing thoughts that deprecate ourselves or any other precious human being. And we must learn to treat all other people with courtesy and respect. After all, we all possess psychokinetic talents, both latent (such as the ability to control the weather) and actual (such as the ability to move our bodies). Perhaps, Ted Owens was sent to us by some higher intelligence for the purpose of measuring whether we were ready to assimilate the powers he exuded. Clearly, we were not. However, we are in a phase of rapid social transition. Perhaps it is not too late to receive other such messengers with greater understanding.

BIBLIOGRAPHY

Adamski, George, *Inside the Space Ships.* New York: Abelard-Schuman, 1955.

Andrews, Lynn V., *Medicine Woman.* San Francisco: Harper & Row, 1984.

Barker, David R., "Psi Phenomena In Tibetan Culture." In W. G. Roll (Ed.), *Research in Parapsychology 1978.* Metuchen, N.J.: The Scarecrow Press, 1979.

Beloff, John, "The Limits of Parapsychology." *European Journal of Parapsychology,* November 1978, 2, 9.

Binder, Otto, *Flying Saucers Are Watching Us.* Dorchester City Publishing Co., N.Y.: 1978.

Boyd, Doug, *Rolling Thunder: A Personal Exploration Into the Secret Healing Powers of An American Indian Medicine Man.* New York: Delta, 1989.

Brown, Courtney, *Cosmic Voyage: A Scientific Discovery of Extraterrestrials Visiting Earth.* New York: E. P. Dutton, 1996.

Castaneda, Carlos, *The Teachings of Don Juan: A Yaqui Way of Knowledge.* Berkeley: University of California Press, 1968.

Chalmers, David J. *The Conscious Mind: In Search of a Fundamental Theory.* New York: Oxford University Press, 1996.

Clarke, Arthur C., *Childhood's End*. New York: Ballantine, 1987.

Corso, Philip J., with William J. Birnes, *The Day After Roswell*. New York: Pocket Books, 1997.

de Mille, Richard, (Ed.), *The Don Juan Papers: Further Castaneda Controversies*. Santa Barbara, Calif.: Ross-Erikson, 1980.

Druffel, Ann and Rogo, D. Scott, *The Tujunga Canyon Contacts*. Englewood Cliffs,: Prentice-Hall, 1980.

Fatunmbi, Awo Fa'lokun, *Iwa Pele: Ifa Quest: The Search of the Sources of Santeria and Lucumi*. Bronx, N.Y.: Original Publications, 1991.

—*Awo: Ifa and the Theology of Orisha Divination*. Bronx, N.Y.: Original Publications, 1992.

—*Iba se Orjisa: Ifa Proverbs, Folktales, Sacred History and Prayer*. Bronx, N.Y.: Original Publications, 1994.

Festinger, Leon, *When Prophecy Fails: A Social and Psychological Study*. Minneapolis: University of Minnesota Press, 1956.

Feyerabend, Paul, *Against Method: Outline of an Anarchistic Theory of Knowledge*. Atlantic Highlands, N.J.: Humanities Press, 1974.

Freud, Sigmund, *Civilization and Its Discontents*. New York: W. W. Norton, 1989.

Fuller, John G., *The Interrupted Journey: Two Lost Hours "Aboard a Flying Saucer."* New York: Dial Press, 1966.

—*Arigo: Surgeon of the Rusty Knife*. New York: Crowell, 1974.

Gandee, Lee R. *Strange Experience: The Autobiography of a Hexenmeister*. Englewood Cliffs, N.J.: Prentice-Hall, 1971.

Gardner, Martin, *Fads and Fallacies in the Name of Science*. New York: Dover Publications, 1957.

Gauquelin, Michel, "The Zelen Test of the Mars Effect." *The Humanist*, Nov./Dec. 1977, 30-35.

Good, I. J. (Ed.), *The Scientist Speculates: An Anthology of Partly Baked Ideas*. New York: Basic Books, 1963.

Holiday, F. W., *The Dragon and the Disc: An Investigation into the Totally Fantastic.* New York: Norton, 1973.

Houston, Jean and Masters, Robert L., *Varieties of Psychedelic Experience.* New York: Holt, Rinehart & Winston, 1966.
—*Mind Games: The Guide to Inner Space.* Wheaton, Ill.: Theosophical Publishing House, 1998.

Hynek, J. Allen, *The UFO Experience: A Scientific Inquiry.* Chicago: Henry Regnery Company, 1972.

James, William, *Varieties of Religious Experience: A Study in Human Nature.* New York: Modern Library, 1994.

Jung, Carl, *Memories, Dreams and Reflections.* New York: Pantheon, 1963.

Kovach, Sue, *Hidden Files: Law Enforcement's True Case Stories of the Unexplained and Paranormal.* Chicago: Contemporary Books, 1998.

Krippner, Stanley and Montague Ullman with Alan Vaughan, *Dream Telepathy: Experiments in Nocturnal ESP* (2nd edition). Jefferson, N.C.: McFarland and Company, 1989.

Kuhn, Thomas S., *The Structure of Scientific Revolutions* (3rd edition). Chicago: University of Chicago Press, 1996.

Laing, R. D., *The Politics of Experience.* New York: Pantheon, 1967.

Leir, Roger K., *The Aliens and the Scalpel: Scientific Proof of Extraterrestrial Implants In Humans.* Columbus, N.C.: Granite Publishing, 1998.

Leroy, Olivier, *Levitation: An Examination of the Evidence and Explanations.* London: Oates & Washbourne, 1928.

Lyons, Arthur and Truzzi, Marcello, *The Blue Sense: Psychic Detectives and Crime.* New York: Mysterious Press, 1991.

Mahoney, Michael J., *Scientist as Subject: The Psychological Imperative.* Cambridge, Mass.: Ballinger Publishing Company, 1976.

Marks, David and Kammann, Richard, *Psychology of the Psychic.* Buffalo, N.Y.: Prometheus Books, 1980.

Maslow, Abraham, *Toward a Psychology of Being.* Princeton, N.J.: Van Nostrand, 1962.

Millman, Dan, *Way of the Peaceful Warrior: A Book that Changes Lives.* Tiburon, Calif.: H. J. Kramer, 1984.

Mishlove, Jeffrey, *The Roots of Consciousness: Psychic Liberation through History, Science and Experience.* New York: Random House, 1975.

—*Psi Development Systems.* Jefferson, N.C.: McFarland, 1983.

Morehouse, David, *Psychic Warrior: Inside the CIA's Stargate Program: The True Story of a Soldier's Espionage and Awakening.* New York: St. Martins Press, 1996.

Morgan, Marlo, *Mutant Message Down Under.* New York: HarperCollins, 1994.

Murphy, Michael and White, Rhea, *The Psychic Side of Sports.* Reading, Mass.: Addison-Wesley, 1978.

Neher, Andrew, *The Psychology of Transcendence.* Englewood Cliffs, N.J.: Prentice-Hall, 1980.

Owens, Ted, *How to Contact Space People.* Clarksburg, W.V.: Saucerian Books, 1969.

Palmer, John, "Parapsychology as a Probabilistic Science: Facing The Implications." Presidential Address, 22nd Annual Convention, Parapsychological Association, John F. Kennedy University, 1979.

Puharich, Andrija, *Beyond Telepathy: With an Introduction by Ira Einhorn.* Garden City, N.Y.: Anchor Press, 1973.

—*Uri: A Journal of the Mystery of Uri Geller.* Garden City, N.Y.: Anchor Press, 1974.

Puthoff, Hal and Targ, Russell, "Information Transmission under Conditions of Sensory Shielding," *Nature,* 252 (October 1974): 602-7.

Radin, Dean I., *The Conscious Universe: The Scientific Truth of Psychic Phenomena.* New York: HarperCollins, 1997.

Ray, Paul, "The Emerging Culture." *American Demographics.* February 1997.

Rhine, J. B., *The Reach of the Mind.* New York: W. Sloane Associates, 1947.

Rogo, D. Scott, *The Haunted Universe.* New York: New American Library, 1977.

Schmeidler, Gertrude, "Research Findings in Psychokinesis," in Stanley Krippner (Ed.), *Advances in Parapsychological Research,* Volume 1, 1977, New York: Plenum Press.

—"PK Research: Findings and Theories," in Stanley Krippner (Ed.), *Advances in Parapsychological Research* Volume 3, 1982, New York: Plenum Press.

—"Psychokinesis: The Basic Problem, Research Methods and Findings," in Stanley Krippner (Ed.), *Advances in Parapsychological Research,* Volume 4, 1984, Jefferson, N.C.: McFarland.

—"Psychokinesis: Recent Studies," in Stanley Krippner (Ed.), *Advances in Parapsychological Research,* Volume 5, 1987, Jefferson, N.C.: McFarland.

—"PK: Recent Publications and an Evaluation of the Quantitative Research," in Stanley Krippner (Ed.), *Advances in Parapsychological Research,* Volume 6, 1990, Jefferson, N.C.: McFarland.

—"PK: Recent Research Reports and a Comparison with ESP," in Stanley Krippner (Ed.), *Advances in Parapsychological Research,* Volume 7, 1994, Jefferson, N.C.: McFarland.

Schnabel, Jim, *Remote Viewers: The Secret History of America's Psychic Spies.* New York: Dell Books, 1997.

Smith, Warren, *What the Seers Predict for 1971.*

Sorokin, Pitirim A., *The Crisis of our Age.* New York: Dutton, 1941.

—*Social and Cultural Dynamics.* New York: Bedminster Press, 1962.

Stanford, Rex, "Concept And Psi." In W. G. Roll, R. L. Morris and J. D. Morris (eds.), *Research in Parapsychology 1973.* Metuchen, N.J.: Scarecrow Press, 1974.

—"Are We Shamans or Scientists?" Full Symposium Papers of the Parapsychological Association 22nd Annual Convention, August 1979, John F. Kennedy University, Orinda, California.

Strieber, Whitley, *Communion: A True Story.* New York: Avon, 1995.

Vasiliev, L. L., *Experiments in Distant Influence: Discoveries by Russia's Foremost Parapsychologist.* New York: Dover, 1976.

Weaver, Warren, *Lady Luck: The Theory of Probability.* Garden City, N.Y.: Anchor Books, 1963.

White, Rhea A., "On the Genesis of Research Hypotheses in Parapsychology." Full Symposium Papers of the Parapsychological Association 22nd Annual Convention, August 1979, John F. Kennedy University, Orinda, California.

Wilson, Colin, *Mysteries.* New York: Putnam, 1978.

INDEX

F

G

H

I

ABOUT THE AUTHOR

Known since 1986 to millions of viewers as the thoughtful, inquiring host of *Thinking Allowed*, a talk show aired on national public television every week, Jeffrey Mishlove, Ph.D., has earned the reputation as a deep and authentic investigator of health, spirituality, and parapsychology. Mishlove is director of the Intuition Network, an organization of thousands of professionals interested in cultivating and applying intuitive skills. The first American to receive a Ph.D. in parapsychology from a major university, he is the author of the classic *Roots of Consciousness*, which recounts the history of parapsychology and served as the basis for his *Psi Development Systems*, a textbook which teaches ways of developing extrasensory abilities. Based in San Rafael, California, Mishlove serves as president of the Intuition Network. He welcomes visitors to his website: www.mishlove.com.

Hampton Roads Publishing Company

... for the evolving human spirit

Hampton Roads Publishing Company
publishes books on a variety of subjects including
metaphysics, health, complementary medicine,
visionary fiction, and other related topics.

For a copy of our latest catalog,
call toll-free, 800-766-8009,
or send your name and address to:

Hampton Roads Publishing Company, Inc.
1125 Stoney Ridge Road
Charlottesville, VA 22902
e-mail: hrpc@hrpub.com
www.hrpub.com